SOCIAL LIFE
UNDER THE STUARTS

Art Repro Co

Mary Ruthven, wife of Vandyck.
holding Viol da Gamba
from the portrait by Vandyck at Munich.

SOCIAL LIFE
UNDER THE STUARTS

BY

ELIZABETH GODFREY

AUTHOR OF 'HOME LIFE UNDER THE STUARTS

ILLUSTRATED

LONDON: GRANT RICHARDS
NEW YORK: E. P. DUTTON & CO.
1904

Printed by R. & R. Clark, Limited, *Edinburgh*

TO

'LUCAS MALET'

MRS. ST. LEGER HARRISON

𝔄 𝔗𝔯𝔦𝔟𝔲𝔱𝔢

OF ADMIRATION TO THE WRITER,

OF AFFECTION TO THE FRIEND

PREFACE

THE study of an historical period from the point of view of the individual reveals a whole range of subjects not strictly belonging to domestic life, yet far from the domain of political history. The way men entertained each other, the pleasures that amused them, the plays they applauded, the pictures and statues they bought to adorn their houses, the portrait painters they patronised, the instruments they played on, the songs they sang, the books they read, the news and gossip of the day, the country sports,—all these belong to private and personal life, and in them the men and women of the day stand revealed in their tastes and preferences, no less than in the graver things that went to build up character—their intimate relations with each other, the way in which they regarded the scientific discoveries of their time, where and how they worshipped, what they believed, and how the faith that was in them affected their lives. These things may be gathered not only from the private lives of the few whose names are written in history, but amongst the scattered records of the cultured many, whose views and propensities are only preserved in the chance survival of letters and journals.

Those who were interested in the *Home Life* of this same period, in the houses and gardens, the dress and furniture, the nurseries and still-rooms, the needlework, the domestic ways that were there described, may care to read of the same people in a wider sphere, and the kind reception accorded to the former volume seems to promise that there is room for this too, especially as not a few reviewers expressed a desire for this kind of continuation or extension.   In the first scheme of that book all these matters were to have been dealt with, but it soon appeared that the book would have grown to excessive bulk, so it seemed best to divide personal life in the home from personal life in the world, and to devote a separate volume to the latter.   To the student much that is here treated of will no doubt be familiar, but for many readers it may not be superfluous to gather together the gleanings from an infinite number of sources into a connected general view of the forty-six years with which it deals—the reigns, namely, of the first two Stuart kings of England.

For in these matters still more than on its domestic side the period has a singular completeness in itself, separated by rapid growth and development from the Elizabethan age, by a chasm from the era of the Restoration.   Whether we look at it from the side of the arts, of science, or of religion, the contrast is sharp both to what went before and to what followed.   To take music: those years saw concerted music emerge from the disconnected crowd of instruments of the lute or mandoline order, and crystallise into the balanced symmetry of violin, viola, and 'cello, with wood-wind, brass, and percussion, forming the band much as we have it now; they saw, moreover, the rise of a school of church music, which is perhaps one of the best things that England has to boast of in that kind, which attained its ripened perfection on the eve of the war, and was by that war and its consequences absolutely cut off.   Other important developments followed later, but they were on distinctly different lines, and owed much more to foreign influences, both German and Italian.

In art we see a school of portrait-painting of singular completeness, dying with Vandyck, whose successors of the Restoration belonged to a totally different order, both by handling and technique, and by the manner in which they envisaged their sitters; with these latter our later school of painters, such as Reynolds, Gainsborough, and Romney, have far more affinity than they have with Vandyck or Janssen. Miniature painting too had its rise, ceasing to be the mere oil-painting in little which it was in the preceding century, and working its way through gouache on vellum to ivory. The enthusiasm for the collection of works of art, Greek marbles, Italian, Spanish, or Flemish paintings, which has enriched England with so many masterpieces, was at its zenith; under Elizabeth men had hardly realised its fascination, and later the war and the subsequent Puritan ascendancy checked it for many years.

The drama had already made a brilliant beginning with Shakespeare and his contemporaries, whose plays held the stage for years after he had passed away, and it is in marked contrast to that which followed the reaction after the Puritan régime. In literature the half century which in poetry may be said to open with Spenser (since he only died in 1599) and close with Milton, and in prose begins with Bacon and Andrewes, and ends with Jeremy Taylor, Clarendon, Walton, and John Evelyn, contains more brilliant names than can here be enumerated, and is, moreover, distinguished by special characteristics, by high tone, lofty ideals, pure diction, so that we seem to enter a different atmosphere with the witty, careless, cynical writers of Charles II.'s day, or the cold, mannered artificiality that succeeded it.

Science had almost a new birth with the great astro-

nomical discoveries which revolutionised the conceptions
of the universe, and with the principles of induction set
forth in Bacon's *Novum Organum ;* and before the end of
the half century the stirrings of newly-awakened curiosity
issued in the formation of the Royal Society for the
encouragement of research.

Religion was passing through a phase distinct from
anything it had yet experienced, though not without
analogies with our own times, when the incompatibility
between the two sections within the Anglican fold showed
itself, and yet the Church escaped the absolute rending in
two that seemed inevitable.

Personal character too stands apart ; the typical men
of the day on both sides showed themselves more serious,
more conscientious, less selfish and overbearing than their
forefathers who had fought for Elizabeth and discovered
the New World, and certainly less so than their grandsons
who hung about the court of Charles II. and lampooned
the king. There is a decided preponderance of noble
ideals of conduct, of a high standard of family life, of
loyalty both to friends and to the chosen cause, whether
it were Church and Throne, or popular rights and liberties,
and a singular spirit of self-sacrifice. On both sides were
faults, but they are not of a degrading order : on the one
side narrowness, obstinacy, a growing spirit of anarchy, an
absolute lack of fairness to opponents ; on the other a
complete failure to grasp the realities of the situation, to
allow for the expansion growth must bring, and a blind
clinging to tradition. Yet no age, I venture to assert,
has finer characters to show.

As in the former volume, my aim has been, wherever
possible, to let the people of the day speak for themselves,
rather than to describe and interpret. It is infinitely more

interesting to read what they said themselves of contemporary books, pictures, plays, than to see them through modern eyes, but it has not been possible to do this as often and as completely as in the study of domestic life, for criticism was in its infancy, and the reviewer of that day was rather a learned commentator than a critic in our modern sense, and the amateur critic was still rare, though Dorothy Osborne occasionally writes to her lover some shrewd and pungent comments on the books they lend each other, and now and then Lady Brilliana Harley recommends some work of piety to her son or his tutor.

The subject of this later study is more ambitious and presents more difficulties than the earlier, and the writer would deprecate being supposed to attempt an exhaustive analysis of the various topics touched on. To do so would require a volume rather than a chapter for each, and a specialist to deal with each subject. It must be borne in mind, especially in the field of art, music, science, or literature, that it is not so much the actual condition and progress of all these that is here attempted to be set forth, as the general view as it would appear to the average man of culture of the day—the environment, in fact, in which he lived. This may be perhaps superficial, but it seemed hardly possible to deal otherwise with so wide-embracing a subject.

In the book on *Home Life* were acknowledgments of the kindness which allowed quotations to be made from letters and autobiographical matter, published of late years and therefore copyright, and I find that this led some of my reviewers to the conclusion that my work was merely a compilation from other books. I should like, therefore, to say that nearly if not quite all quotations made were verbatim from letters or memoirs written during

the seventeenth century, in pursuance of my chief aim of
letting the actors tell their own story in their own words ;
but where, as in many cases, the originals were in private
hands, this could only be done by the permission of the
owners of copyright. Only these were named in the
Introduction. I have therefore thought it well to append
to this a list, approximately complete, of the seventeenth-
century and later books consulted. It is manifest that a
book of this kind must be gathered from older books or
manuscripts, unless it is to be entirely a work of imagination, in which case it would be worthless.

I should like to take this opportunity of thanking
those reviewers, as well as many unknown correspondents,
who kindly brought to my notice things which I regret
not to have made myself acquainted with before. I have
received from two sources the true account of the origin
of the rhyme of Jack Horner, which I, following (I think)
Halliwell-Phillips, had attributed to a satire on the
Puritans. It appears that John Horner, of the Horners
of Fountains Abbey in Yorkshire, was steward of the
Monastic House of Glastonbury at the time of the Dissolution of the Monasteries. He was sent to London
with the title-deeds of the Abbey lands, which were concealed in a pie. Moved by hunger or curiosity he attacked
the pie on the journey and discovered the deeds, which
he thereupon conveyed to King Henry VIII., getting a
considerable 'plum' secured to himself and his heirs.

Another correspondent has kindly sent me the following extract, explaining the expression 'tuck,' taken from
the edition of Wood's *Athenæ Oxonienses*, printed by T.
Combe, Printer to the University, for the Ecclesiastical
History Society, 1848, pp. 34, 35. After describing the
custom of the undergraduates gathering round the charcoal

fires in hall, he continues, they 'would bring juniors or
' freshmen between that time (five) and six of the clock,
' and there make them sit downe on a forme in the middle
' of the hall, joyning to the declaiming desk : which done,
' every one in order was to speake some pretty apothegme,
' or make a jest or bull, or speake some eloquent nonsense,
' to make the company laugh : but if any of the freshmen
' came off dull, or not cleverly, some of the forward or
' pragmaticall seniors would tuck them, that is, set the
' nail of their thumb to their chin, just under the lipp, and
' by the help of their other fingers under the chin they
' would give him a mark, which sometimes would produce
' blood.' The edition from which I made my notes,
differing slightly in wording from this, may possibly have
wanted the explanation, or it may be my own notes were
defective. A reviewer also pointed out an interesting
passage, bearing on the same practice, in the Life of the
first Lord Shaftesbury, by E. D. Christie. He prides
himself on having put down the custom by combining
with some strong young freshmen of his year to resist it,
and describes it in almost the same words as Wood, but
mentions the 'beer glass of salt and water' as though
given purposely to aggravate the pain. Yet another
correspondent suggests another meaning of tuck, a sharp,
slender sword or rapier, which may explain the origin of
the expression, the long, sharp thumb-nail being used
as one.

Two letters supply interesting explanations of the
names of fruit and flowers which have fallen into disuse.
' Melocoton, Spanish for improved nectarine. The un-
' regenerate nectarine is called duragno or prisco ; grafted
' on a quince (membrillo) stem the fruit became thinner-
' skinned, more delicate, etc., and was known as melocoton.'

Another says that in a note to Bacon's *Essays* it is given as a kind of peach, and melocotogno is Italian for quince tree. 'Warden is given as a large baking pear, cornelian ' as the fruit of the cornel tree, sometimes called cornelian ' cherries, which were in some parts of the country used for tarts. Satyrian is given as orchis; "the sweet satyrian ' " with the white flower" is probably the butterfly orchis.'

I am also very grateful for the kindness of many who lent or permitted to be used illustrations, which add greatly to the interest of a book of this kind,—especially to Thomas Longueville, Esq., for so generously lending the plates of Lord Falkland and Elizabeth Lady Falkland— the former, the original of which belongs to Lord Arundel of Wardour, is considered one of Vandyck's finest and most characteristic portraits; also to Ralph Bankes, Esq., for permitting the engravings of Corfe Castle before and after the siege to be used; to Miss Abdy of Southbourne for the loan of the memorial medal of Charles I., and to J. C. Palmer, Esq., for that of the original copy of *Mercurius Rusticus* for 1646 to have the frontispiece reproduced; to A. C. de Lafontaine, Esq., of Athelhampton, for the illustration of the curious sundial in his Jacobean garden. I so much regret I had not seen Athelhampton before the chapters on House and Home and on Gardens in the previous volume were written, as it is a singularly perfect specimen of the house and garden of that day. The house itself dates from far earlier, from Saxon times indeed, but in its present condition is nearly as it must have been in the reign of Charles I., and in its internal fittings, as well as in the gardens, is kept up by the present owner perfectly in the taste of that day, and also contains many precious Stuart relics.

I am greatly indebted, too, to the courteous helpfulness

of Campbell Dodgson, Esq., of the British Museum, for the
choice of prints from that source, and for many hints and
suggestions, both for the former book and this, to Henry
Jenner, Esq., also of the British Museum.   The authorities
of the South Kensington Museum allow photographs of
miniatures and musical instruments from the collections
there.   The copyright photographs of the Vandyck of
Killigrew, and Carew, and of Mary Ruthven, wife of the
painter, as well as of the print of Bacon in his study, are
from Messrs. Mansell, art photographers.

Much help has also been afforded me by loans of books
and suggestions of several I did not know of, for which I
beg to thank my many friends.

ELIZABETH GODFREY.

SOUTHBOURNE, *January* 1904.

AUTHORITIES

HISTORY of the Rebellion. Clarendon.—Clarendon's Life.—Evelyn s Diary.—Walton's Lives.—Life of Lord Herbert of Cherbury. By Himself.—Athenæ Oxonienses. Anthony Wood.—Fuller's Worthies. —Microcosmography. Bishop Earle.—Memoir of Colonel Hutchinson. By his widow, Lucy.—Lady Fanshawe's Memoirs.—The Lady Falkland, her Life. By her Daughter.—Autobiography of Anne Lady Halkett. Ed. by J. G. Nichols (Camden Society).—Liber Famelicus. James Whitelocke. Ed. by J. Bruce (Camden Society).— Diary of John Rous. Ed. by M. A. E. Green (Camden Society).— Diary of Walter Yonge. Ed. by G. Roberts (Camden Society).—Life of Marmaduke Rawdon. Ed. by R. Davies (Camden Society).—Life of Adam Martindale. By Himself. Ed. by Rev. R. Parkinson (Chetham Society).—Proceedings in Kent (Camden Society).—Lismore Papers. Ed. by Dr. Grosart (Camden Society).—Verney Papers. Ed. by J. Bruce (Camden Society).—Hatton Correspondence. Ed. by E. M. Thompson (Camden Society).—Letters of Lady Brilliana Harley. Ed. by Lewis (Camden Society).—The Camden Miscellany.—Historical Notices of Events in the Reign of Charles I. Nehemiah Wallington.—Fragment of Autobiography from the Life of Anthony Ashley Cooper, first Earl of Shaftesbury. By E. D. Christie.—Aubrey's Miscellanies.—Aubrey's Lives of Eminent Men.—The Book of Sports. James I.—Polyolbion. Michael Drayton.—Fumifugium. John Evelyn.—Mundus Muliebris. John Evelyn. — Familiar Letters of James Howell.—The Compleat Gentleman. Henry Peacham.—The Art of Drawing and Limning in Watercolour. Peacham. — The English Schoole-Master. Coote.—The Art of Living in London & The Worth of a Peny. Peacham.—Bacon's Essays. — The Herball. John Gerard.—Paradisi in Sole. John Parkinson.— Kalendarium Hortense. Evelyn.—Acetaria, or Discourse upon Sallets. Evelyn.— The Penyles Pilgrimage. John Taylor the Water-Poet.—A Short Relation of a Long Journey. John Taylor.—The Compleat Angler. Izaak Walton.—Herrick's Hesperides.—Fragmenta Aurea. Sir John Suckling.—Cavalier and Courtier Lyrics. Ed. W. H. Dircks.— England's Helicon.—Works of Bishop Cosins. Cosins' Protestant Hours.—Herbert's Country Parson.—Herbert's Temple.—The Returnes of Spiritual Comfort and Grief in a Devout Soul, & The Holy

Life and Death of Letice Vi-Countess Falkland.   J. Duncon.—Bishop
Jeremy Taylor's Holy Living and Dying.—Religio Medici & Hydrio-
taphia.   Sir Thomas Browne.—Taylor's Golden Grove.—Memoirs of
the Two Last Years of the Reign of King Charles I.   Sir Thomas
Herbert.—The Eikon Basilike of Charles I.—Elegant Epistles.—
Areopagitica and Treatise on Divorce.   John Milton.—Mercurius
Rusticus for 1646.— Pamphlets, Diurnals, and Newsletters from
Collections in the British Museum.—Ornatus Muliebris.   Hollar.—
Theatrum Mulierum.   Hollar.—Journal of the Siege of Lathom House.
—Hornbye's Horn-Book.

OF LATER DATE

General History of the Science and Practice of Music.   Sir John
Hawkins.— Old English Music.   W. Chappell.— Music in the
Seventeenth Century.   Vol. IV. of the Oxford History of Music.
Sir Hubert Parry.—Hutching's History of Dorset.—The Story of
Corfe Castle.   Right Hon. George Bankes.—Memoirs of British
Ladies.   George Ballard.—Home Life of Ladies in the Seventeenth
Century.   By the author of Magdalen Stafford.—Annals of Win-
chester.   T. F. Kirby.—Wykehamica.   H. C. Adams.—English
Schools at the Reformation.   Leach.— Anonymous History of
Winchester published in 1773.—The Child and his Book.   J. M.
Field.—The History of the Horn-Book.   Andrew Tuer.—Popular
Rhymes and Nursery Tales.   J. O. Halliwell-Phillips.—Nursery
Rhymes of England.   Halliwell-Phillips.—Conceits, Clinches, Flashes
and Whimsies.   Halliwell-Phillips.—England as seen by Foreigners.
W. Brenchley Rye.—William Shakespeare.   Karl Elze.   Translated
by Dora Schmidt.—Introduction to Webster and Tourneur (Mermaid
Series).   By J. A. Symonds.—The Age of Milton.   J. Bass Mullinger.
—Masson's Life of Milton.—Characteristics of Cambridge in the
Seventeenth Century.   J. Bass Mullinger.—Original Papers illustrative
of Milton.   W. D. Hamilton.—Letters of Dorothy Osborne.   Judge
Parry.—Five Stuart Princesses.   R. Rait.—Nicholas Ferrar, his
Household and his Friends.   T. T. Carter.—History of Costume.

Extracts from letters and other autobiographical matter were
made by permission from the following :—

Memoirs of the Verney Family.   Lady Verney.—Letters of Mr.
Endymion Porter, Gentleman of the Bedchamber to His Majesty
Charles I.   Mrs. Townshend.—Saccharissa.   Mrs. Ady.—The Life
of Sir Kenelm Digby.   By one of his Descendants.—Falklands.   By
the author of Sir Kenelm Digby.—Mary Rich, Countess of Warwick.
Miss Fell Smith.

CONTENTS

CHAPTER I

COUNTRY PASTIMES

CHAPTER II

THE TOWN

CHAPTER III

THE PLAY

CHAPTER VIII

TRAVELLING

CHAPTER IX

WHAT PEOPLE READ

CHAPTER X

NEWS

CHAPTER XI

THE LITERARY COTERIE

CHAPTER XII

FRIENDSHIP

CHAPTER XIII

RELIGION

CHAPTER XIV

THE RELIGIOUS LIFE

CHAPTER XV

TYPES OF PIETY

CHAPTER XVI

IN TIME OF TRIAL

CHAPTER XVII

WHAT WAS LEFT

LIST OF ILLUSTRATIONS

CHAPTER I

COUNTRY PASTIMES

> I sing of blossoms, birds and bowers,
> Of April, May, of June, and July flowers;
> I sing of May-poles, hock-carts, wassails, wakes,
> Of bridegrooms, brides, and of their bridal cakes.

THUS the cheerful country parson Herrick, and his is
but one voice of a chorus in praise of a country life.
Though towns were neither so big nor so ugly as they
are now, yet the poets unite in contemning the life of
streets and markets, and would fain leave them for the
fields and woods, for ' the sweet contentment the country-
' man doth find.'   Undoubtedly the small house and
large garden of Cowley's desires was to be in the country,
far from 'the crowd, the buzz, the murmurings of this
' great hive, the City.'   But not poets only, who would
naturally appreciate the beauties of nature, extol the
charms of a country life, but the doctors were already
beginning to order their patients into the country, ' for
' better ayre, and to follow the plow by way of exercise.'
Anthony Wood records this prescription of his doctor's
for an ague from which he had suffered all winter.   This
ague, by the way, he had contracted on a rural excursion : in
the latter end of August he had gone on a fishing expedition with his friend Will Stamer of Merton to Wheatly
Bridge, and by the way they went nutting at Shotover,
and the day being warm, got over-heated, which resulted

B

in an obstinate ague which the cold and damp of Oxford increased. So in the spring he went to Cossington and lodged with one Francis Bolton, 'whose house, tho' ' thatched, had a very faire chamber therein with a ' chimney and a place to lay his books in.' Besides the plow, he took exercise practising on the six bells, and for his diversion studied the violin by ear, stringing and tuning by a method of his own.[1]

Plain practical men loved their country homes. Sir Edmund Verney was never so happy as at Claydon ; his heart was in his farm and gardens, and his letters from the Court are filled, not with descriptions of Court functions, but with minute instructions as to the pleaching of hedges or the management of his horses. But of all enthusiastic country lovers none can compare with the retired hosier Izaak Walton, who joyfully turned his back on Fleet Street, where he had made his money, and devoted the autumn of his days to the calm joys of angling.

From the moment when, 'on a fresh May morning,' Piscator encounters Venator and Auceps going towards Ware, and walking with them as far as the Thatched House in Hoddesdon, enters into discourse, he makes us free of their company and transports us through the sweet meadows of Hertfordshire or along by the sparkling trout streams near Winchester till we are ready to say with him, 'No life, my honest scholar, no life so happy and so ' pleasant as the life of a well-governed angler ; for when ' the lawyer is swallowed up with business, and the states- ' man is preventing or contriving plots, then we sit on ' cowslip banks, hear the birds sing, and possess ourselves ' in as much quietness as these silent silver streams, ' which we now see glide so quietly by us. Indeed, my ' good scholar, we may say of angling as Dr. Boteler ' said of strawberries, " Doubtless God could have made a ' " better berry, but doubtless God never did " ; and so, if I

[1] Introduction to *Athenæ Oxonienses*.

' might be the judge, God never did make a more calm,
' quiet, innocent recreation than angling.

'I'll tell you, scholar, when I sat last upon this prim-
' rose bank, and looked down these meadows, I thought
' of them as Charles the Emperor did of the city of
' Florence, "that they were too pleasant to be looked on,
' "but only on holidays." As I then sat on this very grass,
' I turned my thoughts into verse : 'twas a wish which I'll
' repeat to you '—the last stanza of the angler's wish
runs thus :—

> Or, with my Bryan and a book,
> Loiter long days near Shawford brook ;
> There sit by him, and eat my meat ;
> There see the sun both rise and set ;
> There bid good-morning to next day ;
> There meditate my time away ;
>   And angle on, and beg to have
>   A quiet passage to a welcome grave.

Alas! poor Shawford now! Given over to the tender
mercies of the jerry-builder ; its fair hedges replaced by
boards bearing alternate legends of pills and soap. Let
us shut our eyes to to-day, and return to peaceful Hampshire in the olden time.

'But turn out of the way a little, good scholar,
' towards yonder high honeysuckle hedge ; there we'll sit
' and sing, whilst this shower falls so gently upon the
' teeming earth, and gives yet a sweeter smell to the
' lovely flowers that adorn these verdant meadows.

'Look! under that broad beech-tree I sat when I was
' last this way a-fishing. And the birds in the adjoining
' grove seemed to have a friendly contention with an
' echo, whose dead voice seemed to live in an hollow tree,
' near to the brow of that primrose hill. There I sat
' viewing the silver streams glide silently towards their
' centre, the tempestuous sea ; yet sometimes opposed by
' rugged roots and pebblestones, which broke their waves,
' and turned them into foam. And sometimes I beguiled
' time by viewing the harmless lambs ; some leaping

' securely in the cool shade, whilst others sported them-
' selves in the cheerful sun ; and saw others craving
' comfort from the swollen udders of their bleating dams.
' As I thus sat, these and other sights had so fully
' possessed my soul with content, that I thought, as the
' poet hath happily expressed it—

> I was for that time lifted above earth,
> And possessed joys not promised in my birth.

' As I left this place, and entered into the next field, a
' second pleasure entertained me ; 'twas a handsome
' milkmaid, that had not yet attained so much age and
' wisdom as to load her mind with fears of many things
' that will never be, as too many men often do ; but she
' cast away all care, and sang like a nightingale : her
' voice was good, and the ditty fitted for it : it was that
' smooth song that was made by Kit Marlow, now at
' least fifty years ago ; and the milkmaid's mother sang
' an answer to it which was made by Sir Walter Raleigh
' in his younger days.

' They were old-fashioned poetry, but choicely good, I
' think much better than the strong lines that are now in
' fashion in this critical age.   Look yonder ! on my word,
' yonder they both be a-milking again.   I will give her the
' chub, and persuade her to sing those two songs to us.'

There follows a dialogue with the milkmaid and her
mother, in which it appears that their repertoire of songs
was considerable and included such choice favourites as
' At noon Dulcina rested,' 'Phillida flouts me,' 'Chevy
' Chace,' 'Johnny Armstrong,' and 'Troy Town,' as well
as the delightful pair of lyrics he had asked for, 'Come,
' live with me, and be my love,' and ' If all the world and
' love were young.'

Venator, much pleased, remarks that 'it was not with-
' out cause that our good Queen Elizabeth did so often
' wish herself a milkmaid all the month of May, because
' they are not troubled with fears and cares, and sing

'sweetly all the day, and sleep securely all the night;
'and without doubt, honest, innocent, pretty Maudlin
'does so.' No doubt she did, especially if she lived in
the house hard by which so took Venator's fancy for a
resting-place, 'because the linen looks white and smells
'of lavender, and I long to lie in a pair of sheets that
'smells so.'

I am not sure that the Devonshire parson did not
even exceed this dear lover of the country; for while our
well-beloved angler praises early summer and the tranquil
pleasures of angling, interrupted by nothing more serious
than a summer shower, Herrick hymns the whole year
round with its changing seasons, its work and its play,
the toil of ploughman and of shepherd, the joy of harvest
home, the mirth of Christmas games, the mummings and
the junketings with which the country folk solaced
themselves when snow lay thick and ways were foul, no
less than the charm of spring mornings when the maids
went out to the fields laden 'with wicker arks to bear the
'richer cowslips home.'

Mr. Endymion Porter was a dear friend of the poet-
parson, and in his London home often sighed for the
green fields and for the simple farming life at Woodhall,
where his 'little partridges' played about in their grandmother's care, in delightful familiarity with pigs, chickens,
and little lambs. One of Herrick's most charming
descriptive pieces is addressed to him in praise of country
life contrasted to that of the Court. It begins—

> Sweet country life, to such unknown
> Whose lives are others', not their own!

A farmer's life, as here depicted, is indeed idyllic, rising
early—

> When now the cock (the ploughman's horn)
> Calls forth the lily-wristed morn;
> Then to thy cornfields thou dost go,
> Which, though well-soiled, yet thou dost know
> That the best compost for the lands
> Is the wise master's feet and hands.

The verses follow him through all his rounds, after the plough, over the fields, looking to the cattle, and lastly to the sheep feeding on the short sweet grass of the hillside. Then comes a description of country sports which must be quoted entire for its value as a picture of the pastimes of rural life.

> For sports, for pageantry, and plays,
> Thou hast thine eves, and holydays :
> On which the young men and maids meet,
> To exercise their dancing feet :
> Tripping the comely country Round
> With daffadils and daisies crown'd.
> Thy wakes, thy quintels, here thou hast
> Thy May-poles too with garlands graced ;
> Thy Morris-dance ; thy Whitsun-ale ;
> Thy shearing-feasts, which never fail.
> Thy harvest home ; thy wassail bowl,
> That's toss'd up after Fox i' th' hole ;
> Thy mummeries ; thy Twelve-tide kings
> And queens ; thy Christmas revellings ;
> Thy nut-brown mirth, thy russet wit,
> And no man pays too dear for it.—
> To these, thou hast thy times to go
> And trace the hare i' th' treacherous snow :
> Thy witty wiles to draw, and get
> The lark into the trammel net :
> Thou hast thy cock-rood, and thy glade
> To take the precious pheasants made :
> Thy lime-twigs, snares, and pit-falls then
> To catch the pilfering birds, not men.

High-farming with its engines, its ugliness, its dirt, had not yet come in : men still ploughed and sowed and reaped after the manner of their forefathers. Virgil's Georgics would fit as well the operations of those days as of his own, for farmers have always been a conservative race, or at least were so till a time within living memory ; for without doubt there has been more change in the methods of farming within the last fifty years than in all the preceding centuries since the plough was invented. In those days the plough was drawn by oxen, and the sower walked over the furrows strewing his precious grain

from a bag he wore at his waist; the hay was mown
with a scythe and the corn reaped with a hook, while the
gleaners followed the women who bound up the sheaves,
and no man grudged them their leasing cake. The
threshing was done by the flail on the wide barn floor,
and the winnowing with a fan in the fresh wind, as you
may see it done in Brittany to this day.

The work was hard, and the day was long; at
ploughing season or at hay and corn harvest the labourer
was literally up with the lark, if not before, and often out in
the dewy fields between three and four o'clock, and there
was then no talk of an eight-hours' day. Wages were
low, often but sixpence a day, but then provisions were
much cheaper, beef and mutton costing but 2d. or 3d.
a lb., and labourers were allowed to keep a cow or some
geese on the nearest common or green, and on some
estates had a cottage, perhaps we might call it a hovel,
rent free. Also it must be remembered that money must
be reckoned at more than four times its present value. If
labour was hard, care was less; there was still the feudal
feeling of responsibility for an old servant: it was from
the idle, the vagabonds, the masterless men that the
ranks of paupers were so rapidly recruited; and these idle
classes were of course tenfold increased by the Civil War.
Land went out of cultivation, and men who had been
fighting for years had lost the habit of diligent husbandry.

With hard work and freedom from care went along the
mirthful spirit that found or made occasion for rejoicing
in tide-times as the seasons brought them round, or as
each phase of farm work came to its due end. Now,
they say, it is the dulness of country life that drives the
labouring man to the towns, but however hard the life
may have been in those days, at least it was not dull.
Instead of one dreary round of sameness, day in day out,
each man finding his recreation for himself where he can,
or going without, the spells of hard yet sociable labour
were followed by the common pleasures, the wakes, the

mummings, the merry-makings which later the Puritans succeeded in stamping out of country life.

In the *Idyllica* Herrick gives the whole series running the year through.   First comes the New Year, when Wassail, wassail! was sung through the village street, and the lads stopped at each farmer's door to wish him blessings on basket and bin, on larder, dairy, bee-hives, stacks, stocks, and hay-mow, in return for which they received the wassail bowl.   Next follows Twelfth Night with its choosing of kings and queens in memory of the Three Kings of old, its chant of Lavender's blue, and its careful observance of the fairies, especially of Robin Good-fellow, who rewarded the diligent and kind by helping on their work on winter nights.   The old song, ' I saw Three ' Ships,' belongs, of course, to this season.   For Candlemas our poet gives no candle ceremonies—probably the Refor-mation had already put these down—but he mentions the custom of kindling the Christmas brand and letting it burn till sundown, when it was quenched and laid up ' till ' Christmas next return.'   Also the decorations must be changed.

> Down with the rosemary and bays,
>   Down with the mistletoe ;
> Instead of holly, now upraise
>   The greener box for show.

And the box was to ' domineer ' till Easter Day.   Soon follows St. Valentine, which is so frequently alluded to in writings of the time, and which lingered on in the shape of sending amorous verses by post till quite the middle of the last century.   In Herrick's time the observances consisted in the maids drawing by lot the man who should be their esquire for the day.   The swain was expected to make appropriate gifts to his lady ; some trifling fairing or gay ribbon was enough for a country bumpkin, but a choicer present, a jewel, a fan, or a pair of embroidered gloves, would be looked for from an esquire.   If there were any entertainment going forward he would escort her to it, and treat her, perhaps, to curds and cream or syllabub. After these frivolities, Lent, which was very strictly observed, brought a quiet time, broken only by the Rogation ceremonies of going in procession to bless the fields, and by Mothering Sunday, when every one was expected to take the Sacrament in his or her own parish church, and those who had gone into service in a neighbouring parish came home to pay their duty to their parents and have a share in the simnel cake or whatever in their own county was the traditional dainty of the season. From this custom came the pretty old saying, ' Who goes a-mothering finds violets in the lane.' Then Easter brought the Peace-egg, and the poet sighs that the wintry storm of war might pass away, and the dove might ' bring in her bill once more the branch of peace.'

May-Day follows, with its delightful ceremonies, lads and girls going out in the first freshness of morning, to bring in green boughs and snowy white-thorn to deck each house till—

> Each field turns a street; each street a park
>   Made green and trimm'd with trees: see how
>   Devotion gives each house a bough
>   Or branch: each porch, each door, ere this,
>   An ark, a tabernacle is
> Made up of white-thorn neatly interwove;
> As if here were those cooler shades of love.

Then came the choosing of the queen, the rearing of the great pole, richly garlanded, on the midst of the village green, the feasting, the dancing round it till ' Charles's wain came out above the tall white chimney-pots.' No doubt a great day for match-making.

After this was a busy time when the mowers were in the fields from dawn till dusk. But when the hay was safely gathered in, in full summer, in the slack time between hay and harvest came the village Wake, about which, since it is so much less known than May-day, we must needs quote Herrick in full.

> Come, Anthea, let us two
> Go to feast, as others do :
> Tarts and custards, cream and cakes,
> Are the junkets still at Wakes ;
> Unto which the tribes resort,
> Where the business is the sport :
> Morris-dancers thou shalt see,
> Marian too in pageantry ;
> And a mimic to devise
> Many grinning properties.
> Players there will be, and those
> Base in action as in clothes ;
> Yet with strutting they will please
> The incurious villages.
> Near the dying of the day
> There will be a cudgel play,
> Where a coxcomb will be broke,
> Ere a good word can be spoke :
> But the anger ends all here,
> Drench'd in ale, or drown'd in beer.
> —Happy rusticks ! best content
> With the cheapest merriment ;
> And possess no other fear,
> Than to want the Wake next year.

For the next festival, the crown of the year's labour, the Harvest-home or Hock-cart, truly we must go to Herrick once more.

> Come, Sons of Summer, by whose toil
> We are the lords of wine and oil :
> By whose tough labours and rough hands
> We rip up first, then reap our lands.
> Crown'd with the ears of corn, now come,
> And to the pipe sing Harvest Home.
>
> Come forth, my lord, and see the cart
> Drest up with all the country art.
> See, here a maukin, there a sheet,
> As spotless pure as it is sweet :
> The horses, mares, and frisking fillies,
> Clad all in linen white as lilies.
> The harvest swains and wenches bound
> For joy to see the Hock-Cart crown'd.

—Well on, brave boys, to your lord's hearth
Glitt'ring with fire ; where for your mirth,
Ye shall see first the large and chief
Foundation of your feast, fat beef :
With upper stories, mutton, veal
And bacon, which makes full the meal,
With several dishes standing by,
As here a custard, there a pie,
And here, all tempting frumenty.
And for to make the merry cheer,
If smirking wine be wanting here,
There's that which drowns all care, stout beer,
Which freely drink to your lord's health ;—
Then to the plough, the common-wealth ;
Next to your flails, your fanes, your vats ;
Then to the maids with wheaten hats :
To the rough sickle and crooked scythe,—
Drink, frolic, boys, till all be blythe.

Our good parson winds up with an exhortation to remember the return to work, and their duty to the master
—' Feed him ye must, whose food fills you.'

Though this wound up the year's labour, there were
still festivals to make the dark days bright.   With St.
Katharine's day ended the ingathering of the apples, and
collections of beer and apples for a feast were made from
each house ; and later All-Hallow-tide brought quaint,
half-heathenish observances, the household sitting round
the fire in the hall or house-place.   Christmas customs
were many ; there were first the carol-singers and the
waits, coming round to every house and playing on their
antiquated instruments—the lute, guitar, bandore, or ' the
loud bassoon.'   Then came the Morris-dancers, imported
by the Crusaders long ago from the far East, and the
mummers, whose traditional play lingered on in out-of-the-
way places till almost the middle of the last century, and
may have been seen by some now living.   Miss Yonge, in
one of her early stories, gives the rhymes as they had been
handed down in Hampshire, with the various characters,
Father Christmas, the King, the Doctor, St. George, and
the Turkish Knight, and last, Little Johnny Jack with all

his family at his back. The form, however, varied in
different parts of England. These all used to come first
to the great house of the neighbourhood, and show off in
the hall before the whole assembled family, children,
visitors, and servants, and after being regaled and receiving
money, made their rounds to all the farms.

Besides all this, every Sunday afternoon was devoted
to social sports and exercises, to the promotion of good
fellowship and encouragement of manly tastes. The
Puritans, however, in whose eyes the abuses of such
things bulked larger than the advantages, had for long
been endeavouring to put them down, and this was the
occasion of *The King's Book of Sports*, which turned out
such a firebrand. Passing through Lancashire, King
James had been indignant at finding the magistrates
were ' prohibiting and unlawfully punishing Our good
' People for using their lawful Recreations and honest
' Exercises upon Sundayes and other Holy Dayes, after
' the afternoon Sermon or Service.' His son reissued
the same book in 1633, with a preface in which he
explained the old king's intentions. 'Hee prudently
' considered, that if these times were taken from them,
' the meaner sort who labour hard all the week, should
' have no Recreations at all to refresh their Spirits. . . .
' In place thereof they do set up filthy tipplings and
' drunkennesse which breeds a number of idle and dis-
' contented speeches in their Ale-houses. For when shall
' the common People have leave to exercise, if not upon
' Sundaies and Holy daies, seeing they must apply their
' labour, and win their living in all working daies ? ' The
preface, moreover, suggests the bad effect on the minds
of ' Papists,' of whom there were still great numbers in
the North, leading them to think that 'no honest Mirth
' or Recreation is lawful or tolerable in our Religion.'

The king therefore enacts that the churchwardens
shall enforce equal conformity from Recusants, Puritans,
or Precisians, ' so as to strike equally with both hands.'

The sports enumerated are 'Dauncing, either men or
' women, Archery for men, Leaping, Vaulting, or any
' other such harmless Recreation.' From these the people
are not to be debarred, 'nor from having May-games,
' Whitson Ales, & Morris Dances & the setting up of
' Maypoles, and other Sports therewith used, so as the
' same be had in due & convenient time without impedi-
' ment or neglect of Divine Service: And that women
' shall have leave to carry rushes to the Church for the
' decoring of it, according to their old custome. But
' withall We doe here account it still as prohibited all
' unlawfull games to be used on Sundaies onely, as Beare
' and Bull baitings, Interludes, and at all times in the
' meaner sort of people by law prohibited, Bowling.' Why
Bowling? we ask in some perplexity.

'And likewise We barre from this benefite and liberty
' all such known Recusants either Men or Women, as will
' abstain from coming to Church or Divine Service, being
' therefore unworthy of any lawful Recreation after the
' said Service that will not first come to the Church &
' serve God.

'And Our pleasure is, That this Our Declaration shall
' bee published by Order from the Bishop of the Diocese
' through all the Parish Churches, and that both Our
' Judges of Our Circuit, and our Justices of the Peace bee
' informed thereof.'

To his republication of this King Charles adds that he
finds 'there has been, under pretence of taking away
' abuses, a generall forbidding, not only of ordinary
' meetings, but of the Feasts of the Dedication of Churches,
' commonly called Wakes. Now Our express Will and
' Pleasure is that these Feasts with others shall be observed,
' & that Our Justices of the Peace in their severall Divisions
' shall looke to it, both that all Disorders there may be
' prevented & punished, & that all Neighbourhood and
' Freedom, with manlike and lawful Exercises, bee used.'
But he too adds, 'having first done their Duetie to God.'

To enter into the political significance of the storm this raised would be outside our province, but we can see that the social effect of the Puritan victory has been disastrous; to it more than to almost any cause is owing the complete divorce of religion from the daily life of the people. It came to be regarded as a matter for Sunday observance only, and the service of God grew to be associated with all that was gloomy and forbidding. Perhaps James I., whom it is so much the fashion to scoff at as foolish, was in this matter not so unwise after all.

He, as well as his son Charles, was much given to country sports; he loved hunting and hawking, and was an excellent judge of a falcon as well as of a good horse. The races, or 'horsmaching,' as Henry Verney called it, at Newmarket were becoming quite a fashionable pastime, and young Verney sometimes rode as gentleman-rider for the cup for which the officers of his regiment used to subscribe £50. But the stag hunt seems to have been the favourite amusement and to have drawn most fashionable gatherings into the country. Readers of the volume on 'Home Life' may remember the yearly run in the neighbourhood of Winchester, in which the scholars were allowed to join; and in the *Letters of Endymion Porter* we read of one at Hatfield when Lord Salisbury's guests, including the Countess of Arundel, Sir John North, and Sir Tobie Matthew, rode out to meet Mrs. Porter, who was to dine and sleep at Lord Boteler's at Hatfield Woodhall.

When Robert Dover, an old-fashioned country squire, friend and neighbour of the Porter family, revived the ancient Cotswold Games, he met with much encouragement from the royal family. These took place at Whitsuntide on a rising ground above Mickleton, about a mile from Chipping Campden. In the same book there is a charming description of the gathering of all the countryside, gentle and simple, to share in or witness the sports which Mr. Dover 'trusted would imbue the people with a chivalrous valour.' Endymion himself was there of

From a print in the British Museum.

THE COTSWOLD GAMES.

In costume of the reign of James I.

PLATE II.

course, with his two friends, Davenant and the great Ben
Jonson, and a tribe of Porter cousins and his handsome
wife, the party no doubt distinguished amongst the country
bumpkins by their courtly elegance ; while the Master of
the Revels hurried to and fro, gorgeous in a crimson suit
which had belonged to no less a person than the king,
and had been presented through Mr. Porter.   There was
dancing, racing, singing, wrestling, throwing the hammer,
and all such true old English sports as you may witness
in a Cornish Parish Revel to this day.

In Peacham's *Worth of a Penny* is a charming catalogue
of the country sports proper to the gentry.   ' Walking,
' riding upon pleasure, shooting, hunting, hawking, bowling,
' ringing, Paille-Maille, and the like ; but the truth is, the
' most pleasing of all is riding with a good horse and a
' good companion in the spring or summer season into
' the country when blossoms are on the trees, flowers in
' the fields, corn and fruit are ripe ; in autumn what
' sweet and goodly prospects shall you have on both sides
' of you uppon the way, delicate green fields, low meadows,
' divorces of christall streames, woody hills, parkes with
' deere, hedge-rows, orchards, fruit-trees, churches, villages,
' the houses of gentlemen and husbandmen, severall habits
' and faces, variety of country labour and exercises, and
' if you happen (as it often falleth out) to converse with
' country men of the place, you shall find them for the
' most part understanding enough to give you satisfaction,
' and sometimes the maids and market wenches will give
' you as unhappy answers as they be asked knavish and
' uncivill questions ; others there be who out of their
' natural simplicity will afford you matter of mirth if you
' stay to talk with them.   I remember once, riding by
' Horncastle nere to Stikeswold in Lincolnshire, in the
' heat of summer, I met a swineherd keeping his hogs
' upon a fallow field.   My friend (quoth I), you keep here
' a company of unruly cattell.   I, poore soules, they are
' indeed (quoth he).   I believe, said I, they have a language

' among themselves, and can understand one another as
' well as you or I : were they ever taught ?   Alas, poore
' things, they have not a letter of the booke, I teach them
' all I have.   Why, what says that great hog with red spots ?
' (quoth I) that lies under another, in his grunting language.
' Marry, he bids him to lie further off.'   With this lesson
in the pig's language our Compleat Gentleman goes on
his way, as well entertained with his swineherd as the
Compleat Angler with his handsome milkmaid.   And we
too must turn our backs on the fields and bend our steps
to ' that busy hive the city.'

CHAPTER II

TOWN LIFE

IF we may to a certain extent realise the beauty of the country as it must have been some three hundred years ago, it is well-nigh impossible to reconstruct in our mind's eye the London of our forefathers. Instead of a huge amorphous town, swallowing up in its ever-stretching advance suburb, village, hamlet, it was then a small, compact city with walls and gates lying upon the river with the adjacent city of Westminster, surrounded east, north, and north-west by the open country, separated by green fields and lanes with an occasional farm or country house from the neighbouring villages of Chelsea, Kensington, Paddington, or Finsbury, while even Holborn was described as 'near London.' The heights round about were crested with windmills and dotted here and there with a clustered hamlet between sloping woods : as to such outlying districts as Hampstead or Shepherd's Bush, they were divided from town by stretches of heath and moorland which were the haunt of highwaymen, and over which it was dangerous to ride alone after nightfall. Near the river, where the principal theatres stood, were gardens and groves of trees. Lincoln's Inn Fields, Covent Garden, and other open spaces in the immediate vicinity were just beginning to be built over ; new and handsome houses were rapidly springing up, and that neighbourhood was quite in the van of the march of fashion which was then, as for long after, westward. The Strand was, however, still quite a fashionable quarter, and on the south side were very good houses with large gardens running down to the river. In the year 1610 the population was estimated by the Venetian Ambassador, Marc Antonio Correr, as about 300,000 souls.[1]

In Milton's boyhood[2] the city was not merely the place of business to which men resorted by day, but the abode of merchants, shopkeepers, scriveners, and the like, while the poor for the most part lived herded together in close alleys behind the better streets, in such insanitary conditions that periodically the plague swept through the town, reducing the population to an alarming extent, and driving the fashionable world off in dismay to Oxford or Winchester. The Great Fire made almost a clean sweep of these wretched quarters, which were chiefly built of wood, and in burning out these nests of plague was probably a blessing in disguise, much as we must lament the destruction of many ancient city churches and fine old houses.

With all its drawbacks it must have been a beautiful city, this London of old, with its picturesque houses standing gable-end on to the street, with deep eaves and carved corbels, projecting upper stories, lattice windows, and a sign swinging over the door. For it was by the sign, not the shop-front, that people knew what manner of goods were to be found inside: shops were low and dark, with but little display in their narrow windows, and it was by the Golden Fleece, the Flowerpot, the Three Lutes, the Three Bibles, or some such device that customers could find the dealer in the commodity they needed, or by the cry of the 'prentice, 'What d'ye lack, gentles? What d'ye lack?' Of all these signs the barber's pole, the golden balls, and the Highlander alone survive. Not shops only, but all who exercised any public calling displayed signs; the father of Milton, who was a scrivener, lived at the sign of the Spread Eagle in Bread Street.

[1] Rye's *England as seen by Foreigners.*   [2] Masson's *Life of Milton.*

Bread Street, the birthplace of the great poet, was in the very centre of the city, running from Cheapside to the river, and was inhabited principally by well-to-do merchants, drapers, silk mercers, and the like, while gold-smiths chiefly congregated in Cheapside. At the corner of Watling Street stood the church of All Hallows, which was attended by the Milton family, and close by was the Mermaid tavern, where, not long before, Sir Walter Raleigh had started a kind of literary club. Old St. Paul's was still standing, and its broad middle aisle was the chief resort of business men—a kind of general meeting-place. Bishop Earle thus describes the gathering there : [1]—

'Men of all professions, merchants, gentry, courtiers, 'used to meet by 11, walk in the middle aisle till 12, and 'after dinner from 3 to 6. . . . The noise is like that of 'bees, a strange humming or buzz mixed of walking 'tongues and feet : it is a kind of still roar or loud 'whisper. It is the great exchange of all discourse, 'and no business whatsoever but is here stirring and 'a-foot . . . the general mint of all famous lies.'

On the pillars were posted advertisements of servants out of place or all manner of persons wanting employment. In *The Gul's Horn-booke* there is a reference to it : 'A 'horne-booke have I invented because I would have you 'well schooled : Powles is your Walk, but this your Guid.'

All round the Churchyard as well as in Paternoster Row swarmed the booksellers, and on the north side stood the famous covered pulpit of wood raised on stone steps from which every Sunday forenoon sermons were preached by some learned divine. On the east side was St. Paul's School.

The streets must have been quite as busy and as noisy as now, for though coaches were as yet far from common, drays, pack-horses, sumpter-mules, and porters jostled each other as they do to-day in the narrow streets

---

[1] Earle's *Microcosmography*.

of some Eastern town, and the street cries must have
been deafening in their number and variety.   They were
not unmelodious, however, for the musicians adopted a
good many of them as the basis of rounds and catches.
'Hassocks for your pew!' was a favourite, and was no
doubt often heard at the corner by the Puritan church
of All Hallows, varied by 'Sweet lavender!' and 'Cherry
'ripe!' in their season.

Hackney coaches, though to be had from the beginning
of the century, were only becoming a regular institution
in the reign of Charles I.   About the year 1634 a retired
sea-captain of the name of Bailey started the then novel
idea of placing them on stands for hire at important
centres of traffic ; previously they could only be hired
privately at the house of the owner.   In this year he
'erected, according to his ability, some four hackney
'coaches, put his men into livery, and appointed them to
'stand at the May-pole in the Strand, giving them in-
'structions at what rates to carry men into the several
'parts of the town, where all day long they may be had.'
This new departure was greatly appreciated, and soon
appeared so lucrative to the promoters that a patent was
applied for, and many gentlemen of position invested
money in the business, amongst others Sir Edmund
Verney.   Another project started about the same time
was one for 'carrying people up and down in closed
'chairs,' sedans as they were called later.   Formerly a
cloak and a slouch hat were the pedestrian's sole defence
against rain or shine ; now umbrellas occasionally made
their appearance in the streets, having been introduced by
travellers from China, where they were of very ancient use.

Not only pleasure but business brought many country
gentlemen up to town to listen to the talk on 'Change or
in Paul's Walk, for men of position were beginning to
dabble in trade, and company-promoting had made its
appearance.   New schemes for making money were almost
daily set on foot, and the granting of monopolies became

a very lucrative source of revenue to the Crown. Into the political bearing of this, important as it proved, it is no part of our business to enter, but the change it brought about in private life was enormous. To support the ever-increasing expense of fashionable life men needed to make money faster than they could by farming their estates or going to the wars as their fathers did before them, and the colonising or buccaneering expeditions, which the discovery of the New World had made an opening for, were no longer so lucrative as they had been in Elizabeth's reign.

The fashion now was to apply to the Patent Office for the sole right of carrying on some manufacture, and the capital one man could put into the concern being usually insufficient, a company was got up; as in former years trading companies were formed to fit out fleets for the East or West Indies. The glass-blowing factory in which James Howell was for some years employed belonged to two men of title, Sir Robert Mansell and Lord Pembroke, and there were but few peers who had not shares in some trading concern. The monopoly, of course, enabled the companies to force up prices to the detriment of the consumer, which, like the American Ring, became an intolerable grievance, especially in the case of such necessaries of life as salt. It occasionally happened that a monopoly was granted twice over, as with the soap about which such a pother was raised : King James had granted the right to a number of gentlemen who had formed themselves into a company, and his successor rashly granted another patent to a new company consisting chiefly of Catholic noblemen, which was, of course, an infringement of the former, and a cry of Jesuit intrigue was at once raised. The amusing part of it was, that the case being brought before the Council, two laundresses were summoned, and ordered to wash some linen in their presence with the rival soaps, that they might decide by results.

These business interests naturally caused men to congregate increasingly in London, and moreover the times were such that men longed to be near the heart of things ; then, no less than now, it was the capital, the centre, the place where things happened, where the news that travelled so slow was soonest known, where the pulse of life beat strongest.   No wonder that the good Devonshire parson, Herrick, London-born as he was, when he found himself there again after long absence, forgot for a moment his enamelled meads, his vaunted country peace, and cried in his enthusiasm—

> London my home is ; though by hard fate sent
> Into a long and irksome banishment !

Never were politics of a keener, more absorbing interest than during that half century ; never was news from town more breathlessly waited for ; yet it is not with the doings at Westminster, with the talk on the Exchange or in Paul's Walk, that we must concern ourselves, but rather with the plays, the masques, the pageants, the shows, the various arts with which men killed time.   These were many and suited to a wide variety of tastes, for London was a city of pleasure no less than a city of business ; indeed, business seems to have been considerably less encroaching as to hours than it is now, since plays, balls, and pageants took place in the afternoon by daylight. The long Court function given in honour of the Constable of Castile by James I. at Whitehall in the year 1604, and so amusingly described by his secretary or gentleman-in-waiting,[1] must have begun quite early in the day, as there was a succession of entertainments and the whole was over by supper-time—six o'clock at latest—and the distinguished guests were suffered to sup in private, worn out with amusement no doubt.   It began with a banquet, which was followed by a dance in the audience-chamber. The writer was much entertained by watching the dancing

---

[1] Rye's *England as seen by Foreigners.*

of the young Prince Henry, then quite a boy. The king
commanded him to dance a galliard with a certain lady
whom he pointed out, which the prince did 'with much
' sprightliness and modesty.' Then four couples danced a
brande, probably a square dance, a forerunner most likely
of the quadrille. The prince presently stood up in a
corrente in which the Earl of Southampton danced with
the queen. It may perhaps be remembered that it was
a corrente or coranto, a dance somewhat similar to the
polonaise, in which Venetia Stanley, afterwards Lady
Digby, so distinguished herself at a Court ball. A
custom which so greatly astonished a visitor from abroad
in the previous reign, of gentlemen being permitted to kiss
their partners, seems by this time to have been dying out.
Shakespeare has a passing reference to it in Henry VIII. :—

> Sweet, I were unmannerly
> To take you out and not to kiss you.

But the guest from Castile makes no reference to it, nor
to the custom of visitors being expected to kiss the ladies
of the house on being received or on taking leave.
Readers of Gibbon will recall the scandalised astonish-
ment of the Greek Chalcondyles at this on his visit to
England in the fifteenth century. It was probably
regarded as no more of a familiarity than a shake of the
hand in these days, for Englishwomen were at least as
correct in manners and morals as those of foreign
countries. At any rate, by the seventeenth century it
must have been entirely discontinued in fashionable circles,
though it probably survived much longer round the rustic
maypole, for Venetia Stanley was furiously indignant with
Kenelm Digby when he ventured to kiss her on meeting
again after long absence and estrangement. Anne Murray
also, when she permitted her lover, from whom she was
parting for good, to kiss her, expressly says, 'which
' was a libertye I never permitted before, nor should not
' then——.' So that clearly these ladies would not have
allowed it as part of the courtesies of the dance.

Dancing was certainly a far more modest, dignified, and graceful pastime than it has since become. Waltz, galop, polka were quite unknown ; and the dancing was of two sorts, the stately minuet, pavane, or coranto of the Court balls, varied with an occasional galliard danced to a more lively measure, or the merry country dance of the May games or Christmas festivities, with the jig or hornpipe. The country dance was either danced in two long lines, *contre-danse*, with various figures, up the middle and down again, each couple taking it up in rotation, or it was a round, in which the dancers stood in a circle, men and girls alternate, and all joined in some interlacing figure, sometimes with long ribbons, which were plaited and unplaited to the tune of Sellenger's Round.

But we have wandered a long way from King James's Court ball. Dancing being ended, the company took their places at the window of the room which looked out upon a square where a platform had been erected, and a vast crowd assembled to see the king's bears fight with greyhounds, which afforded great amusement. Presently, a bull tied to the end of a rope was fiercely baited by dogs. After this certain tumblers came, who danced upon a rope and performed various feats of agility and skill on horseback. With this the entertainment ended, and the distinguished guests departed to their private rooms for supper.

Besides the circus, which still holds its ground in popular favour, these rather savage amusements were greatly appreciated. Even Charles I., whose refined taste was proverbial, is represented in a curious old print, from a drawing said to be by Van Dyck, but of doubtful authenticity, seated in the royal cockpit, surrounded by his courtiers, watching a set-to between the birds. Taste in these matters has changed, yet, after all, from the sportsmanlike point of view, the matching of game-cocks does not compare unfavourably with pigeon-shooting at

From a sketch signed 'Vandyck, pinxit.'

THE ROYAL COCKPIT AT WHITEHALL.

PLATE III.

Hurlingham, or with a great battue of practically tame pheasants. With the ruder populace, bull and bear baiting were tremendously popular: there were bear gardens at Southwark, where dwelt the famous bear Sackerson, whose fame is alluded to in *The Merry Wives of Windsor*.

Active amusements were many. There were tent-pegging in the tilt-yard; the then fashionable game of paille-maille, now fallen into such oblivion that the very nature of it is forgotten; it seems to have been something of the description of hockey, and was played on the broadway leading from town to Hyde Park, in which the name survives in the form of Pall Mall; and lastly, the numerous bowl-alleys, of which Bishop Earle remarks: ' It is the school of wrangling, for men will cavil here for ' a hair's-breadth. It is the place where three things are ' thrown away besides bowls, to wit, time, money, and ' curses, and the last ten to one.' The mention of Hyde Park reminds us of the many pleasant gardens and open-air resorts with which the London of that day abounded. Hyde Park itself was then a wooded stretch of country some three or four miles beyond the town, which we may picture to ourselves as not unlike the wilder parts of the Bois de Boulogne, where the fashionable world loved to drive or ride in the spring mornings to take the air and hear the birds sing. We may remember Sir Kenelm Digby's meeting with his Venetia there after his long absence abroad. Pleasant walks abounded through green fields or lanes, with blossoming hedgerows, as in the neighbourhood of some small country town. The river was, of course, a very favourite resort, and was indeed one of the main arteries of traffic, which was the reason that most of the theatres were built on or near Bankside. One might then take a boat at the Tower stairs and row up past all the shady gardens of Westminster or Chelsea. A little later, indeed, people were beginning to complain bitterly that the river was getting spoilt. In his *Fumi-*

fugium, or protest against smoke, Mr. Evelyn laments
that 'the Wharfes and Magazines of wood and coales,
' &c., are taking up the noblest situations on the goodly
' River.' His pamphlet was designed to induce Charles II.
to legislate that wood should be burnt instead of coal, for
by that time London was already growing black and
grimy. But at the time of which I speak, though the
great waterway was thronged, there were no huge
steamers belching forth clouds of smoke and churning up
the water, no groves of tall chimneys with their over-
hanging clouds of soot blackening the sky ; but in the
clear sunshine sailing vessels went to and fro gaily, with
broad barges both for freight and pleasure, and innumerable wherries that plied for hire like the hansoms of
to-day. For water-parties, richly decorated and cushioned
barges, with awnings overhead, were to be had, and often
the king's barge appeared with gilded crown on the prow
and watermen clad in the royal liveries. One of these
royal barges, belonging to the latter part of the seventeenth century, was to be seen at Tims' Yard at Staines,
where it was refitting, during the Coronation summer.

Sometimes water-parties would carry professional
musicians for their entertainment, or one of the company
would bring his lute, and voices were uplifted in madrigal
or villanelle, for music on the water had not fallen into
disrepute. On an occasion when Sir Kenelm Digby and
his friend Nugent were 'entertaining themselves for their
' pleasure upon the river,' they met a boat in which were
Sir Kenelm's unacknowledged wife and her bosom friend,
who were 'listening to a song accompanied with excellent
' music that they had brought out with them, having
' allotted this pleasant and calm evening to their recreation
' in this kind'; and rowing up to them, Sir Kenelm
introduced Mr. Nugent, with the result that the latter
paid his court to Venetia's friend, no doubt greatly to
the contentment of the other pair, whose meetings were
restricted by the secrecy so foolishly maintained. One

would like to know whether these gallants rowed themselves, as their successors of to-day would have done, or
whether they employed a boatman.

There were many gardens close to the town where
the fashionable world used to congregate, as it did later
at Ranelagh or Vauxhall. There was the Paris Garden
at Southwark, where the bears were kept ; and Blackfriars,
which is satirically described by Henry Fitzgeffery in his
Notes from Blackfryars Spring Gardens, seems to have
been the one most patronised by people of position, and
ladies occasionally visited it, as Anne Murray mentions
having liked to go there 'before it grew something
'scandalous.'

But it was not always summer nor the season for
excursions on the river or rides in the Park, and for men
there was always the tavern, the ordinary, the barber's or
tobacconist's shops, where invariably gossip and sometimes
music was to be had ; and at the latter instruction was
given in the art of smoking, which was becoming extremely
popular. In the better class of tavern, clubs, sometimes
literary, were formed, as at the renowned Mermaid, where
wits, poets, dramatists, and actors forgathered. There
were others at the Mitre, the Falcon, the Apollo, or the
famous Boar's Head in Eastcheap, which Shakespeare
has immortalised in placing Falstaff there. The ordinary
was a somewhat meaner place of entertainment, and Mr.
Peacham, who loved to play mentor, both in his *Worth of
a Penny* and in his *Art of Living in London*, gives much
sage advice to the young man from the country as to his
behaviour there. Dice was much played, and he advises,
'Do not play with strangers ; do not borrow ; never
'venture more than a third of your money, and avoyd
'quarelling.' He recommends the newcomer to lodge
in a private house rather than in a tavern, where there
are so many temptations to excess, and also suggests,
'You shall not do amisse if you send for your diet to
'your own chamber ; an hot joint of meat of mutton,

' veale or the like, what you have, covered with a faire
' napkin, will serve you to breakfast the next morning or
' when you please.'   He warns his pupil against extrava-
gance in ' visits, cloathes in the fashion, this or that new
' Play, play at Ordinaries, Taverne-feastes and meetings,
' horse and coach hire to Kingston, Winsor and other
' places with the like——'   Also against the ' crafty
' Daughters of the Sun.'

In their seasons there were the great fairs,
Bartholomew Fair or Smithfield, which did not then, as
they did later, attract the lower orders only with their
plays and puppet shows, exhibitions of curiosities, dancing
horses, or performing dogs.   Punch and Judy began to
be seen in the streets, having been introduced in Naples
in the year 1600, and quickly becoming popular in
England.   Then the streets were often gay with processions, royal progresses to Westminster, weddings and
Guild processions, though the great Church functions of
Corpus Christi and the like had been done away in the
previous century.

A fair notion of the sights of London may be gleaned
from the same entertaining book from which the description of a Court ball was taken.[1]   The secretary of one
foreign visitor relates in his journal how he, with his
Excellency, ' passed through the suburb of Watterlambet,
' and went to see the tombs of the kings at Westminster.'
He makes no mention of the wax effigies, which is rather
singular.   On another day he went to Eltham Park to
see various curiosities : the Perpetual Motion, which was
the invention of one Cornelius Drebbel, a native of
Alkmaar, also virginals that played of themselves.
Eltham would seem to have been a kind of Polytechnic.
Another traveller about the same date does mention ' the
' wax-works at Westminster,' especially one of ' the late
' Prince of Wales ' (Prince Henry).   The same visitor
also gives a lengthy catalogue of the pictures at White-

[1] Rye's *England as seen by Foreigners.*

hall, St. James's, Somerset House, Theobald's, and Green-
wich. Both James I. and Charles I. were great connoisseurs and collectors of pictures. In one of the
galleries a sea chart is mentioned and a map of England,
drawn with the pen, showing the Wars of the Roses, and
the first English Bible printed for Henry VIII. There
were also magnificent tapestries both at Theobald's and
Hampton Court.

Many cheap sights for the common people are
enumerated by the indefatigable Mr. Peacham in his
Worth of a Penny. 'For a peny,' says he, 'you may see
' anie Monster, Jackanapes, or those roaring boys the
' Lions.' Or you may go to the top of St. Paul's, or see

The Fleete-Streete Mandrakes, that heavenly Motion of Eltham,
Westminster Monuments, and Guildhall huge Corinæus.
That horn of Winsor, (of an Unicorne very likely)
. . . . . .
Saint James his ginney hens, the cassowary moreover,
. . . . . .
Drake's ship at Deptford, King Richard's bedstead i' Leyster,

and many more such things.

This enumeration serves to show how very similar was
the taste in sights to that of our own day. The cheap
tripper was evidently not unknown, and liked much the
same things as he likes to-day. A very popular excursion was down the river to Deptford to see Drake's
ship *The Golden Hind*, which, after he had made his
voyage round the world in her, was by Queen Elizabeth's
command anchored there as a lasting memorial. A note
on this subject from Professor Elze's book on Shakespeare
is worth quoting entire :—

'Londoners frequently went in holiday parties to the
' ship, where the cabin served as a tavern, but, according to
' Peter Eisenberg, it was already almost wholly destroyed
' in 1614 (Rye, *England as seen by Foreigners*). In *East-*
' *ward Ho!* iii. 2 (*The Works of George Chapman :*
' *Plays*, ed. by Richard Herne Shepherd, p. 469), are the

' words : "We'll have our supper brought aboard Sir
' " Francis Drake's ship, that hath compassed the world ;
' " where, with full cups and banquets, we will do sacrifice
' " for a prosperous voyage "—hence a farewell banquet
' before starting on a voyage.'

Indoor games ought perhaps rather to have been
mentioned with country pastimes, for winter evenings in
the country were great times for chess, cards, forfeits, and
the like.   King James said of chess that it was 'an over-
' Philosophicalle Follie,' but his son was extremely fond
of it.   In one of the charming letters which Lewis Boyle,
in the field with the king at York, wrote to his father,
he says : 'The King when he is neither in the Field
' (where he constantly is every fair day), nor at the Council,
' passes most of his time at chess with the Marquis of
' Winchester.   Some three days since, the King long
' studying how to play a bishop, the Marquis of Win-
' chester blurted out, " See, Sir, how troublesome these
' bishops are in jest and earnestly."   The King replied
' nothing, but looked very grum.' [1]

Mr. Peacham's list of town games includes ' Chesse,
' Tables, Cards, Dice, Billiards, Gioco-d'oco or the like.'
Various card games were played ; gleek is frequently
mentioned ; in one of Endymion Porter's letters to his
wife he says, 'I have sent you a hundred sixpences for
' counters to play at gleek.'   Mrs. Townshend describes
this as a game of cards for three players, and says the
name is probably derived from the German word *Glück*
(luck), which was said when a player held four of a sort,
as in bezique.   Beggar-my-neighbour is a game of some
antiquity, and may have been played at this time.
People usually played for money ; during the Christmas
family reunions at Stalbridge or Lismore, the daughters
and daughters-in-law were continually appealing to the
old Earl of Cork to help them make up their losses.
Counters were often used ; silver boxes of counters be-

[1] *Mary Rich, Countess of Warwick*, by C. Fell Smith.

longing to Charles I. and his queen are still in existence.
Draughts were played from an earlier date, as a silver
draught-board belonging to Queen Mary Stuart was shown
at the Stuart Exhibition.

We can hardly leave the town without some mention
of the manners of the day, the urbanity for which the
city dwellers were supposed to be distinguished. From
the frequent mention of tavern brawls, quarrels, and duels,
we might perhaps infer that this urbanity was somewhat
mythical ; yet from the very fact that a man was swift to
draw his sword in defence of his honour, and was looked
on askance if he did not, we may draw the conclusion
that the general level of good manners was high. A
man thought twice before he said or did a rude thing
that might put his life in pawn, and the sense that it was
practically impossible for one with any sense of self-
respect to pocket an affront caused considerably fewer to
be offered than in more easy-going days.

The practice of this age in duelling stood midway
between the sudden onset which in the days of chivalry
followed instantaneously on the offence, and the
punctilious arrangement of a meeting with pistols which
belonged to the eighteenth century. Every one wore a
sword in those days as naturally as a cane later, and with
hot-blooded youth it was soon out of the scabbard, and a
quick affront might be quickly avenged ; but more often
a challenge was sent and a meeting appointed, generally
in the fields behind Montague House now covered by
Woburn Square, and while the principals were engaged
the seconds usually had a set-to of a milder character
between themselves. A very curious challenge is extant,
written by Lucius Cary in his young days to a young
man to whom had been given an appointment promised
to himself, by which he conceived himself affronted.
The matter coming to the king's ears, the challenger was
promptly put in the Fleet, and only released on his father
becoming surety for his good behaviour.

For Charles discouraged the practice for any but the most serious offences. The Spaniards, whose dignified manners commended themselves to his tastes, considered duelling vulgar, and put it down by the weight of a public opinion more potent than regulations. If the ruffling young gallants of the Inns of Court were too prone to pick a quarrel, and too ready to display their prowess with the sword, the manners of the Court and those who frequented it well deserved the epithet urbane.

CHAPTER III

THE PLAY

OF all the amusements which London offered so liberally to pleasure-seekers, none was more highly esteemed than the play, and no wonder when such a galaxy of talent, with Shakespeare in its midst, held the stage. For a half century past a wonderful development of the drama had been taking place, which found its culmination in the production of *Hamlet* at the Globe in 1602, the year before the death of Queen Elizabeth. Many things contributed to this ; the Reformation with its secularising of life, the Renaissance with its humanist conceptions as well as with the classical models it brought within reach, the widening of the horizon, the thrill of vivid self-conscious life, the individualism, if by individualism we mean personal initiative, which characterised ' the spacious ' times of great Elizabeth,' all helped on the movement ; life itself had grown dramatic, and it reflected itself upon the stage as, in our own more introspective days, it reflects itself in the novel.

The stage had always been popular, but for long it had been entirely in the service of religion. In days when few read, the best way of teaching Bible stories was by the presentation of mysteries and miracle plays, which were soon followed by moralities in which symbolical characters of virtues and vices were represented. These were at first acted by the priests themselves, but later by the children—that is, by the choirs or monastery

D

schools attached to the church. By degrees these plays passed into the hands of the guilds, who kept their companies of paid actors, and managed the entertainments for Corpus Christi and other great festivals, until the Reformation put down such observances. The dramatic spirit, however, was bound to find an outlet, and stories from history or adaptations from the classics begin to make their appearance. Translations from the plays of Seneca became very popular, but soon an independent school of English comedy arose, and opened with *Ralph Royster Doyster* by Nicholas Udall, an Eton master.

By Shakespeare's time Kyd, Lilly, Peele, Greene, and Marlowe had all written or were writing for the stage. Shakespeare's own work belongs, indeed, half to the sixteenth century, but it was in the opening of the seventeenth that it arrived at its completeness, and until the Civil War it held the stage in undisputed preeminence. Round about him stood a band of dramatic writers enough to shed glory on any other age; there were Beaumont and Fletcher, who shone in idyllic fancy, in graceful pastoral conceptions; there was Ben Jonson, Shakespeare's rival in learning and in industry; there were Webster and Tourneur, who were at their best in what Symonds has described as the Tragedy of Blood. Yet Shakespeare excels all these in the amazing breadth of his view of life, which includes tragedy and comedy, romance and farce; he can give us clown or lover, fool or philosopher, a Touchstone or an Imogen, a Jaques or a Romeo, a Falstaff or a Hamlet, each with the same unerring touch. No less does he excel in the genius which fires these creations with life; not only with 'the ' very form and body of the time,' but with the reality which holds its own through all change of time. Put upon the stage the *White Devil*, *Every Man in his Humour*, the *Tragedy of Edward III.*, or *The Faithful Shepherdess*, you will be interested, but you will feel that it is a revival; but Shakespeare is never revived, for while human nature is what it is his work cannot die.

Those must have been stirring days for play-goers. How much we wish that the dramatic critic had been in existence that we might read some account of the first night of *Hamlet*. That Shakespeare's work was very highly esteemed among his fellow-dramatists, we gather as much from the restless jealousy Ben Jonson from time to time betrayed as from the praise they continually lavish upon it. Laborious, painstaking, learned as Jonson was, and inordinately greedy of praise and ambitious of making his way with great men, it must have sometimes vexed his soul to see genius soar while talent painfully climbed. In the learning of the schools he knew himself Shakespeare's superior; the great dramatist had, said he, ' small Latin and less Greek,' and it annoyed him to see himself so easily passed in the school of life. It is always a trial to plodding industry to see genius sweep ahead, and the ease and fulness of the great poet's inspiration was a thing no pains could rival. So sometimes Jonson spoke sneeringly of the man who ' never ' blotted a line,' and inferred that his own work was to be taken more seriously ; but no doubt he spoke his true mind in the lines which he wrote when the poet's work was done and the rivalry quenched in death, ' To the memory of my beloved Master William Shakespeare, and what he hath left us.' There is a very genuine ring about

> Soul of the age!
> The applause, delight, the wonder of our stage!
> My Shakspeare, rise! I will not lodge thee by
> Chaucer or Spenser, or bid Beaumont lie
> A little farther off to make thee room :
> Thou art a monument without a tomb,
> And art alive still, while thy book doth live,
> And we have wits to read, and praise to give.
>
>   .   .   .   .   .
>
> Triumph, my Britain, thou hast one to show
> To whom all scenes of Europe homage owe.
> He was not of an age, but for all time!

Jonson's own attitude towards his rival we can very well understand from Drummond's description of him :—
' He is a great lover and praiser of himself, a contemner
' and scorner of others ; given rather to losse a friend than
' a jest ; jealous of every word and action of those about
' him (especiallie after drink, which is one of the elements
' in which he liveth) ; a dissembler of ill parts which
' raigne in him, a bragger of some good, that he wanteth ;
' thinketh nothing well but what either he himself or
' some of his friends or countrymen hath said or done ;
' he is passionately kynde or angry ; careless either to
' gaine or keep ; vindictive, but if he be well answered, at
' himself.   For any religion, as being versed in both.
' Interpreteth best sayings and deedes often to the worst.
' Oppressed with his fantasie, which hath ever mastered
' his reason, a generall disease in many Poets.   His
' inventions are smooth and easie, but above all he
' excelleth in a Translation.   When his play of a *Silent*
' *Woman* was first acted, there was found verses after on
' the stage against him, concluding that that play was
' well named the *Silent Woman*, there was never one man
' to say Plaudite to it.'
This rather uncharitable sketch sets before us the irritable self-centred man who carped at the supremacy which all the time his judgment endorsed.   Shakespeare does not seem to have resented if he were aware of Jonson's strictures ; his large-minded genial nature won him friendships among the dramatists, among his fellow-actors, and with his patron, the Earl of Southampton ; between whom and himself, even if the much-disputed identification of the sonnets is set aside, a very warm personal relation seems to have existed.   Good fellowship must have been wonderfully fostered by those meetings at the Mermaid, where both dramatists and actors resorted, and which have been immortalised by Beaumont in lines which, well known as they are, one cannot but quote in this place :—

> What things have we seen
> Done at the Mermaid! heard words that have been
> So nimble, and so full of subtle flame,
> As if that every one from whence they came
> Had meant to put his whole wit in a jest,
> And had resolved to live a fool the rest
> Of his dull life.

Of all that merry company those who live in written words alone survive effectively ; the actor's art is gone like the breath on a mirror—a list of names, and that is all.[1] There were the two Burbages, who came from Shakespeare's county and were large shareholders in the Globe Theatre. Of Richard Burbage we hear that he was great in the part of Richard III. Heminge and Condell must both have been friends of Shakespeare—indeed, the former is supposed to have come from Shottery near Stratford—and they joined in editing the First Folio after his death. Condell acted in several of Ben Jonson's plays, and represented the Cardinal in the *Duchess of Malfi*. Unluckily the record of the parts played by Shakespeare himself is very meagre and fragmentary. He is known to have played the Ghost in *Hamlet* ; there is also a tradition that he played King Henry IV., during which performance Queen Elizabeth, crossing the stage, dropped a glove, which he picked up and handed to her with the improvised line—

> And though now bent on this high embassy,
> Yet stoop we to take up our cousin's glove.

Whether this be true or no, it seems undoubted that he acted Adam in *As You Like It*, for his brother in extreme old age ' had a vague recollection of seeing his brother ' Will act a part in one of his own comedies, where he had ' to appear a decrepit old man, so unable to walk that he ' was forced to be supported and carried by another ' person to a table, at which he was seated among a ' company who were eating, and one of them sang a song.'

[1] *William Shakespeare*, by Karl Elze.

His name is mentioned among the actors who performed Ben Jonson's *Every Man in His Humour*, and it is thought that he took the part of old Knowell, as his portrait by Droeshout is supposed to represent him in that character. His name is prefixed to others of Jonson's plays, but unluckily the custom of that day was to give a list of the actors without specifying the parts taken by each ; indeed, since companies usually consisted of from eight to twelve men, it is obvious that the parts must have been doubled, and tradition has it that the Ghost, the First Player, and the Priest in *Hamlet* went together. Shakespeare would seem to have been a player of great versatility ; indeed, he who could create such varied characters may well have been able to present them on the stage.

There were in those days no independent companies ; actors were always attached to some princely household. The one to which Shakespeare belonged was the royal company, which was called the Lord Chamberlain's Servants, and acted at the Globe Theatre alternately with the Lord Admiral's Servants. These companies occasionally acted in the provinces, or even abroad ; on one occasion the Earl of Leicester's Servants went to Italy to act, and it has been imagined that Shakespeare may have been amongst them, as so many of his plays reflect Italian influences so vividly. English acting was very highly thought of, and travelling companies are frequently heard of giving performances in various cities on the Continent. On the occasion of a dramatic and musical performance at Stuttgart it was said :[1] 'England produces many ' excellent musicians, comedians, and tragedians, certain ' companies of whom are in the habit of visiting foreign ' countries at particular seasons, exhibiting and representing ' their art, principally at the Courts of Princes.' Foreign companies also seem to have appeared in London, as there is an old print representing a company of French actors performing before Charles I.

[1] *Equus Auratus;* Collins.

Great harmony and good fellowship must have prevailed amongst them, for there is no record of jealousy or ill-feeling, and in their wills they not only frequently bequeath small legacies, rings, swords, etc., to each other, but often appoint each other as executors and trustees. Their social position, which had been a somewhat anomalous one, was gradually improving. In former days they were legally classed with vagabonds, and Bishop Earle makes slighting mention of the profession. He is commenting with disapproval on the habit amongst the young lawyers of taking up actors and making friends of them—'Your Inns of ' Court men make of actors and acting their chief guest ' and employment. . . . He is masked still in the habit ' of a gentleman.' That actors resented this tone towards them is shown in a passage in *Bartholomew Fair*, where Leatherhead, the owner of a puppet show, is invited to a supper, and it is said : ' Marry, then, they must not set him ' at the lower ends ; if they do he'll go away, though he ' fast : but put him a-top of the table, where his place is, ' and he'll do you forty fine things.' If this could be said of the owner of puppets, how much more of those actors who were poets as well, and frequent guests at the houses of such men as the Earl of Southampton and Lord Falkland, Shakespeare and Jonson, Davenant and May ; these men associated with the first in the land and adorned their company.

Actresses as yet did not exist ; the female characters were always taken by boys or men slight and beardless enough to pass for women. Ladies of position, however, did not disdain to take part in the private theatricals which, in the form of masques, were so extremely popular. Milton's *Masque of Comus*, which was so charmingly set to music by Henry Lawes, was written purposely to be performed by the children of the Earl of Bridgewater, the composer being their music master, and the principal part was taken by Lady Alice Egerton, the eldest. The piece commemorated a little adventure which had befallen her of being lost in a wood. We do not, however, hear until after the Restoration of plays being performed at Court by the Ladies-in-Waiting. Mrs. Margaret Blagge, later Mrs. Godolphin, was induced, much against her will, to take part in one, which she did in a most serious and self-sacrificing spirit. But by that time actresses were appearing on the public stage.

King James was extremely fond of masques; he loved gorgeous scenery and dresses as well as music, and the masque gave scope for considerable scenic display, and in some respects answered both to the pantomime and to the musical comedietta of our own day. It also made less demand upon the actors, and was therefore suitable for the amateur performances which were so much in vogue. The gentlemen of the Inns of Court presented a masque before the king and queen on Candlemas Day 1633, under the direction of Noy the Attorney-General and Mr. Edward Hyde, who had not yet come to look so gravely on these frivolous pursuits as he afterwards did. No doubt an infinity of time and money was wasted over the business, for on this occasion the whole charge for scenery, costumes, etc., came to a thousand pounds.

Professor Elze supposes the children's companies to have been formed in the preceding century; but if so, it was the revival of an earlier custom, for the children of the choir schools had always been in the habit of acting in the mysteries and moralities. Interludes, though more old-fashioned than masques, were still in much favour, and were frequently performed by the gentlemen and children of the Chapel Royal. The Westminster School play was regularly given, having been instituted long before. Two old accounts for expenses incurred in the production have been recently unearthed, and are given in the *Athenæum* for 14th February 1903. The first is for the year 1564, the other for 1606; they contain some quaint entries such as the following :—' At ' the playing of Miles Glor: in Mr. Deanes howse for

'pinns halfe a thowsand vi*d*: Bestowed uppon three
'gentlewomen that did attyre the childrene iii*d*.—for
'suger candee for the childrene iii*d*:—for buttered beere
'for ye childrene being horse xii*d*.' In the other 'Hayres
'and Beards' and 'Fidlers Coates' are specified as well as
tenter-hooks either for scenery or curtains.

In the same number appears an interesting account of
a play by Arthur Wilson, lately come to light, called *The
Swissers*, which, according to an endorsement on the MS.,
was played at Blackfriars in 1631, though it was entered
in the Stationers' Register, together with another by the
same author, called *The Corporall*, in 1646, fifteen years
later. The writer of the article says : 'We learn from
'Anthony à Wood that Wilson's plays were acted at the
'Blackfriars in London by the King's Players, and in the
'act time at Oxford "with good applause, himself there
'"present." A few notes as to the character of the play
'will be of interest. The scene is laid in Lombardy ;
'the plot, though carefully worked out and varied with
'many incidents, is by no means elaborate. On the
'other hand, the characterisation is strongly marked and
'full of vitality, and the tone of the play, as a whole, is
'in distinct contrast to much of the dramatic writing of
'the time—it is moral, generous, and manly. The comic
'touches—for the play may be considered a tragi-comedy
'—are witty without being in any way coarse.' The
names of the original cast are given, and the writer
adds : 'It is of interest to note that of the names
'included in the cast, John Lowin, in the title-rôle,
'and Joseph Taylor are named in the list of principal
'actors prefixed to the First Folio of Shakespeare ;
'moreover, they took over the management of the
'King's Players after the retirement of Heminge and
'Condell about 1623.'

The two earliest theatres in London were the Theatre
and the Curtain. The former was pulled down in 1599,
and the material used in the erection of the famous Globe

in Bankside. Blackfriars Theatre was also in existence
by the beginning of the seventeenth century, as well as
Whitefriars, the Red Bull, the Fortune in Golden Lane,
the Newington Butts, and the Cockpit or Phœnix, while a
little later arose the Swan, the Rose, and the Hope, all
near the river, for convenience of being reached by wherry,
when cabs were not, and it was inconvenient to have a
horse, which must be held during the whole performance.
Most were built of wood, and only roofed over the stage,
the audience sitting in the open ; but the 'private'
theatres, of which Blackfriars was one, were roofed entirely
over, so that they could be used in winter, but performances, though always given in the afternoon, had to
be by candles or torches.[1]   'Outside, the Globe was
' hexagonal in shape, and, like all the theatres of that
' epoch, was open at the top, excepting the part immedi-
' ately over the stage, which was thatched with straw.
' The interior of the theatre was circular.   The per-
' formances took place by daylight, and while they were
' going on, a flag with the cross of St. George upon it
' was unfurled from the roof. Originally in place of
' scenery, the names of the localities supposed to be
' represented were inscribed on boards or hangings for the
' information of the audience. The sign of the theatre
' was the figure of Hercules supporting the globe, beneath
' which was written "Totus mundus agit Histrionem."
    ' In 1601 the Globe Theatre was used as a place of
' meeting by the conspirators engaged in Essex's rebellion,
' and next year Shakespeare's *Hamlet,* following upon
' other of his plays, was here produced for the first time.
' In subsequent years plays by Shakespeare, Webster,
' Ford, and contemporary dramatists were performed at
' the Globe, until in 1613 the theatre was burnt to the
' ground owing to some lighted paper, thrown from a
' piece of ordnance used in the performance, igniting the

[1] Prefatory note to Webster and Tourneur, Mermaid Series, edited by
J. A. Symonds.

THE GLOBE THEATRE.

On the   Bankside.

As it appeared in the reign of King James I.

The Globe Theatre was originally erected in the reign of Qu. Elizabeth, and was at first a rude, inartificial building, thatch'd with reeds. It is supposed to have acquired its name of the GLOBE, from its nearly circular form, or rather from its sign, which was Atlas, bearing a Globe on his shoulders. In the year 1603, King James I granted a patent to Shakespeare and others, (his associates) to play plays, as well within theire then usuall house, called the Globe, in the Countie of Surry, as elsewhere. Under whom it continued to flourish until the year 1613, when it was accidentally burnt, and the following year a more stately Theatre built on its site. Taylor, the Water poet, notices this event in the subsequent Epigram.

> *'As Gold is better that's in fire tried,*
> *So is the Bankside Globe, that late was burn'd,*
> *For where before it had a thatched hide,*
> *Now to a stately Theatre 'tis turn'd.*
> *Which is an emblem that great things are won,*
> *By those that dare through greatest danger run.'*

The above view represents the Globe previous to the conflagration above alluded to. The Rose, another Theatre in its immediate neighbourhood, is mentioned by the same poet (Taylor) in his 'True cause of the Watermans suit concerning Players' (1613).—And the site was, untill of late years, called "ROSE ALLEY."

London, Published Oct. 2d 1810, by Rob.t Wilkinson, N.o 58 Cornhill.

From an engraved view of London circa 1612.

THE GLOBE THEATRE.

PLATE IV.

' thatch. The theatre was rebuilt in the following spring
' with a tiled roof, and, according to Howe's MS., quoted
' by Collier in his life of Shakespeare, "at the great
' "charge of King James and many noblemen and others."
' Ben Jonson styled the new theatre "the glory of the
' "Bank and the fort of the whole parish."

'The Globe Theatre was pulled down in 1644 by Sir
' Matthew Brand, with the view to tenements being
' erected on its site, a portion of which is at the present
' day occupied by Barclay and Perkins's brewery.'

Inside, a balcony ran round three sides of the building,
which was reserved for the better portion of the public,
at prices ranging from sixpence to half-a-crown ; at some
theatres there were some seats as low as twopence, and
standing-room in the pit cost a penny. There were a
few covered boxes close to the stage, which were known as
Lords' rooms, but there were no stalls, all the arena was
occupied by the 'groundlings,' as those who stood in the
pit were called. There was a higher gallery for the
orchestra above the stage boxes. The stage was
separated from the audience by palings and a silk or
woollen curtain on a rod, which was drawn apart instead
of being raised. The stage was usually strewn with
rushes, but matting was used on special occasions. It
was hung round with tapestry, such as covered the walls
in all private houses of any pretension. It was of course
behind this arras that Polonius was lurking when Hamlet
ran him through the body. At the back of the stage
was a balcony some eight or ten feet above the floor.[1]
' It would be from this balcony that Christopher Sly in
' *The Taming of the Shrew* witnessed the play with the
' disguised page ; it would also have formed the Capitol
' on which Julius Cæsar was murdered ; it was there that,
' in *Richard III.*, the ghosts of the murdered persons
' would present themselves ; it was there that, in *King*
' *John*, the negotiating citizens of Angers would enter ;

[1] Elze's *Shakespeare*.

' and again, it was from this balcony—in the same drama
' —that Prince Arthur leaped down, whereas Romeo
' made use of it for climbing up to Juliet's chamber.
' Upon occasions when an inner balcony on the stage was
' not wanted in the play it was concealed by a traverse
' or curtain. There must also have been some such
' contrivance as trapdoors ; also trees, rocks, and other
' objects to effect a change of scene, and also some means
' for raising and lowering objects from above, but no
' moveable decorations, and the scenic apparatus was, in
' fact, so imperfect that the scene of the action had to be
' written up on a board, an arrangement which is even
' met with at the time of the Restoration.' We may
remember the apology in the mouth of the chorus in
Henry V., before the battle : ' Can this cockpit hold the
' vasty fields of France?' with its appeal to the imagination of the audience, which they, unjaded by marvellous
spectacular illusions, probably responded to far more
readily than we should do, as children who depend on
their own make-believe have a far more vivid fancy in
their games than those whose nurseries are filled with
mechanical toys.

But if scenery was lacking in gorgeousness, dress made
amends ; large sums were spent on costumes, and it was
quite a common thing for actors to purchase the cast-off
clothes of king or courtiers, and on one occasion it is said
that the coronation robes were actually lent for a performance. As much as sixteen or twenty pounds would
be given for a velvet mantle, whereas the author of the
play had to content himself with about four to six pounds.

The performance was announced by play-bills posted
in the principal thoroughfares. It took place always in
the afternoon, and in the open theatres by daylight. A
trumpet, sounded thrice, as is done to-day at Baireuth,
gave the signal that the play was about to begin, and a
flag was hoisted on the flagstaff which crested the stage
roof. In Queen Elizabeth's day it was the custom for all

the actors to cross the stage in costume before the piece
began, but it is doubtful whether this was still done in
the seventeenth century. The prologue was read by a
personage in long black velvet mantle and a laurel wreath,
supposed to represent the poet. There were frequently
intermezzos in which clowns played the fool and improvised after the manner of harlequin, clown, and pantaloon
in the traditional part of a pantomime. In one old play
is found the stage direction : ' Here the two talke and
' rayle what they list.' But Shakespeare preferred that
his clowns should keep to what he had written for them,
as Hamlet exhorts—' Let those that play your clowns
' speak no more than is set down for them.' Jigs also
were introduced, corresponding to the modern ballet, but
there were no girl dancers, so the jig was danced by the
clown, who accompanied himself with tabor and pipe.
There was always an orchestra consisting of violins,
hautboys, flutes, drums, horns, and trumpets ; lutes too
in all probability.

The play usually lasted from two to two and a half
hours ; the time being sometimes specified as 'two short
' hours.' By this it is evident that plays must have been
more mercilessly cut than even in our own day, for
Hamlet would take nearly twice as long to play *in
extenso*. In *Bartholomew Fair* Cokes asks : ' But do you
' play it according to the printed book ? ' and Leatherhead
replies : ' By no means, sir.' Cokes : ' No ! How then ? '
Leatherhead : ' A better way, sir ; that is too learned and
' poetical for our audience.' The public of that day,
however, had a very keen relish for tragedy, especially
for tragedy of the ' blood and thunder ' order. The plays
of Webster and Tourneur are steeped in gloom and
abound in murders, suicides, and hideous blood-curdling
crimes, and though the interest of Shakespeare's stories
is so much wider, saner, and more full of beauty and
pathos, he so far yielded to the popular taste as to sweep
off his characters at the end in batches of corpses. It

is considered doubtful whether the curtain was drawn between the acts, as it is invariably provided that the bodies were carried off by the other actors, but at the conclusion they could be left lying there for the spectators to gloat over.

In 1610 Hans Jacob Wurmser, who came to England in the suite of Ludwig Friedrich, Duke of Wurtemburg, witnessed *The Moor of Venice* at the Globe, and the next year Dr. Simon Forman reports the performance of *The Winter's Tale*, *Richard II.*, *Macbeth*, and *Cymbeline*. On the marriage of Princess Elizabeth in 1613 to the Prince Palatine several plays were given at Whitehall: *Much Ado About Nothing*, *The Tempest*, *The Winter's Tale*, *The Moor of Venice*, and *Cæsar's Tragedy*. Sir John Falstaff is also mentioned; this was probably *The Merry Wives of Windsor*.

The audience was composed of various classes, much as in the present day. There were, of course, a certain number of the looser sort of characters who always haunt any place of public entertainment, and the 'groundlings' may have indulged in rough jokes, as well as in drinking beer, eating fruit, and playing cards between the acts, but we must beware of taking the strictures of the Puritans on the subject without allowance. The reserved seats would be occupied by the respectable middle class, merchants and so forth, as well as by people of fashion. There was a good deal of smoking and drinking among the young men of rank who were accommodated with seats upon the stage, but at any rate there were no actresses for them to flirt with. That ladies of refined taste appreciated the theatre we learn from many a casual mention. The elder Lady Falkland was exceedingly fond of the play, both in her early married life, and later when she was living in London with her second son Lorenzo. So, too, was Anne Murray; and it may be remembered that in a passage from her memoir, quoted in the earlier volume, she mentions that she was the first to attempt being independent of a man's escort, going with her sister and girl friends under the charge of the footman, and paying for themselves, so as to spare the purses of their friends. Lady Mary Boyle, in her early and frivolous days, delighted in going to the play with her young sister-in-law, as she subsequently deplored ; but we may be very sure that those giddy young women did not dispense with an escort ; Mary, when she was in disgrace with her father, was always hard up, and was probably quite willing that Charles Rich or young Mr. Howard should put his hand in his pocket for her.

The attack of the Puritans on all forms of amusements was especially bitter as regarded the theatre ; they not only brought against it the stock charges of its leading to immorality, but maintained that fiction and poetry were lies, and therefore to be utterly condemned ; they used no discrimination between what was high and noble and what was base ; but if for a time they succeeded in closing the theatres, the Restoration reopened them with a license formerly unknown. During the first half of the century theatres were always closed during Lent, and a very strict censorship was exercised over any kind of profanity. If certain subjects were treated with an out- spokenness which to a more refined age seems coarse, there was a tone of nobler and higher morality in the plays of Shakespeare and his contemporaries than the stage has seen since. Taste in the latter half of the century compares very unfavourably with that before the Puritan régime, and even Shakespeare himself went for a time quite out of fashion. Pepys records in his Diary that he finds *The Moor of Venice* 'a mighty poor Play,' after seeing *The Adventures of Five Hours*.

It is difficult to avoid the conclusion that the Puritans did more harm than good by their attack on all theatrical representations. While respecting the conscientious protest of men who took life very seriously and would fain see all men think as they did themselves, we must certainly admit that, as with Sunday observance, the stage lost more than it gained. The reaction that set in at the Restoration brought in a more unbridled license than had been known before ; as to-day the revolt against the Puritan Sabbath has brought about the widespread neglect of public worship.   Under Elizabeth, James I., and Charles I., the stage, though, like all human institutions, mingled of good and bad, had elements of high thought, of noble poetry, of inspiring examples, and on the whole it made for righteousness.

CHAPTER IV

MUSIC

MUSIC at the time of which I write was so universally taught, practised, and beloved, that it is quite startling to read in Sir Hubert Parry's new volume of *The Oxford History of Music* that 'The seventeenth century is ' musically almost a blank, even to those who take more ' than the average interest in the Art; and barely a score ' of composers' names during the whole time suggest ' anything more than a mere reputation to modern ears.' Turning to Chappell's *Old English Music*, we find a picture the very reverse of this, all classes of the community taking in music their chiefest recreation and delight. Art might be the pleasure of the rich, playhouses and gaming-tables the resource of the idle, but music was for all; it heightened pleasure and made labour light; the weaver sang at his loom, the blacksmith at his forge; the milkmaids carolled rounds and catches, the girls chanted ballads to the hum of the wheel; the travelling tinker and the chapman carried new tunes from village to village; a cobbler was actually counted an impostor because 'he could neither sing, sound the ' trumpet, play the flute, nor reckon up his tools in ' rhyme.' Godfrey Colton, a tailor of Cambridge, was better remembered for his skill with pipe and tabor and singing of northern songs than for the fashionable suits he cut. As to the barber, whose shop was always full of loiterers, waiting to be served their turn, or dropping in to hear the news of the day, his place of business was invariably furnished with lute, cittern, viol, or virginals, that customers might have wherewith to pass the time. The barber, moreover, was the dentist of those days, and truly it must have been much more raising to the spirits to make music while waiting for the tortures he would inflict than to turn over piles of stale illustrated papers.

And all this is fully borne out by the continual mention in letters and journals of lute, guitar, or virginals, of madrigal, catch, or villanelle, of music for dancing or music at meals. This last was a very old custom, and though by this time falling a little out of fashion, we still read of it in great households, such as that of the Earl of Cork, who kept his own harpers and his blind fiddler at Lismore Castle. The wandering minstrel is with us always, but those were palmy days for him ; instead of the organ-grinder, haunting the streets and picking up an uncertain penny, usually given rather to buy him off as a nuisance than for any pleasure in his tunes, the tramping fiddler roamed from fair to fair or from farm to township, sure of his welcome, which generally included bed and board, and found himself in great request for Wakes, May-games, or Whitsun-ales. Sometimes the rover would be a singer who chanted long ballads of adventure to the accompaniment of his lute or bandore ; or he might be a blind fiddler with a vielle, a small fiddle played upon with a rosined wheel instead of a bow ; or perhaps a harper such as the one mentioned in Carew's *Survey of Cornwall in 1604.* Speaking of Tregarrick, at that time the residence of the sheriff, the writer says, ' It was some ' time the Wideslades' inheritance, until the father's rebellion ' forfeited it, and the son then led a walking life with his ' harp, to gentlemen's houses, wherethrough, and by his ' other active qualities, he was entitled Sir Tristram.'

The explanation of this conflicting testimony probably is that the two musical historians are looking at the subject from two totally different points of view—the one in its wider aspect, as it affects ordinary folk ; the other with the eye of the professional musician who, seeing none of the highly developed forms, the symphony, the opera, the oratorio, the intellectual richness, the elaborate orchestration which the enormous advance of the eighteenth century was to bring, hastily writes down a blank. Sir Hubert, however, admits that there was considerable musical activity. It was a time of change and transition, and he notes that the foundations of modern art were being laid. In Italy, especially in Venice, opera was making its first tentative steps, but England until the Restoration was barely touched by the new movement.

There was nevertheless movement of a sort, and signs of change setting in. The Reformation had, of course, deeply affected Church music, substituting anthems of a more tuneful character, and metrical Psalms by Sternhold and Hopkins set to rhythmical melodies, for the old plain-song with its concomitant fugue. Everywhere was 'a tendency towards unsophisticated tunefulness, ' simplicity of harmonisation, and definiteness of rhythm,' which, of course, rendered the new madrigals or songs for solo voices with easy accompaniments more popular with the general public. This increasing love of rhythm was largely due to the spread of dance measures to which words were often set, so that they could be either sung or danced, or both at once.

In those days music was considered quite as integral a part of education as reading and writing, instead of being an 'optional subject.' We have seen what value Mr. Peacham set upon it in his training for 'a Compleat ' Gentleman'; but it was not only for persons of quality that it was held essential—every one learned to sing as a matter of course, and it was reckoned among the qualifications expected in servants, either men or maids. Tusser, writing at an earlier day, recommends the 'huswife' to choose by preference such as are musical—

Such servants are oftenest painful and good
That sing in their labour as birds in the wood.

Sir Ralph Verney certainly acted on this principle when
he selected a maid-servant in his wife's absence, for her
skill in lute-playing, 'though she was raw to serve and
' had the itch.'[1]

In all descriptions of the education of young gentlewomen the mention of lute, guitar, or virginals invariably
appears, and we may remember the musical training of
little Mistress Apsley, who was 'tabled,' that is, boarded
in the house of her music master at Richmond, that she
might pursue her study of the lute in her mother's absence
from home, and who there attracted the kindly notice of
her future brother-in-law, Colonel Hutchinson, who himself
had 'great mastery on the viol.'[2]

Singing was, of course, almost universal, and the
musical training of pupils was not considered complete
until they could read prick-song, that is, written music at
first sight, so as to be able to take their part in madrigals
or catches.   There is an interesting passage on this in
Morley's *Introduction to Practical Musick*, a book which,
no doubt, was in general use during the reign of James I.,
though it was published in the previous century.   The
book was written in dialogue form, as was very usual
with educational works, and the pupil is made to express
himself as follows :—

' But supper being ended and musicke bookes according
' to custom being brought to the table, the mistress of the
' house presented me with a part, earnestly requesting
' me to sing, but when after many excuses I protested
' unfeignedly that I could not, every one began to wonder ;
' yea, some whispered to others demanding how I was
' brought up, so that upon shame of my ignorance I go
' now to seeke out mine old friend Master Gnorimus, to
' make my self his scholar.'

[1] *Home Life under the Stuarts ;* same author.   [2] *Ibid.*

Music books were many, especially Tutors. Another, written in the same quaint dialogue form, in which the speakers were a knight who had children to be taught, and a fictitious master named Timotheus, was brought out in 1603 by Thomas Robinson, and was entitled, *The School of Musicke, the perfect method of true fingering of the Lute, Pandora, Opharion, and Viol da Gamba.* After the dialogue comes an eulogium, the tablature or method of notation, succeeded by a collection of easy lessons for the lute, rules for singing, and a few Psalms set in tablature for the viol da gamba.

Less was written for the guitar; the professional musician looked down upon it somewhat as being too easy to learn, and it lent itself rather to slight improvised accompaniments for singing than to elaborate harmonies, but its facility recommended it to the amateur. Mention of Mary Lady Verney's guitar is frequent in the *Verney Letters;* it was a very good one, we learn, bought in Paris, ' the most beautiful that could be found, for it was of ' ebony enlayed with mother pearle.' The gracefulness of its shape made it a favourite with women; it was much less awkward to hold than the lute, which was formed like the section of a gourd or pear. The guitar, however, lacked the richness and fulness of tone which the deep body of the lute could give. This last held the field up to the rise of the violin, and a box of lute strings was considered a most desirable present for Valentine's Day or the New Year. The cittern was another solo instrument much played; it was like the guitar, but had four double strings of wire tuned to G, B, D, C, on the treble staff. The method of tuning was to draw the treble string as high as it would go, and tune the others from that; pitch was not regarded unless for playing concerted music. New ' Citherne Lessons ' were brought out by Robinson in 1609, and new lute books were continually appearing.

The music master was a person of great consequence. Henry Lawes, who set the *Masque of Comus* to music,

was music master to Lady Alice Egerton, daughter of the
Earl of Bridgewater, the same young lady whose adventure
in the wood was the occasion of the Masque being written.
He was apostrophised by Milton in a sonnet as—

> Harry, whose tuneful and well-measured song
> First taught our English music how to span
> Words with just note and accent.

He was (to quote from Sir Hubert Parry) 'a child of the
new music,' and not well versed in counterpoint; his
anthems show a tendency towards secularisation, and are
full of tuneful and melodious solos with choruses in the
newer taste.   There is an interesting account of him and
of his brother William in Fuller's *Worthies*.   They were
the sons of a vicar choral of Salisbury, and showing great
talent, were placed by the Earl of Hertford with Coperario,
an Italian, says Fuller, and a most exquisite musician.
An Italian he was not, however, but an Englishman bred
in Italy who had Italianised his name of Cooper according
to a custom which is still followed.   William, of whom
Fuller says, ' the Scholar did equal, yea exceed his Master,
' was made one of the Private Musick to King Charles, and
' was respected and beloved by all such Persons as cast any
' looks toward Vertue and Honour.   Besides his Fancies
' of the 3, 4, 5, and 6 parts to Vyol and Organ, he made
' above 30 several sorts of Musick for Voyces and Instru-
' ments, neither was there any Instrument then in use, but
' he composed to it so aptly as if he had only studied that.'
His master Coperario (to give him the name of his
choice) had a royal pupil in King Charles while Prince of
Wales, whom he taught to play excellently on the viol da
gamba—an instrument similar to, but smaller than the
violoncello.   Charles was an enthusiast of music as well as
a discriminating patron of musicians, and in later, sadder
days found solace in the playing of his chief lutenist,
John Wilson, who faithfully followed his master, and on
whose shoulder the king would lean while he played his
favourite airs.

The days before the war were rich in sacred music, for though the Reformation had banished much of the old, Puritanism had not yet laid its destroying hand on organs and music books, and Charles, a devoted lover both of the Church and of music, delighted to use the one to serve and adorn the other. He always liked to choose the anthem and services for his private chapel himself, and he had a rich and abundant store to choose from. At his accession Orlando Gibbons, who was accounted, says Anthony Wood, one of the rarest musicians of his time, was organist of the Chapel Royal, to which he had been appointed in 1604. He attended the marriage of King Charles at Canterbury, having composed special music for the occasion, and while there was seized with smallpox, of which he died. He left behind him much valuable work. Many of his compositions figure in the ' Noble collection ' of church music,' as Hawkins in his *History of Music* calls it, which was issued in 1641 by John Barnard, minor canon of St. Paul's, entitled, *First Book of Selected Church Music, consisting of Services and Anthems, such as are now used in Cathedrals and Collegiate Churches of this Kingdom, never before printed. London, printed by Edward Griffen, and are to be sold at the signe of the Three Lutes in Paul's Alley. 1641.* The book contains Matins and Evensong, Communion Office, Preces and Responses, the Litany by Tallis, and Motets and Anthems in four, five, and six parts by several composers, among whom were Tallis, Byrd, Gibbons, Hooper, Farrant, Will Munday, Tye, Morley, Bull, etc. It was dedicated to the king. Within a few years it was followed by another with the title, *Musica Deo Sacra et Ecclesiae Anglicanae,* by Thomas Tomkins. The *Cantica Sacraria* and *Gradualia* by Byrd were accounted particularly fine; ' they abound with fugues ' of the finest contexture, and such descant as entitle them ' to the character of angelical and divine.' [1]

This was the last of such publications for many a long

[1] *History of Music;* Hawkins.

year. In 1644 the Puritans, by that time in power, forbade the use of the Book of Common Prayer in the churches, and all instrumental music, as being both Jewish and Popish. Organs were taken down, in many cases broken up and totally destroyed, music books were burnt, whereby many unpublished treasures existing only in manuscript were entirely lost to posterity ; and the injury done to music by the complete break of the traditions of the old English style of contrapuntal writing is beyond all estimation. Instead of the dignified and restrained beauty of anthem or motet, it was ordained that nothing should be sung but metrical versions of the Psalms, and that after a manner hopelessly destructive of all musical effect, as the preacher was to read out the verse, line by line, the congregation following.

Sir Hubert Parry thanks the Puritans for doing service to the cause of music in the home by banishing it from the churches ; but long before their influence became paramount, both part-singing and chamber music had become extremely fashionable, while the more popular amusements of rounds sung and danced, catches, and ballads hardly found much favour in their sight.

The vocal music in fashion was very rich and varied, and compares well with that of our own day. The principal varieties were the madrigal, the canon, the catch or roundelay, all for several voices. The canzone or canzonet was written sometimes for one voice, sometimes for three ; it was less elaborate than the foregoing, and more in the nature of a modern drawing-room song. The villanelle was the lightest kind of air, suitable for singing with a thrumming accompaniment on the guitar or bandore ; just the airy trifle with which a lover might amuse his mistress over her needle or sitting in an arbor. Then there was the ballet, a tune to a ditty or ballad that might likewise be danced to. Airs for dancing often had words to them, especially those for the country dance or *contre-danse*, or the round. This latter must not be

confused with the roundelay or catch, although either
might be sung. The round, such as ' Sellenger's,' a very
popular favourite, or ' The Beginning of the World,' would
be danced and sung together round the maypole with
interlacing figures, while the *contre-danse* was better suited
for a hall or long room, with its two long lines of dancers,
men and girls facing each other. These rounds are often
mentioned in old plays or rhymes ; ' an old hop-about
called ' " Sellenger's Round "' is referred to by Heywood,
Ben Jonson, Taylor, the water-poet, and a host of others.
' The Beginning of the World ' is to be found in Lady
Neville's lute book with several other old dancing tunes.
These tunes were always written in $\frac{6}{8}$ time.

While madrigals were most in favour among the
cultivated, the canon was popular with the common
people. Drinking songs and catches called freemen's
songs were printed in black-letter and sold on stalls in
the streets or hawked about by wandering chapmen.
One of these collections, *Robin Hood's Garland*, seems to
have been a universal favourite.

A more refined album of vocal music was *England's
Helicon*, a volume of songs by Sidney, Spenser, Drayton,
Bolton, Greene, Lodge, and others, set to music by some
of the ablest masters of the day, chiefly in the form of
madrigals. This was dedicated to Lady Elizabeth Carey.
There were at that time three of the name living, two of
whom were likely to have that kind of compliment paid
them ; Mr. Bullen, in his recent edition, gives it in favour
of the wife of Sir Henry Cary or Carey, afterwards Lord
Falkland, on the ground of a reference to her authorship
of the tragedy of *Mariam the fair Queen of Jewry*. It
may well be so, for she, like her eldest son Lucius, Lord
Falkland, was eminent in her taste for poetry and music,
and a constant patron of poets, though her own verses,
like most of his, were not of first-rate quality.

Another very popular music book was *Pammelia,
Musicke's Miscelanie or mixed varietie of pleasant Rounde-*

*laies and delightful Catches of 3, 4, 5, 6, 7, 8, 9, or 10
parts in one. None so ordinarie as musical, none so
musical as not to all verie pleasing and acceptable. London,
printed by William Barley for R. B. and H. W., and are
to be sold at the Spread Eagle at the great North doors of
Paule's. Quarto. Reprinted in 1618.* This was full of
humorous catches and vulgar songs, several of them
made on the street cries, some of which were very musical,
as ' New oysters,' ' Have you any wood to cleave ? ' ' Sweet
' lavender,' ' Buy a broom,' or ' Cherry ripe.'

In the same year appeared *Deuteromelia*, containing
three-part songs more in ballad form, each verse to the
same tune. One of these was—

> Wee be souldiers three,
> Pardonnez moi je vous en prie ;
> Lately come forth of the Low Countree,
> With never a penny of money.

This with its scrap of French suggests the cosmo-
politanism of the men who through the long reign of
Elizabeth were continually to and fro, fighting the battles
of the Protestants in the Netherlands.

Lute books and albums of songs abound. How much
one would like to know which were those left by Endymion
Porter on the cupboard shelf together with ' Cousin Meutys
' his papers.' Chappell's *History of Old English Music*
contains a fine collection of songs with accompaniments
for the lute or viol da gamba taken from private MS.
books, Lady Neville's lute book, Dorothy Weld's lute
book, and many another. Thomas Morley's *First Booke
of Ayres or Little Short Songs*, to sing and play to the lute
with the bass-viol, is a charming collection. Amongst
others, it contains ' It was a lover and his lasse,' with many
an old favourite, which so lately as the middle of the last
century were still heard and appreciated, though now
fallen into undeserved neglect. Towards the end of the
reign of James I. the madrigal went a little out of favour
in the fashionable world, owing to the increasing popularity

THEORBO, LUTE, AND DULCIMER.

PLATE V.

of the masque with music ; but in the country it still held
its own till Puritan strictness on the one side, sorrow and
misfortune on the other, silenced the singers, and all the
daughters of music were brought low.

Instrumental music was by no means behind in quality,
though it had not yet developed into what we now have,
and great orchestras as well as pianos of wide compass
and powerful tone were quite unknown. The variety of
instruments in common use at the time are quaintly set
forth by Michael Drayton in his extraordinary poetic
survey of England, called the *Polyolbion.* He thus
enumerates them :—

> All quickly at the hint as with one free consent
> Struck up at once, and sung each to th' instrument,
> (Of sundrie sorts that were, as the musician likes)
> On which the practised hand with perfect fing'ring strikes ;
> Whereby their height of skill might likeliest be exprest.
> The trembling lute some touch, some strain the violl best
> In setts which there were seene, the musick wondrous choice ;
> Some likewise there affect the gamba with the voice,
> To shew that England could varietie afforde.
> Some that delight to touch the sterner wyerie chord,
> The Cithron, the Pandore, and the Theorbo strike ;
> The Gittern and the Kit the wandering fidlers like.
> So there were some again in this their learned strife,
> Loud instruments that loved, the Cornet and the Phife,
> The Hoboy, Sagbut deepe, Recorder, and the Flute ;
> Even from the shrillest Shawm, unto the Cornemute.
> Some blow the Bagpipe up that plaie the country round,
> The Tabor and the Pipe some take delight to sound.

This sounds like a pandemonium, but it was the
ferment out of which the two lines of orchestral and
chamber music were presently to be evolved, for this
period saw the rise of the violin and the constitution of
the string band, the root of all orchestral music. It will
be necessary before we trace this, that we examine a little
the nature of the instruments in use at the beginning of
the century, and how they were developed, and for this
the most valuable authority is Martin Mersenne or

Mersennus, a French monk who studied at the Sorbonne, and was a friend of Descartes. He was described as ' scholar, philosopher, mathematician, musician,' a combination which enabled him to write on the nature of music and musical instruments with an insight beyond that of the merely practical performer. In 1638 he published his *Harmonie Universelle,* a collection of treatises, *On the Nature of Sound, On Stringed Instruments, On Percussion Instruments, On Organs, On Composition,* and *On Various Kinds of Music.* Twelve years later the same work was brought out in Latin. The treatise on stringed instruments is especially useful as showing those in general use in his day, and how the lute, theorbo, and cithern, the whole class played by hand, were gradually superseded for concerted playing by those played with the bow, the violin, viola, and viol da gamba, though the others still retained their place as solo instruments or accompaniments for the voice until ousted by the piano, which was developed from the clavicymbalum, virginals, or spinet.

The theorbo was a kind of lute with two necks, or rather with a bent neck and two sets of strings ; it was an instrument of deeper tone than the lute proper, and its part would answer to that of viol da gamba or 'cello. The lute itself, with its pear-shaped belly and long neck, has been already described, and the pandora or bandore was of similar character with a slightly differing shape. The cithern or guitar is mentioned with some contempt as well enough for the amusement of idlers in barbers' shops, but too poor in tone and easy of execution to be worth the study of the serious musician. These instruments, being played by the fingers, were none of them capable of giving a sustained note such as the long-drawn bow could bring out from the viol tribe.

With the growth of the century came the gradual slow perfecting of the violin and its congeners, the viol dividing into violin and viola, the viol da gamba and bass-viol developing into violoncello and double-bass. While the

Cremona workshops were by repeated experiments bringing
the violin to its highest perfection, Germany was already
in the field, and the most popular instruments of the kind
in England were those by Jacob Stainer of Innspruck,
one of which is described in *John Inglesant*, bearing the
inscription, 'Jacobus Stainer in Absam prope Œnipontem
' 1647.'

These four instruments formed the basis of the four-
part string bands of the day, and with six performers to
each part, were the 'four-and-twenty fiddlers all in a row'
which constituted the famed string band of the Grand
Monarque, and were so much admired by his nephew
Charles II. that on the Restoration he organised a similar
band in his own Court. 'Whoever,' says Mersenne, 'hears
' the twenty-four fiducinists of the King, with six barbitons
' to each part, namely, the viol da gamba, viola, contra-
' tenor and treble violin, perform all kinds of Cantilenes
' and tunes for dancing, must readily confess that there
' can be nothing sweeter and pleasanter.' The violone, as
the Italians called the double-bass, is not here mentioned,
but the bass parts of Corelli's Sonatas, printed at Bologna
towards the end of the century, were written for it, though
in the later edition printed at Amsterdam they were given
to the 'cello. There was also a small kind of violin called
the lesser barbiton, the precursor of the 'kit,' which was
used by dancing-masters as it could be carried in the
pocket in a sheath.

Although this band seems to have contained neither
wind nor percussion instruments, several were already in
use, which in another treatise Mersenne enumerates. Of
wood-wind there were Pan's pipes or syringa, a row of
little pipes of graduated lengths. Then there were flute,
flageolet, and fistula, tibia Helvetica or fife, hautboy, and
bassoon. Of brass or silver there were the horn-shaped
cornet, the much-twisted serpent, the hunting-horn, 'that
' noble instrument the trumpet,' the tuba tractilis or sack-
but. Amongst drums he mentions a curious novelty sent

him by Cardinal Barberini's secretary from Rome, made of half an Indian fruit, of the melon kind, scooped out and covered with a serpent's skin ; to this was affixed a handle made of an Indian reed about twice the length of the body.

Of the constitution of ' the King's Music ' under James I. and Charles I. it is difficult to speak precisely. Full lists of the performers are given in Hawkins's *History of Music*, but, except in the case of first or second lutenist, the instruments played by each are not specified. We know that both viol and viol da gamba were played, and the part taken by the lute in the full orchestra would probably answer to that of first and second violin. The Master of the King's Music, Nicholas Laniere, received a salary of £200, the band receiving from £20 to £40 each.

Chamber music was in great favour, and there are frequent references to it in Wood's *Athenæ Oxonienses*. He describes how he and his friends used to ' meet for ' practice at the house of Will Ellis, Bachelor of Music, ' who played the organ or virginal.' Wilson, the king's favourite lutenist, was often there, and in speaking of the compositions of Rogers for instrumental music in three or four parts, Wood observes that Dr. Wilson, ' the greatest ' and most curious judge of music that ever was, usually ' wept when he heard them well performed, as being ' wrapt up in an extacy or, if you will, melted down, ' while others smiled or had their hands and eyes lifted up ' at the excellency of them.' Jenkins is also praised as another composer of chamber music who did much to introduce the violin. At these practices Ellis himself usually conducted, but if Edward Low came, would leave the baton to him and would take up counter-tenor or viol. Thomas Jackson played the bass-viol.

Wood was a great connoisseur ; he makes an interesting comparison of the playing of David Mell, a very eminent violinist, and Thomas Battorzan, who had been at one time Bandmaster to King Charles. The latter, says Wood, was quicker at stopping, but he found more sympathetic

IACOBO GOVTERO INTER REGIOS MAGNÆ BRITANNIÆ ORPHEOS ET AMPHIONES
LYDIÆ DORIÆ PHRYGIÆ TESTVDINIS FIDICINI ET MODVLATORVM PRINCIPI
HANC E PENICILLI SVI TABVLA IN ÆS TRANSSCRIPTAM EFFIGIEM IOANNES LÆVINI
FIDÆ AMICITIÆ MONIMENTVM L. M. CONSECRAVIT.

Ioannis Livius fecit et excudit.

From an etching by Livens—British Museum.

JAMES GAULTIER, OF THE KING'S MUSIC.

PLATE VI.

quality in the playing of Mell. One would much like to know whether the king took any part in chamber concerts, or only played his viol da gamba as a solo instrument. It was used sometimes as an accompaniment for the voice, and was occasionally played by women. Mary Ruthven, who became the wife of Vandyck, is represented holding one in her portrait; but it was thought by some 'an ' unmannerly instrument for a woman.'

The study of the theory of music had hitherto received but scant attention. 'Before the publication of Morley's ' *Introduction,* the precepts of musical composition were ' known to few, existing only in MS. treatises, which, ' being looked upon as inestimable curiosities, were trans- ' mitted from hand to hand with great caution and diffi- ' dence ; so that for the most part the general precepts ' of music and that kind of oral instruction which was ' communicated in schools belonging to cathedral churches ' and other seminaries of music, were the only foundation ' for a course of musical study.' [1] Morley's work was followed by Ravenscroft ; but the greatest impetus given to the study was by the foundation, towards the end of James's reign, of a Music Lecture in the University of Oxford by Dr. William Heyther. He was an intimate friend of the famous Camden, who, having a few years before his death determined to found a History Lecture, sent his friend Heyther with the deed of endowment to the Vice-Chancellor, Dr. Piers. He and Mr. Orlando Gibbons, wishing to take degrees in music, were suffered to accumulate both degrees, and having been made bachelors, were both created musical doctors the next day. There was an ancient professorship of music in Oxford founded by King Alfred, but the chair had not been filled by practical musicians till 1626, when it was new consti- tuted, and certain monies to be employed in paying a music reader who should lecture on the theory once every term at least.

[1] Hawkins's *History of Music.*

Musical discussions seem to have been the fashion of the day, and a public debate was proposed between Heyther and Dr. Nathaniel Giles:—'First: Whether discords may be 'allowed in music?—affirm.   Second: Whether any arti-'ficial instrument can so fully and truly express music as 'the natural voice?—negat.   Thirdly: Whether practice be 'the more useful part of music or theory?—affirm.'

Just before the close of the preceding century, Sir Thomas Gresham's College had been established in the city, and in it provision was made for the teaching of music.   John Bull, the favourite organist of Queen Elizabeth in her latter days, and reputed composer of 'God save 'the Queen,' was appointed first professor of music.   The passage from the constitutions relating to music ran thus: —'The solemn music lecture is to be read in the manner 'following; that is to say, the theoretic part for one half-'hour or thereabout, and the practical part, by the help of 'voices or instrument, for the hour.'   The requirement that all lectures should be in Latin was waived in the case of Bull, who was no scholar.   He was succeeded in his professorship by Byrd.

The musicians were, almost to a man, loyal, though one, John Hingston, of the King's Music, was tempted by the offer of a hundred a year to become organist to the Protector and instructor of his daughters.   He used to give concerts at his own house, which were attended by Cromwell himself and his family.   For though the Puritans showed themselves such enemies to church music and also to music at merry-makings, many of them were assiduous in the private practice of it—Milton, Bulstrode White-locke, and Colonel Hutchinson were all notable lovers of the lute.   But the two Lawes, the Gibbon family, Wilson the lutenist, and many another preferred following the fallen fortunes of the king to the loaves and fishes which awaited turncoats.

Edward Gibbon, brother of the more famous Orlando, who was organist of Salisbury at the outbreak of the war, assisted the king with a thousand pounds, for which he afterwards paid dearly when the town fell into the hands of the Parliament; for they thrust him out of his house with his three grandchildren, being then above eighty years of age, and he died in extreme penury. Another brother was Christopher, the distinguished organist of Winchester Cathedral. He threw up his appointment in 1644, being succeeded by John Silver, that he might join the Royalist forces. Whether he lost his life or met so sad a fate as his brother we do not learn.

Both the Lawes brothers were entirely devoted not only to the royal cause but to the person of the king. Of William, Fuller says, 'He ingaged in the war, and by his 'venturesomeness was shot at the siege of Chester where 'Lord Bernard Stuart lost his life. . . . Nor was the 'King's soul so ingross'd with grief for the death of so 'near a kinsman and so noble a lord but that hearing of 'the death of his dear servant William Lawes he ordered 'a particular mourning for him when dead, whom he had 'loved when living, and commonly called the Father of 'Musicke.' His brother Henry, in spite of his early association with Milton, was no less loyal; indeed betwixt the two brothers—to quote again from Fuller—'was no 'difference, either in eminency, affection, or otherwise.'

F

CHAPTER V

ART

IF on the Continent the high tide of painting was in the seventeenth century already beginning to recede, in England the enthusiasm for art was at its highest. The refined and kingly tastes of Charles I. included a great love for pictures and a high idea of the duty of royal patronage of painters and right royal collections of art treasures. His predecessor, if he had a less discriminating taste, was fond of encouraging painters, and treated Rubens with distinguished honour, presenting him with a magnificent diamond hat-band. This, however, may have been an attention intended rather for the ambassador than for the painter, for Rubens, as many did in his day, combined politics and painting, and represented the Court of Spain in this country.

In the anxious days which preceded the outbreak of the war, Charles was believed to make use of the pretext of picture-buying to send his emissaries abroad on more delicate diplomatic negotiations. This idea probably arose from the fact that two of his most faithful servants, his Gentleman of the Bedchamber, Mr. Endymion Porter, and Mr. Nicholas Laniere, Master of the King's Music, were both great connoisseurs; indeed, Mr. Laniere was himself also a painter, and they frequently went abroad to secure some treasure that the king desired for his collection. Neither were in the least given to dabbling in politics: Mr. Porter's correspondence betrays no trace of any diplomatic confidences, in fact his attitude towards politics was, for such a time, amazingly detached ; and Laniere, though he might possibly have conveyed letters, never took any part in public affairs ; his name survives as musician, painter, picture-buyer ; in history he has left no record. However, when in 1628 Porter was abroad buying pictures for the king, the suspicions of the popular party became very acute. He was always more or less a *persona suspecta* with them, being the friend and protégé of the great Duke of Buckingham, whose kinswoman he had married.

The Duke shared to the full his royal master's taste for art, and when in 1632 Rubens came again as ambassador to London he was entertained in the house of Gerbier, who was attached to the Duke's household as Painter-in-Ordinary. It was on this occasion that Rubens undertook to decorate the new banqueting-hall at Whitehall for the sum of £3000. This payment was sent through Porter, and by him transmitted to two Catholic merchants named Wake, his agents at Brussels. Rubens was treated with most distinguished honour, knighted, and loaded with magnificent gifts. A little later, Gerbier was made English Resident at Brussels, and when in 1634 Mr. Porter was sent on a mission thither, he stayed in his house and made acquaintance with his 'large family of handsome sons and daughters.' But it is Rubens' great pupil Van Dyck whose name is most closely associated with the Court and Charles, and it must have been on an earlier visit that Porter made his acquaintance and purchased his 'Rinaldo and Armida' for the king, as by 1632 he was settled in England and had been made Painter in Ordinary to his Majesty.

The three great rival collections of pictures — the king's, the Duke of Buckingham's, and the Earl of Arundel's—were growing apace. In 1627 Laniere had succeeded in securing for the royal galleries the whole collection of the Duke of Mantua, which included twelve

Emperors by Titian, the 'Mercury instructing Cupid' by Correggio, now in the National Gallery, a Madonna by Raphael, and paintings by Michael Angelo, Andrea del Sarto, and Tintoret—a treasure well worth the £15,000 which it cost, though one can understand Parliament looking askance on such an outlay at a time when money was so scarce, and imagining some deep-laid scheme to lurk beneath.

It was not only pictures which excited the zeal of collectors; every day fresh treasures of Greek art were being unearthed in Italy or in the islands of the Archipelago, and the agents of the Earl of Arundel were ever on the watch ready to pounce upon them and carry them off before they should be absorbed into the overflowing galleries of the Roman cardinals. Mr. Petty, his principal agent, was busy searching for precious marbles among the Greek Islands, but on one occasion Sir Peter Wych was too quick for him, and secured two statues which 'Mr. Petty desired infinitely,' and shipped them off from Scio for his Majesty's collection, announcing at the same time that he had nineteen more on their way from Smyrna, 'some of them very rare peeces.'

Mr. Evelyn was also a collector in a smaller way, and something of a connoisseur. When in Holland he was much struck by the cheapness of Dutch pictures, and made large purchases, 'chiefly Landskips and Drolleries, ' as they call these clownish representations.' They were on sale at the annual mart or fair at Rotterdam, and it was said to be usual for farmers to lay out quite large sums in them as a good investment, land being scarce.

To the enlightened appreciation of such men for the precious things of antiquity England owes, not only the possession of a vast amount of art treasures, but also the fashion which was set in high places of caring for these things. There may have been ostentation, especially among those who followed the fashion for novelty's sake and because it was the thing to do, rather than because they shared the whole-souled enthusiasm of Arundel, but it resulted in the enriching of the great houses all over the country with treasures which not even the widespread destruction of the war wholly scattered or destroyed.

This collecting craze was, however, a thing for the great ones of the land alone to indulge in. It needed a long purse, and was beyond the reach of the average well-to-do Englishman ; but for him there was the special fashion of the age—his own or his wife's portrait by the king's prime favourite, Van Dyck. Portrait-painting had already become popular in the preceding reign. Van Somers had left many stiff records of the worthies of his time, which have the air of being staringly like, and in which every detail of the dress, still Elizabethan in fashion, is painstakingly given. His portrait of Lady Tanfield in her stiff stomacher, thickly plaited ruff, and rouged cheeks, gives a vivid idea of that redoubtable lady. William Dobson, too, was highly thought of by King James, and dubbed the English Tintoret. Janssen was another portrait-painter who was much esteemed, and his picture of Lettice Lady Falkland, might almost be taken for a Van Dyck. The fame of the English painter, Robert Walker, stands deservedly high, but he for some reason seems to have been more popular among the Parliament men than with the Royalists. However, the loyal John Evelyn sat to him, as he records under date July 1, 1648 : —' I sat for my picture in which there is a Death's head, ' to Mr. Walker that excellent painter.'

But it was reserved for Van Dyck to portray for us a whole generation in their habit as they lived ; to give us their grace, their dignity, their beauty, their plainness, the seemly fashion of their clothes, almost their very souls. Hardly any one since Titian has ever seen so deeply into the character of his sitters, so caught for us the aroma of their life, as has Vandyck. It was no wonder that the whole fashionable world flocked to ' the ' Beauty Shop' at Eltham to be immortalised.

His gift is the more striking as, unlike the great portrait-painters of the Venetian school, when he strayed from his especial line and essayed subject-pictures he became at once cold, mannered, and artificial, partaking of the decadence which so quickly followed on the renaissance in Continental art. This is more particularly noticeable in his sacred subjects : his Crucifixions, Entombments, Pietas, are conventional and entirely devoid of religious feeling. His mythological subjects, too, are as artificial as eighteenth-century pastorals, but when we stand before such a canvas as his Lord Wharton, from the Hermitage in St. Petersburg, we feel that the subject lives and breathes before us. And this is not only the case when he had a handsome sitter ; such a portrait as that of Lucius, Lord Falkland, with keen, eager glance, plain-featured face, yet beautiful countenance, exercises the same sort of charm as the man himself, short in stature, with his rough hair and harsh-toned, eager voice, always did upon his contemporaries. It may be easy to make the beholder admire the 'lovely sweet-turned face' of a Venetia Digby or the three beautiful children who lean on the Duchess of Buckingham's knees ; but when we are made to feel the charm of one who had only the inward beauty of mind and character, then we know the painter for a true revealer of men.

Certainly he was not a flatterer; he painted Lady Sussex for her friend Sir Ralph Verney, and she is very amusing about the result. She was to be painted in a ' blew gowne with pearl buttones,' and it was to be a full length. When at length it arrives, she remarks,[1] 'The ' pictuer is very ill-favourede, makes mee quite out of ' love with myselfe, the face is so bige and so fate that it ' pleses mee not att all. It lookes lyke on of the windes ' poffinge—but truely i thinke it tis lyke the original.' For this she was to pay fifty pounds, a copy to cost eight pounds. Perhaps it was the copy that was for Sir Ralph.

[1] *Letters of the Verney Family.*

There was an immense difficulty in arranging for the transit of this precious package from London down to Claydon. 'The cole wagon,' she writes, 'will be in 'London this weke, but I doubt he cannot cary the 'pictuer and the glase (a Venice glass which she had 'bought for forty pounds). If he cannot I thinke that 'may be sent safe by the wagen of sentarbones (St. 'Albans). I am very glad if a coppell of porters would 'undertake to bring it done carefully for any reasonable 'matter, suer that is the saffest way. But if the will not 'I will send a hors for it with paniers.' It arrived eventually with the frame 'a littell hurt, the gilt beinge 'robbede off.'

Of course not every portrait signed by Van Dyck was entirely from his own hand; with so prolific a painter inevitably there was a good deal of studio work turned out, bearing the impress of his style, very likely in a measure his work, but in the main executed by pupils. Notably is this the case with the immense number of replicas of the portraits of the king, which after his murder would be produced and reproduced by pupils trained under Van Dyck, and were eagerly bought by the Royalists and treasured in their families with almost the honour paid to a saint. In one old Devonshire family (and doubtless in many another) the children, now middle-aged, can remember when they were little being lifted up to kiss the king's hand on every 30th of January. But the revered portrait in its wooden solemnity bears little resemblance to the graceful vivid work of the great master.

It is not a little singular that the fascinating painter, lover of many women, whose studio became known as the Beauty Shop, should have been so much more successful as a painter of men than of women. Beautiful and charming as many of his female portraits are, there is a certain shallowness of treatment in them all; not one is worthy to stand beside his Lord Wharton, the two matchless Straffords, his Sir John Suckling or the two Stuart brothers, Lords John and Bernard. Perhaps because he loved widely rather than wisely, so a true insight into feminine nature was never granted him. With children, however, he was incomparable. His well-known pictures of the royal children, so solemn and dignified, his little Miss Campion with her horn-book, his family groups of Porter children or Villiers children, are one and all delicious revelations of baby nature showing through the stiff and antique fashions of the day.

In spite of the peccadilloes of the painter, and the king's usually rigorous attitude in such matters, the latter loved the wayward artist well, and often visited him in his home at Blackfriars. In the long conversations carried on during his sittings, Charles endeavoured to lead him from the error of his ways, and induce him to settle down and make a prudent marriage. The match between him and Mary Ruthven was of the king's making, it was said, and she looks in her portraits such a charming creature that very likely she would have reformed him, but his married life was sadly brief; he paid for a fast life by an early death, and so dying escaped the ruin which soon involved his royal master and all who followed him.

As the musician Laniere dabbled in painting, so the painter practised music, and his wife's musical tastes may have been a bond between them, for she played the viol da gamba, and they may very probably have met not only at Court functions, but at the house of Mr. Porter in the Strand, where musical parties were frequent. One of Van Dyck's most successful portraits of himself is the one at Madrid where he has painted himself and Endymion Porter together. It is hard to connect the stories of his dissolute life with a face so refined; possibly gossip, especially rampant about those in any way connected with the Court, may have exaggerated youthful wild oats.

PRINCE RUPERT.

(*Ascribed to Samuel Cooper.*)

J. THURLOE, SECRETARY OF STATE.

(*After Samuel Cooper.*)

SIR SAMUEL MORLAND.

(*Isaac Oliver.*)

South Kensington Museum.

PLATE VII.

Miniature-painting was also in great favour, although the exquisite art of painting on ivory was not yet introduced. The method in vogue was *gouache*, that is body-colour on fine vellum.[1] John Hoskins was one of the earliest of these painters in little, but his two pupils, Alexander and Samuel Cooper, are more celebrated than he was, especially Samuel, who was as much in fashion among the Roundheads as Van Dyck among the Cavaliers. Whether they thought it less frivolous to be painted in miniature than life-size, or whether they preferred the economy of the thing, it would be difficult to say. One of the finest of Samuel Cooper's works is his small portrait of the Protector, plain, resolute-looking, with a good deal of rugged force in both brow and jaw. Another of John Lilburne is very interesting as a study of character. It is a fine face, but with the look of a visionary, a fanatic, an impossible man as his contemporaries found him. Excellent ones of Fairfax and Sir John Maynard show the miniaturist at his best; Colonel Duckett is coarse-looking, with a fierce expression; Thurloe looks keen and harsh. The Earl of Southampton and Thomas May, the latter with a delicate boyish face, show that the painter could deal with gentler characteristics; but, on the whole, a collection of Cooper's miniatures gives a sense of ruggedness out of harmony with a style suited for delicacy and refinement, and there seems a lack of finer qualities in both painter and sitters, which seems to make miniature-painting less suited to the subjects than rougher larger canvases would have been.

Samuel Cooper had one fair sitter in the person of Dorothy Osborne, for in one of her letters she mentions she had been sitting to him for her miniature. Although herself belonging to an ultra-royalist family, she was on friendly terms with the Cromwells, who may have introduced the painter to her notice. She frequently

[1] *Samuel Cooper, Miniaturist*, by Lumsden Propert, Connoisseur, Oct. 1901.

mentions the Protector's second son Henry ; indeed he
was among the many aspirants to her hand, and when he
was in Ireland sent over for her acceptance two beautiful
Irish greyhounds, she being a great lover of dogs. Her
portrait by Sir Peter Lely, which must of course have
been painted later, gives the impression of a pleasant-
looking rather than a beautiful woman ; perhaps the
miniature, done when she was younger, may have been
more flattering, but it is not reproduced in the delightful
volume of her correspondence to which such frequent
reference has been made.

But it was not only as sitters nor as connoisseurs that
the people of the day concerned themselves with art.
They were just beginning to dabble in it as amateurs,
and drawing, especially the drawing of flowers, began to
be recommended as a part of education. Mr. Peacham
not only advises it as a suitable occupation for a ' compleat
' gentleman' upon a wet day, but he devotes an entire
volume to the *Art of Drawing and Limning in Water-
colour.* This little treatise is really most interesting as
one of the earliest hand-books extant. It was published
in 1606 ' For the behoofe of all young Gentlemen or any
' els that are desirous for to become practitioners in
' this excellent and most ingenious art.'

It begins with an address to the reader in which is
set forth the position of drawing in the curriculum.
Mr. Peacham places it third. First, Grammar ; second,
Gymnastic; third, Writing and Drawing; fourth, 'Musique.'
He then goes into a long dissertation upon the history
and antiquity of the art, after which he reaches more
practical matters, and the reasons why he would recommend it.

' I would have my scholler take it when he is wearied
' at his books, forced to keepe home by reason of foule
' weather, or solicited by idlenesse to some worse busi-
' nesse ; having chosen such a convenient time, let him
' make or buy him a fayre paper booke for the nonce, to

' begin to practice in, and keep very carefully that he
' hath done, by which he shall see how he profiteth
' daily.' He is very urgent that his pupil shall 'avoyd
' scribbling in loose papers, and keep his hand from wall
' and wainscot.'

The instruments necessary are ' black lead sharpened
' finelie and put fast into quills, some ten or twelve for
' your first rough draught. Sallow coales sharpened at
' the end, they are more blew and finelie grained than
' other coles; smooth like latten. Sharpen them upon
' one of your fingers.' These 'sallow coales' are the same
as the *fusain* used by French artists, which makes such
soft grey shadows. He continues, 'A small pair of
' brazen compasses and a Brasil rule for taking the
' distance if you follow a print. Broome pencils sharpened
' with the teeth. Thirty or forty goosequill pens.'

Thus equipped you were to practise for a week
' circles, squares, a cylinder, ovalls, other solids and plain
' geometrical figures, till you can do them indifferent well.
' After you are cunning in these figures . . . a cherry
' with a leaf, the shaft of a steeple, or a rose.' With the
third stage the pupil reached the human face in three
positions; 'full face, as you may see King Henry 8
' drawne, 3 quarter face, as our Flanders or ordinary
' pictures are, or onelie half-faced, as the pictures of
' Philip and Mary upon a twelvepence.' After briefly
explaining the rules of proportion, he continues with the
whole figure, shading, and foreshortening.

Next we come to 'Landskip,' which is rather briefly
disposed of, and finally to birds and beasts, heraldic or
otherwise. The remainder of the book is devoted to very
full directions as to the choice and preparing of colours, a
serious business, as the painter had it all to do for himself;
there were no ready-prepared tubes or pans of moist
colour to be had in those days. The materials had all to
be bought at a druggist's, and if we want to know what
the druggist's shop of those days was like, we may see

just such an one in a bazaar in the East, with great piles
of yellow ochre, scarlet vermilion, or lovely cerulean
cobalt lying ready to be weighed out, and these having
been carried home in separate packets must be ground
fine, rubbed smooth, mixed with a medium, and then blent
in whatever proportions were needed.   The directions how
to do this and the enumeration of the various colours to
be obtained are well worth more study than can be
afforded them in this brief chapter.   Altogether, limning
in water-colour involved so much labour, it was likely to
keep its votary out of mischief, as Mr. Peacham foresaw,
for many a wet day ; and as if all this were not enough
an extra treatise is appended, dealing with 'the true
' manner of Painting upon Glasse, the order of making
' your Furnaces, Annealing, etc.'

It does not appear whether this accomplishment was
part of the usual course at girls' schools ; but most
women must have had some knowledge of drawing and
colouring to have been able to design such wonderful
pictures in needlework as they produced.   The more
elaborate compositions could not possibly have grown up
under the needle ; they must have been either drawn
beforehand upon the canvas or copied from a painted
pattern.   Mrs. Evelyn and her daughters were excellent
artists, but she had had a foreign education, and we do
not read much of women as painters.   However, whatever
was taught to boys at this time was usually taught to
girls too, so probably they were not behindhand with the
pencil.   But whether or no the practice of it was as widespread as it is to-day, the sense of beauty, the instinctive
feeling for form and colour, must have been almost
universal ; we see it in all that they have left behind—in
furniture, in needlework, in dress, in the commonest
utensils of daily living, as well as in the ordered loveliness
of their gardens and the solid dignity of the homes they
dwelt in.

CHAPTER VI

SCIENCE AND SUPERSTITION

To treat seriously of the science of the first half of the seventeenth century would be a bold undertaking ; this is not the place for it, nor am I the person to attempt the task : what I have in view is rather a slight sketch of the science of the day as it appeared, I will not say to the man in the street, but to the ordinary cultivated man or woman as they met with it in everyday life. The science of the philosopher in his study, of the chemist in his laboratory, of the astronomer in his observatory, must be sought elsewhere ; here is no place for it.

I have called this chapter Science and Superstition, because it appears that the distinguishing mark of the time was that it was a meeting-ground between the two : the acceptance of facts because they were traditional, the dogmatic teachings of the schoolmen were yielding before the advance of experimental knowledge, of the trained observation of men of the newer light. It was not very long since men of science had arrived at the conclusion that the world was round instead of flat, as had been hitherto supposed, and, acting on the inference that if so ships could sail round it, explorers trying to discover the North-West Passage had found the New World. Thither some three generations of Englishmen had been flocking, bringing back with them wonderfully enlarged notions of many things. Still more recently had the whole conception of the universe been turned upside down by the new theories of Galileo, whereby the system of Copernicus had been established upon a sound basis, and the ancient idea of sun, moon, and stars existing round and for the sake of the earth been finally shelved.

The new ideas were so new, so startling, that it is not wonderful that those to whom was committed the guardianship of religion shrank dismayed, and imagined that faith must be imperilled if such subversive doctrines were allowed to be taught. Truth, however, could not be stamped out; the teachings of Galileo steadily gained ground, and were established as the century wore on, and presently it was found, as in our own day it has been found by some who were terrified at the discovery of evolution, that it was not faith which was destroyed, but human conceptions of the universe. The parallel is wonderfully close; only in our own more tolerant days no measures of persecution were taken against the discoverer.

Galileo, however, did not have such hard measure dealt him as we are apt to fancy. When Sir Kenelm Digby visited Florence, then in the zenith of its glory under Cosmo II., brother of the Queen Dowager of France, he found the great astronomer living and working there quite undisturbed, though six years earlier he had been summoned to Rome, and his theories formally condemned. At this time he was engaged on his *Dialogues on the Ptolemaic and Copernican Systems of the World*, and no doubt he found great pleasure in discussing his novel theories with a man of so much intelligence and culture. Twelve years later he was again brought before the Inquisition and condemned to a quasi-imprisonment, but it could have been scarcely a hardship, for he wrote, 'I have as a prison the delightful ' palace of the Trinita di Monti,' and of his second jailer he speaks as 'my best friend the Archbishop of Siena at ' whose house I have always enjoyed the most delightful ' tranquillity.' His third and last prison was his own

TERTIVS
A PLATONE
PHILOSOPHIÆ
PRINCEPS

QVOD FELICITER VORTAT REIP: LITERARIÆ.
V.C. FRAN: DE VERVLAMIO PHILOSOPH: LIBERTATIS
ASSERTOR AVDAX, SCIENTIARV REPARATOR FELIX

From a print in the British Museum.

BACON IN HIS STUDY.

PLATE VIII.

villa near Florence.   When he made his formal submission with the reservation ' e pur si muove,' he was no
doubt well aware that though he might consent to keep
silence, his ideas were already in the air ; truth had
germinated in many minds and was bound to come to
the surface.

Minds were stirring, new ground was being broken up
every day, new views were gaining acceptance, and no
authority could stamp them out.   Every one was talking
of the *Laws* of the German astronomer Kepler, which he
had partly founded on the discoveries of the Dane Tycho
Brahe.   In England the labours of Bacon—who had
something else to do than write Shakespeare's plays—
had completely reconstructed the whole body of natural
science.   His *Novum Organum*, in which he ' took all
' knowledge for his province,' was laying deep in men's
minds a conception of the universe founded solidly on
observation and experiment, on laws deduced from
knowledge, instead of on groups of facts forced into
conformity with unproven dogma, and on the lines thus
laid down has arisen the complete structure of Natural
Philosophy as the modern world knows it.

Sir Kenelm Digby stands well for the type of man
between the scientist and the layman ; over-rated in his
own day, under-rated probably since, he did no little to
popularise the great discoveries of others.   It has been
asserted that he ' gave form and birth to many of Bacon's
' mighty conceptions,' but this would claim too much for
him ; he may have talked of them, written of them,
brought them down within the ken of the average man,
but great discoveries were not for his fly-away brains ; he
was an intelligent dabbler, keenly interested in scientific
discovery, and quick to follow new trains of thought.
Certainly in his person science and superstition met as
they did in his age.   We find him at one moment discoursing with Galileo of the motions of the heavenly bodies
or of the grand theories of Lord Bacon ; at another he is

entering in his precious book of recipes the secret of the Sympathetic Salve, which he had from a Carmelite monk who came from the Indies and Persia, and having refused to divulge it to the Grand Duke of Florence, imparted to Sir Kenelm in gratitude for some service rendered.[1]   The recipe exists in the Ashmole MS., and is entitled :—

'TO MAKE A SALVE YT HEALETH THOUGH A MAN 'BE THIRTY MILES OFF.

'Take mosse of a ded man's hed 2 onc., man's greace
' 1 onc., mummia, man's blood of each half an onc.,
' linseed oyle 22 onc., oyle of roses, bolearminick of each
' an onc., bet them together in a mortar till it be fine
' leeke an oyntment, keep it in a box ; and when any
' occasion is to use it, take the weapon wherewith a man
' is wounded, or for want thereof take another iron or
' peace of wood and put it in the wound, and so far as it
' is bloody anoynt it with that salfe.'

The recipe for the famous Venice Treacle which Sir Ralph Verney bought when he was in Italy and despatched to his aunt Mrs. Isham, and which is also mentioned by Evelyn, is worthy of a place beside this.[2]   'Hee that is
' most famous for treacle,' notes Sir Ralph, 'is called
' Signor Antonio Sgobis, and keepes a Shopp at the
' Strazzo Or Ostridge, sopre il ponte de' Barreteri, on the
' right hand going to St. Mark's.   His price is 19 livres
' (Venize money) a pound, and hee gives little leaden potts
' with the Ostridge sign upon them and papers both in
' Italian and Lattin to shew its virtue.'   According to tradition, this wonderful concoction was composed by Nero's physician, and was made of vipers steeped alive in white wine, opium, spices from both the Indies, liquorice, red roses, germander tops, juice of rough sloes, seeds of treacle mustard, tops of St. John's wort and some twenty

---

[1] *Life of Sir Kenelm Digby.*   [2] *Verney Memoirs.*

other herbs, to be mixed with honey, triple the weight of
all the dry species, into an electuary. The recipe is given
in Dr. Quincey's *English Dispensary*, published in 1739.

Personal acquaintance with Galileo did not prevent
Sir Kenelm Digby, like many another learned man of his
day, having a profound faith in the occult systems of
Astrology, nor from consulting the great Astrologer Lilly,
and having his horoscope carefully cast. We smile now
at the apparent childishness ; yet perhaps after all the
men of that day had a wider grasp of verities than had
the materialists who succeeded them. These last were
bounded by the things they could see, hear, touch, measure
with instruments of great yet not unlimited power, and
beyond those limits they acknowledged nothing but a
blank. It may have been childish to assume that man's
little life was written in the stars, yet behind these futile
calculations of the astrologers lay the perception that
man's fate was governed by the same laws that ordered
the planets in their courses ; the working of God's
ordinances that kept the heavenly bodies true to their
unchanging march ordered no less the fall of the sparrow
and the end of man's little day.

Sir Kenelm's credulity included the easy acceptance
of all manner of unexamined marvels which show him to
have had at any rate a very unscientific habit of mind ;
in Lady Fanshawe's *Memoirs* an absurd story of him is
related :—' When we came to Calais, we met the Earl of
' Strafford and Sir Kenelm Digby, with some others of
' our countrymen. We were feasted at the Governor's of
' the Castle, and much excellent discourse passed ; but, as
' was reason, most share was Sir Kenelm Digby's, who
' had enlarged somewhat more in extraordinary stories
' than might be averred, and all of them passed with great
' applause and wonder of the French then at table ; but
' the concluding one was that barnacles, a bird in Jersey,
' was first a shell-fish to appearance, and from that, sticking
' upon old wood, became in time a bird. After some

G

' consideration, they unanimously burst into laughter,
' believing it altogether false ; and, to say the truth, it
' was the only thing true he discoursed with them : that
' was his infirmity, though otherwise a person of most
' excellent parts, and a very fine-bred gentleman.'

'The Pliny of our age for lying,' as one of his contemporaries called him, it was always his hap to be believed
when he romanced, and laughed at when he spoke the
sober verity.   Lady Fanshawe and many others accepted
the barnacle story in all good faith ; but there was another
wonderful story that found no credence which later investi-
gation proved literally true.   When travelling in Barbary
he discovered a petrified city, and his description of it was
received with a scoffing incredulity ; but nearly a century
later it obtained a striking confirmation : a paper was read
before the Royal Society by Mr. Baker, English Consul
at Tripoli, who said that about forty days' journey S.E.
from Tripoli, and seven from the sea coast, there existed,
at a place called Ongila, a petrified town of which the
description tallied exactly with that of Sir Kenelm Digby.
He was a great traveller, and from all his journeys brought
back all manner of curiosities and travellers' tales ; not
long after his marriage, when one would have expected
the claims of home to have been paramount, he fitted out
and commanded a kind of privateering expedition to
Scanderoon and the East ; and later he travelled a good
deal in Germany, at that time much less familiar to
Englishmen than Italy or Spain.

Clever as he was, he certainly did not fulfil the high
expectations formed of him by his Oxford tutor, the
learned Alleyne.   Perhaps his studies were too many and
too varied for depth.   He studied Philosophy at Oxford,
Paris, Florence, and under many great savants, yet never
attained the true philosophic temper ; he was 'rather
' curious, showy, broad - minded than profound.'   John
Evelyn called him frankly a charlatan ; his biographer
and descendant, with sympathetic insight, has more

happily summed him up as ' a brilliant amateur ; a person-
' age rather than a great man.'[1] He stands for the restless
enquiring spirit which made the pursuit of knowledge
fashionable ; he shows the eager interest which the man of
the world took in the great discoveries in Science and
Philosophy which were to revolutionise thought.

For science had become the fashion ; experiments in
chemistry—more practical ones, too, than the search for
the Philosopher's Stone, that *ignis fatuus* of so many ages
—had become quite the rage. Already the Royal Society
held its informal meetings both at Oxford and in London,
and, but for the outbreak of the great Rebellion, would
probably have been incorporated during the reign of
Charles I. As it was, inventive genius was turned into
other channels ; no one had leisure for the peaceful
arrangement of a society for research, so it had to wait till
the Restoration brought back tranquil days and a king
who was inclined to patronise, if sometimes to make game
of, the experiments and discussions of learned men. In its
early unchartered days, which are all with which we have
to do, it was merely the friendly meetings at each other's
rooms of men like-minded in trying to apply Bacon's great
cardinal principle of deducing laws from experiment, and
verifying experiment by careful and accurate observation.
Among these men were Mayow, the young doctor whose
promising career was so quickly cut short, and Robert
Boyle, the 'sweet Master Robert' of the Eton letters.[2]
For his early promise of diligence and love of learning were
amply fulfilled, and his quiet studious temper found its
congenial work in scientific research. The very antithesis
of 'the great amateur' Digby, his work, which made little
noise in his lifetime, gained an enduring value, and the
Society owes as much to him as to any of its promoters.

I do not know that Chillingworth's name is mentioned
in connection with these meetings, but we may be sure
his speculative and enquiring temper would lead him

[1] *Life of Sir Kenelm Digby.*   [2] *Home Life under the Stuarts.*

often from Great Tew to assist at them, but when the
war broke out he turned his mind to applied mechanics,
and busied himself with the construction of an engine of
assault on the principle of a Roman testudo, which was
thought so well of that Lord Sunderland wrote of him
that he had evidently mistaken his vocation, and was
fitter for an engineer than for a divine, since Lord
Falkland easily demolished his arguments on the Socinian
heresy.   Whether the enemy would have had more
difficulty in demolishing his engine was never proved, for
before it was ready for use the siege of Gloucester was
raised, and in the following January the inventor died
while a prisoner in the hands of the Roundheads ; it was
thought from the privations and hardships which he
suffered during the siege of Arundel.

It was only amongst the cultured that the scientific
habit of mind—that is to say any perception of the relation
between cause and effect—had gained any hold at all ;
with average minds the belief in charms and spells was
almost universal.   If they were in any difficulty they
consulted a wise woman ; if it were enmity against a
neighbour that tormented them, they got her to overlook
his cattle ; if a girl desired to win the love of some man
who had not looked her way, she bought of the witch a
love-philtre with as profound a belief in its virtue as any
pagan ancestress in the days of the Druids might have
had.   Witchcraft was a singular mixture ; wisdom in
herb-lore or midwifery, sometimes in bone-setting, handed
down and kept as occult secrets, a cunning which knew
how to trade on the fears and spites of the ignorant, with
perhaps in some cases an exceptional hypnotic influence
which even yet we but dimly comprehend, gave the witch
a power in the countryside which probably she thoroughly
enjoyed while she wielded it ; though she must often
have gone in fear of the cruel laws against her craft
which the Puritans were always ready to put in force,
and she would not often meet with a Justice of the Peace

as wide-minded as Sir Lawrence Tanfield, who cleared
and released the witch at his little daughter's suggestion.

The beliefs of the Puritans included a very active and
vivid realisation of the personality of the devil, and it is
always easier to see his works in the concrete form of
outward practices than in the hidden activities of the
sinful heart ; but the mingling of cruelty and fear which
prompted the torturing of many a poor old hag, whose
old age and ugliness were very likely the most damning
pieces of evidence against her, seem to us far more
devilish than her half-comprehended abracadabras.
They imported this witch-baiting into the New World
with them, and Cotton Mather's sketches of the early
days of New England abound in grisly stories of the
cruel treatment of those suspected of witchcraft.

There were, however, already some who protested
against the practice ; a very interesting letter written by
Wilson, the steward of Lees, about the year 1642, on the
subject of witches, shows that more enlightened ideas
were beginning to gain ground.[1]

'There is nothing on the stage of the world acted by
'publick justice comes so cross to my temper as putting
'so many witches to death.   About this time in Essex
'there being a great many arraigned, I was at Chansford
'(Chelmsford) at the trial and execution of eighteen
'women.   But could see nothing in the evidence that did
'persuade me to think them other than poor melancholy,
'envious, mischievous, ill-disposed, ill-dieted, atrabilious
'constitutions, whose fancies working by gross fumes and
'vapours, might make the imagination ready to take any
'impression, and they themselves by the strength of this
'fancy may think they bring such things to pass which
'many times unhappily they wish for and rejoice in when
'done, out of the malevolent humour which is in them :
'which passes with them as if they had really acted it.
'And if there be an opinion in the people that such a

[1] *Mary Rich, Countess of Warwick.*

' body is a witch, their own fears (coming where they
' are) resulting from such dreadful apprehensions, do make
' every shadow an apparition ; and every rat or cat an
' imp or spirit, which makes so many tales and stories in
' the world which have no shadow of truth.'

The night before the battle of Newbury was spent by
Cromwell's troops in ducking a poor old woman whom
they found on a plank in some water, and therefore
concluded to be a witch. As they succeeded in drowning
her, her character was cleared, but at the expense of her life.

If a belief in witches has given way before the advance
of knowledge, belief in ghosts has been much more
tenacious, and the ghost stories related in Lady
Fanshawe's *Memoirs* and in Aubrey's *Miscellanies* are
very much the same as those sent nowadays to the
Society for Psychical Research ; only in those days no
one tried to account for them. One experience shall be
related in Lady Fanshawe's own words : she was on a
visit in Ireland, to Lady Honor O'Brien. 'There we
' stayed three nights. The first of which I was surprised
' by being laid in a chamber, when, about one o'clock, I
' heard a voice that wakened me. I drew the curtain,
' and in the casement of the window, I saw, by the light
' of the moon, a woman leaning into the window, through
' the casement, in white, with red hair and pale and
' ghastly complexion : she spoke loud, and in a tone I
' had never heard, thrice, " A horse " ; and then, with a
' sigh more like the wind than breath, she vanished, and
' to me her body looked more like a thick cloud than
' substance. I was so much frightened that my hair
' stood on end, and my night clothes fell off. I pulled
' and pinched your father, who never woke during the
' disorder I was in ; but at last was much surprised to
' see me in this fright, and more so when I related the
' story and showed him the window opened. Neither of
' us slept any more that night, but he entertained me
' with telling me how much more these apparitions were

' usual in this country than in England ; and we concluded
' the cause to be the great superstition of the Irish, and
' the want of that knowing faith, which should defend
' them from the power of the Devil, which he exercises
' among them very much.   About five o'clock the lady
' of the house came to see us, saying she had not been to
' bed all night, because a cousin O'Brien of her's, whose
' ancestors had owned the house, had desired her to stay
' with him in his chamber, and that he died at two
' o'clock, and she said, "I wish you to have had no
' "disturbance, for 'tis the custom of the place, that, when
' "any of the family are dying, the shape of a woman
' "appears in the window every night till they be dead.
' "This woman was many ages ago got with child by the
' "owner of this place, who murdered her in the garden,
' "and flung her into the river under the window, but
' "truly I thought not of it when I lodged you here, it
' "being the best room in the house."   We made little
' reply to her speech, but disposed ourselves to be gone
' suddenly.'   Lady Fanshawe's other ghost story is a grisly
one, but not being first hand is not so well worth relating.

England was getting old enough to look back upon
her past, and an interest in antiquities was beginning to be
felt. Anthony Wood mentions a visit to Dorchester Abbey
in Oxfordshire, and speaks of the glories of its tombs and
crusaders as being, even in his time, much decayed.   Sir
Thomas Browne took a deep interest in the discovery of
some ancient Roman cinerary urns in Norfolk, and wrote
a curious treatise on them, called *Hydriotaphia*, full of
out-of-the-way learning on old customs of urn burial.
He was a man of many learned tastes and pursuits, and
his work in the domain of natural history was much
thought of in his own day.   Not long ago was published
Letters and Notes on the Natural History of Norfolk, from the
MSS. of Sir Thomas Browne, M.D.   This was a common-
place book, written at the instigation of a friend who
wished to have his observations on the natural history of

the county. 'Which,' says he, 'while I was doing, my
' good friend died.' It does not seem to have occurred
to him to publish them in his lifetime, but afterwards
they were placed in the hands of his contemporary, Ray,
with a number of coloured drawings. It was said of this
book that, 'for accuracy and shrewdness of observation,
' it has never been surpassed.' It contains many valuable
notes on the habits of cootes, haggards, and kites.

Sir Thomas Browne's house at Norwich was described
by Evelyn as 'A paradise and cabinet of varieties, and
' that of the best collections, specially medals, plants,
' books, and naturall things.'

Mr. Evelyn was himself a very good instance of the
intelligent interest taken by the cultivated amateur in
things scientific ; his diary abounds in passing mention
of learned men and their discoveries. Though not
himself exactly learned, he liked to keep abreast of what
was going on. When at Leyden he notes : 'I was much
' pleased with a sight of their Anatomy Schole, Theatre
' and Repositary adjoyning, which is well furnished with
' natural curiosities, skeletons from the whale and elephant
' to the fly and spider, which last is a very delicate piece
' of art, to see how the bones (if I may so call them) of
' so tender an insect could be separated from the mucil-
' aginous part of yt minute animal.' There was a still
earlier Anatomy Theatre at Bologna, which I do not
think he mentions, curious in being panelled and fitted
throughout with cedar wood.

What may be described as scientific toys were very
fashionable, and King Charles took great pleasure in such
things. He had a curious telescope of parchment, made
by William Longland at the Ship in Cornhill, which was
shown at the Stuart Exhibition some years ago, as was
also a microscope mounted in gilt leather. A ring he
specially valued and bequeathed to the Duke of Gloucester,
his youngest son, contained a miniature sundial in silver.
These portable dials were quite a fashion of that day ;

ATHELHAMPTON.

SUNDIAL AT ATHELHAMPTON.

PLATE IX.

some were made to carry in the pocket, some set in rings or other ornaments, and, when watches were rare and costly, were of course very useful, with the drawback that the possessor could not always command the essential assistance of the sun.

The whole science and practice of dialling had been quite a hobby with those who liked to dabble in abstruse calculations since the preceding century, and was discussed at great length in all astronomical works. In 1612 an immense treatise on the subject was published by Clavius in a quarto volume of 800 pages, in which the far more recondite theory of moon-dialling was also fully set forth.

In one of the quadrangles of Queen's College, Cambridge, there is an elaborate sundial of the seventeenth century surrounded with a series of numbers which make it available as a moondial when the moon's age is ascertained. A fine example of a dial with brazen rings stands in the Italian garden at Athelhampton in Dorsetshire, a garden which reproduces all the characteristic features of the Paradise or Pleasaunce of our forefathers, with its pleached yew hedges, its clipped peacocks, pinnacles, and little ships in finest topiary art; its fountains of goldfish, its filbert walk, its statues and alcoves, above all in its fragrance and old-world tranquillity.

But wandering in this 'haunt of ancient peace' has led my pen astray from science and its popularity. Even the common people began to take some interest in the wonders science had to show, and would travel down to Eltham to see the Perpetual Motion of Cornelius Drebbel and other curious things, as has already been related among the sights of London. It was an age of alert curiosity—a curiosity which was unhappily checked and thrown back many years by the civil war. When settled times came again, the spirit of enquiry stirred once more, and the Royal Society was able to lift its head, and, encouraged by kingly patronage, address itself once more to the business of research.

CHAPTER VII

DOCTORS AND ILLNESSES

MEDICAL science shared the transitional character of all other science at the opening of the seventeenth century: the blind following of tradition was beginning to yield to the advance of experimental knowledge. Early in the century Harvey announced to the world his grand discovery of the circulation of the blood, and anatomical knowledge was continually being added to by the researches of Hook, Lower, and Mayow. The enormous advance in surgery which later days were to see had not yet begun, and in spite of the stirring of new ideas already germinating, empirical learning still held its ground. The 'meer dull Physitian,' whom Bishop Earle sketches,[1] whose one panacea was cupping, and who 'was ' sworn to Galen and Hippocrates as university men to ' their statutes though they never saw them,' was still a familiar figure, with 'his discourse all aphorisms, though ' his reading be only Alexis of Piemont.'

The old-fashioned knowledge of the properties of herbs and simples, which had been carried to great perfection, was now beginning to be considered a little out of date, and yielding to such new nostrums as the ' bezoars ' and 'orampotabily,' of which Lady Brilliana Harley thought so much. A note to her *Letters* thus explains the properties of these discoveries, new in her day and highly prized : 'Bezoars—concretions met with

[1] *Microcosmography.*

90

' in the bodies of ruminant animals and considered highly
' alexipharmic : their virtues now considered imaginary.
' "Orampotabily," Aurum potabile — another medicine
' rejected from the Materia Medica, but formerly much
' vaunted by empirics as a powerful tonic.' Herbalist
lore was indeed less in the hands of the physician than
in those of the wise woman, or more or less in those of
the mistress of every household.

For in those days people who lived in the country
could not be sending off for the doctor on every little
emergency.   Every mother or nurse knew what to do for
whooping-cough, measles, or croup ; could dress a wound
or set a broken bone if needful, and her store of recipes
comprised medical prescriptions, and these carefully-
hoarded manuals were handed down in families for
generations.   The old one in my own possession, alluded
to in *Home Life under the Stuarts*, contains not only
prescriptions for cough and gout and all manner of minor
ails, but for such serious maladies as smallpox, the plague,
and the evil.   Dame Margaret Verney bequeathed her
' Cookery and medisable Boockes' by will to her
daughters ; but in spite of them the delicate ones seem
to have required the doctor often, for amongst the old
bills and account books are continual entries for pills and
potions.   Poor Pen in especial was continually dosed,
and so was Cary, when, as a sorrowful young widow, she
returned to her old home.   Perhaps the Turkey rhubarb
which was so constantly administered to Mary Verney's
two little boys may have tended to make them weak and
rickety, and was responsible for Edmund's curvature of
the spine and little Jack's crooked legs.

The favourite remedy for any and every ail then and
for long after was cupping.   Some ladies were competent
to inflict it upon members of their household, but, as a
rule, it was done by the barber-chirurgeon, who was also
tooth-drawer, and whose methods and instruments for
the latter branch of his art were of a primitive barbarity.

Occasionally the blacksmith was resorted to as an extractor of teeth, and for some occult reason bone-setting seems to have been numbered among the gifts of a blacksmith ; for Anthony Wood relates that having fallen from his horse and put out his shoulder, after a week of suffering he resorted to Adams, a locksmith in Cat Street, who was a noted bone-setter.   This worthy practitioner ' gave ' him sweet words and told him all was well,' and therewith wrenched it in ; ' whereupon he fell into a sown.'

Surgery was quite in its infancy : antiseptic treatment was absolutely unknown, and the use of anæsthetics was hardly yet introduced, though opium was occasionally given.   Lady Warwick, in her *Meditations*, refers to the practice of giving opium to stupefy the person who takes it that he may not be sensible of pain.   The account of the treatment of the first Lord Falkland's injured leg gives a distressing idea of what people had to suffer at the hands of the surgeons of those days.   He had met with an accident while out shooting in attendance on the King at Theobalds, and it appears to have been a compound fracture, for we gather it was from a fall, not a gunshot wound.   It was so mismanaged in the beginning that it gangrened, and the leg had to be amputated—in those days a horrible operation, not only on account of the absence of chloroform, but from the antiquated instruments used.   He bore it ' without a change of ' countenance,' but shortly after, hemorrhage set in while the surgeons were absent at tables.   When summoned, they do not seem to have hurried themselves, and when at length they arrived they said it was too late to do anything ; there was no hope, and they calmly suffered him to bleed to death.   These were no obscure practitioners, but the royal surgeons whom the King had desired should attend upon the patient.

Over against such as these we may set the portrait of more than one delightful doctor of the day.   Besides those distinguished men of science who were adding to the

resources of their profession, and to whose researches
modern medicine owes so much, there were general
practitioners who would have remained unknown but
for the private letters and journals in which their names
occur. It is with these that our chief concern lies, as it is
from the point of view of the patient that the doctor has
his place in these pages.

Amongst the many interesting characters which the
Verney letters depict, there is hardly one more attractive
than the doctor uncle, William Denton, younger brother
to Margaret, Lady Verney, who was a Denton of Hillesdon.
He was but seven years senior to his eldest nephew Sir
Ralph, and between the two existed a very warm and
durable friendship, unbroken even by their finding themselves arrayed on opposite sides in the war. Dr. Denton
was one of the physicians-in-ordinary to the King, and
was in attendance on his person during the Scotch cam-
paign. He remained faithful to the Royalist cause, but
he was a wide-minded man, and not improbably among
the many on either side who were alive to the good in
those who opposed them, and sensible of the faults and
follies on their own side. His friendship and kindness
for Ralph and his wife never faltered ; indeed to Mary
he was absolutely devoted, and when she came to England
on her tedious and difficult mission he was like a brother
to her, aiding and sustaining her in every way, helping
her to get access to the people it was important she
should see, finding her suitable lodgings, looking after her
health, and making arrangements for her journeys, and at
last undertaking the distressing task of breaking to her
the woeful tidings of the loss of her two children.

He was a good friend, too, to the orphan girls at
Claydon, and did his best for poor Mall, the unsatisfactory
one, when she got into trouble, and arranged the marriage
which should save her good name. His influence on the
younger nephews, too, was always exerted for good, and
when young Edmund, in disgrace after leaving Oxford,

was sent into a kind of banishment at his grandmother's, it was intercourse with his young uncle that set him in a better way and brought out the nobler side of his character. He was a highly-educated man, and had preceded his nephews at Magdalen Hall; he studied medicine under a famous physician, Henry Ashworth, taking his doctor's degree at the age of twenty-nine. He had a great fondness for general literature as well as for the studies proper to his profession, and his letters to Ralph are full of mention of books, either sending or recommending them to him. When growing old and sick of a fever, he writes of himself as 'an old, old man with a bed full of 'books.'

Like his contemporary, the celebrated Norwich physician, he did not find that his profession tended to make him less a Christian. He was, in fact, a deeply religious man, though with a vein of shrewd humour and worldly common-sense ; his letters to his nephew, who was growing morbid in his distress at the loss of his adored young wife, breathe no less genuine Christianity than good sense and tender-heartedness. He was almost as fond of horses as of books, and very knowing about them, but he did not share his younger nephew Henry's passion for the turf. His contemporaries described him as 'an ingenious and phasetious 'man, who for his Polite Conversation among the Ladies 'of the Court was called the Speaker of the Parliament 'of Woemen.'

It is almost more as a Christian than as a doctor that the name of Sir Thomas Browne has come down to posterity : the work by which he is best known, his *Religio Medici*, is invaluable as setting forth the attitude of a certain type of mind in his day towards religion. He writes neither as theologian nor as saint ; a man of the world, in a way a man of profound learning, yet of the old school rather than the new, he stands nicely balanced on the meeting-point between science and superstition. His professional views were of the most antiquated cast,

F. H. Van Houe sculp

From an engraving in 'Religio Medici,' 1672 edition.

SIR THOMAS BROWNE OF NORWICH.

PLATE X.

his religious ones rarely enlightened ; he was the most
tolerant of men in a day when toleration was well-nigh
unknown. The consideration of this his chief book may
more fitly be left to the chapter on the religious attitude
of the day, but in his *Letter to a Friend on the Death of a
Friend* we see him more as the doctor, although the divine
peeps out occasionally.

And yet how unlike a modern doctor: so little of
symptoms or of means employed, so much that reads like
old-wives' fables. It is not by the pulse, the tongue, the
temperature that he judges of the condition of his patient,
but by a singular likeness to one of his relations which
appeared with the approach of death. 'Upon my first
' visit,' says he, 'I was bold to tell them who had not let
' fall all hope of his recovery that in my sad opinion he
' was not like to behold a grasshopper, much less to pluck
' another fig ; and no long time after seemed to discover
' that odd mortal symptom in him not mentioned by
' Hippocrates, that is, to lose his own face, and look like
' some of his near relations ; for he maintained not his
' proper countenance, but looked like his uncle, the lines
' of whose face lay deep and invisible in his healthful
' visage before : for as from our beginning we run through
' a variety of looks before we come to consistent and
' settled faces ; so before our end, by sick and languishing
' alterations, we put on new visages : and in our retreat to
' earth, may fall upon such looks which from community
' of seminal originals were before latent in us.' May has
always been held a fatal month for consumptive patients,
and so thought Sir Thomas, for he adds, 'He lived not
' unto the middle of May, and confirmed the observation
' of Hippocrates of that mortal time of the year when the
' leaves of the fig-tree resemble a daw's claw.' Moreover,
he refers to the ancient belief about the dead time of the
night or the ebbing tide. 'I was not so curious to entitle
' the stars onto any concern of his death, yet could not
' but take notice that he died when the moon was in

' motion from the meridian ; at which time an old Italian
' long ago would persuade me that the greatest part of
' men died : but herein I confess I could never satisfy my
' curiosity ; although from the time of tides in places upon
' or near the sea, there may be considerable deductions ;
' and Pliny hath an odd and remarkable passage concerning
' the death of men and animals upon the recess or ebb of
' the sea. However, certain it is, he died in the end and
' deep part of the night, when Nox might be most appre-
' hensibly said to be the daughter of Chaos, the mother of
' sleep and death, according to the old genealogy ; and
' so went out of this world about that hour when our
' blessed Saviour entered it, and about what time many
' conceive He will return again to it.' The doctor then
describes with the feeling of a poet, 'his soft departure, so
' like unto sleep that he scarce needed the civil ceremony
' of closing his eyes ; contrary unto the common way,
' wherein death draws up, sleep lets fall the eyelids.'

A dissertation follows upon consumption and 'pleurisies'
which he thinks were rare in England formerly, according
to Polydore Vergil who lived in the reign of Henry VIII.
Some think there were fewer, he says, when men lived
more upon milk, and many hold that in ancient times,
when men went naked and slept in caves, coughs were
unknown, a view borne out by the gipsies in our own
day ; such as have taken to town dwelling in the winter
will often tell you they never knew what a cold was till
they slept under a roof. From describing the autopsy,
from which it appeared that the lobes of the lung were
adhering to the side, he suddenly takes an excursion into
the land of dreams, holding that dreams may be a useful
indication of physical condition, and so afford hints towards
the preservation of health or prevention of disease, on which
subject he again quotes Hippocrates. Certain dreams he
held to belong exclusively to good health, for he says,
' He was now past the healthful dreams of the sun, moon,
' and stars, in their clarity and proper courses. 'Twas

' too late to dream of flying, of limpid fountains, smooth
' waters, white vestments, and fruitful green trees, which
' are the visions of healthful sleeps, and at good distance
' from the grave.' The remainder of the letter is chiefly
occupied with discourse upon death, and upon the preparation of a good life, which belongs rather to the divine
than to the physician.

Although, according to this writer, a comparatively new
disease, consumption seems to have been already terribly
common, and as with us its victims were generally young.
All Sir Kenelm Digby's strange concoctions of snail broth
and extracts of all manner of meats could not avail to
save Venetia. It is perhaps little wonder that after all
she had gone through of sorrow and fatigue Mary, Lady
Verney, should have fallen into a decline, and the same
fate ended the widowhood of Lettice, Lady Falkland ; but
those in happier surroundings were not exempt. Three
of the Earl of Leicester's daughters, in their sheltered
home life at Penshurst, fell victims to this sad malady.
First Mary, then, two years later, Elizabeth, one of the
younger ones, died in her eighteenth year. Her father's
account of her death in his journal is very touching. He
writes : ' She had such divine assurance of her future
' happiness that she left the world with more joy than if
' she had gone to be marryed to the greatest Prince upon
' earth. And not above half an houre before her death
' she took her leave of me, smiling, and when I told her,
' " Betty, I have prayed for you, I desyre you to pray for
' " me," she, holding me by the hand, said, " I do pray for
' " you heartily, and God be with you," which were the
' last words I heard her say.' Only a year after, Frances,
another sister, two years older, died of the same illness.

Lady Sussex writes to Ralph Verney a quaint ill-spelt
letter from the bedside of her aged husband, dying of
paralysis : ' Now i must tell you that which may bee you
' will hardly belive, that i hartily cuffer for my good olde
' lord who truly growes so very weke that i fear hee will

H

' not holde out very longe.'   Later she says : ' He eats his
' meat as well as he used to do and slipes well ' ; but in a
few days the bulletin is, ' He is grown so infinit weke, not
' able to put on anything, but lapede in a shete and a
' blanket, and so lade upon his palet.'

Although the plague was from time to time rampant
up to the terrific outbreak in Charles II.'s time, we rarely
meet with any mention of it in private letters or memoirs.
Probably as a rule its ravages were confined to the large
towns, and in them chiefly to the quarters where the poor
were herded together under frightfully insanitary conditions.
A far worse dread among the upper classes was the smallpox.   When we recall the scare of 1901, and compare
the tens out of a population of millions with the hundreds
out of a population of thousands, we realise a little what
we owe to vaccination.   I think it may be safely asserted
that there is not one volume of letters or memoirs of the
time of which I speak in which there is not some distressing story of smallpox, it may be several.   It seemed like
a fiend lurking in secret places, ready to pounce upon its
victim at the most cruel moment.   It has already been
related how Mrs. Hutchinson nearly lost her life, and for
a time did lose her beauty on the very eve of her marriage,
and a precisely similar misfortune befell Dorothy Osborne
when she was in London choosing her wedding clothes.
In both these cases the loyalty of the lover rose superior
to the changed looks of his mistress, but in how many
may not the loss of beauty have meant the loss of the
promised husband and the hopes of happiness.

Our forefathers had their share too of most of the ills
which modern flesh is heir to ; in the early days of the
Commonwealth they set up the influenza, much as we know
it, and it seems to have appeared suddenly after so long
an immunity that the doctors did not know what to
call it.   We find Dr. Denton summoned to Claydon to
prescribe for the servants and tenants, amongst whom it
was spreading rapidly, and one wonders whether seven-

teenth-century constitutions were able to stand the heroic remedies in the way of cupping and emetics which he prescribed.

Agues and intermittent fevers were much more rife than now, which is not to be wondered at, as there was a great preference for low and sheltered situations for houses, and drainage was but lightly regarded. Lady Brilliana Harley's letters are full of the mention of it. On one occasion she writes: 'Mr. Ballam is very sike; I think it ' is an ague, but he eates, and so makes his fits violent; ' he will take nothing of Wodowes nor Morgan, but is ' resould to send to-morrow for doctor Rwit, but he feares ' he will not stay longer with him than 3 pounds will ' hoold out; that he is willing to give, but he can spare ' no more, he says: this two dayes he has bine debating ' of it as they tell me; but now in his fitte he resoulfes ' to send for him and does not reckon the charges.' But Dr. Wright, it appears in another passage, was not one to stand upon his fees, for she says: 'Mrs. Yates is upon ' recovery. Doctor Rwit dealt very kindely with them & ' tooke much paines, and tooke but halfe his feese.'

Lady Brilliana herself was a great invalid, and both Sir Nathaniel Wright and Dr. Diodati make frequent appearance in her letters. The former, indeed, was a very loyal friend, standing up for Sir Robert in Hereford when he was in the black books of the royalist town, and during the troubles of the war he took up his abode at Bramton in order to aid and support Lady Brilliana in her husband's absence. In one letter both are mentioned: 'I did not send for doctor —— to take phisick, for I ' thanke God I was not sike, but I knwe I had need of ' cordials, and thos I toucke of doctor Deodate and not ' of doctor Rwit. I thanke God I am now able to site ' up a littell. This day I sat up out of my beed allmost ' an ower.' Her second son suffered from fits, which seem to have slightly affected his mind, or at least his temper, for she writes to his brother: 'Your brother Robert has

' had no fite this fortnight. I thanke God he is not
' alltogeathor so stubborne as he was.' And on another
occasion : ' Your brother Robert had one fite a weak sence
' but sence that he has bine very well but alas! he cares
' not to gaine any jentile corage, comes littell to me, but
' when I exacte it from him ; but your brother Thomas
' is of another minde.'

Rheumatism and gout are frequently alluded to, and
the Bath waters had a great reputation. Sir Edmund
Verney often went there for a time to try and get rid
of the sciatica from which he suffered greatly. It was
becoming the fashion too to take the waters at Epsom,
Barnet, or Tunbridge Wells ; the latter place, the virtues
of which were only discovered in 1606, became very
fashionable after Queen Henrietta Maria's visit in 1630.
When she went the accommodation was so scanty that
she and her suite had to live in tents on the banks of
the spring.

We occasionally read of minor ailments, headache,
depression of spirits, and the like. Lady Sussex writes :
' I toke some fissicke hopinge it woulde have made my
' sperets somethinge cherfuller, but truely i finde myselfe
' still so doll and sade that i take littell ioy in anythinge
' in this worlde ; i pray God give me a cherfuller hart.'
The ' fissicke ' does not seem to have been a success, for
again she says : ' My fissicke made me so out of tune in
' my hede that truly i dorst not right.'

She probably suffered from what they used to call the
spleen, which Frenchwomen know as a *migraine*, and for
which we seem to have no name, though we are familiar
enough with the complaint. When it becomes much
aggravated our doctors generally call it nervous depression,
which sounds well and consoles the sufferer. Dorothy
Osborne had it rather badly, and thus complains : ' They
' do so fright me with strange stories of what the spleen
' will bring me to in time, that I am kept in awe with
' them like a child ; they tell me 'twill not leave me

' common sense, that I shall hardly be fit company for
' my own dogs, and that it will end either in a stupidness
' that will make me incapable of anything, or fill my head
' with such whims as will make me ridiculous. To prevent
' this who would not take steel or anything—though I
' am of your opinion that 'tis an ill kind of physic. Yet
' I am confident that I take it the safest way, for I do
' not take the powder as many do, but only lay a piece of
' steel in white wine overnight and drink the infusion in
' the morning, which one would think were nothing, yet
' 'tis not to be imagined how sick it makes me for an
' hour or two, and which is the misery, all that time one
' must be using some kind of exercise. Your fellow-
' servant has a blessed time on't that ever you saw. I
' make her play at shuttlecock with me, and she is the
' veriest bungler at it that ever was. Then I am ready
' to beat her with the battledore, and grow so peevish as
' I grow sick, that I'll undertake she wishes there were no
' steel in England.'

The 'fellow-servant' who had to bear with Mistress
Dorothy's humours was Jane Wright, the waiting-gentle-
woman, whom she often playfully alludes to in her letters
to Sir William under this title.

Hysteria makes a very infrequent appearance, never
under that name ; but undoubtedly the mysterious malady
that attacked Lady Warwick was some form of that complaint. In spite of the various severe diseases which were
prevalent, it appears probable that the general level of health
was higher, judging from the amount of hardship and fatigue
which the people of that day were able to undergo without
serious consequences. Although everything that we know
as sanitary science was set at nought, yet it must be
remembered that our ancestors had the advantage of us
in being infinitely better fed ; adulteration was practically
unknown, and the difference that must have made in
building up a sound constitution is beyond all calculation.
Cancer, that hideous scourge of modern life, was rarely if

ever heard of. It has been supposed to follow a high state of civilisation; it is far more likely it follows on the ingenuity that has learned to substitute all manner of cheap mischievous ingredients for the food we suppose ourselves to be eating, if, as some think, it is not directly brought on by the substitution of German yeast for barm in our daily bread.

Nervous depression and religious mania, though not common, were not unknown, and were treated in the same manner as to-day by rest-cure in a doctor's house. In the *Liber Famelicus* by James Whitelocke occurs this passage :—

'An, wife of John Seele and sister to my wife, having 'layen long at phisick to be cured of a distraction of her 'minde which held her with a kind of mopishnesse and a 'religious desperateness, still crying out on her sins, and 'shewing fear of God's judgments against her, dyed in 'October 1611, at the house of on Panton in Sussex, 'where she lay at cure, and being brought to more quiet- 'nesse of mynde and to hope of recoverye. She was a 'very modest, religious gentlewoman as ever I knew any, 'and ever lived a most godly and virtuous life.'

The great increase of nervous and mental maladies since then is usually attributed entirely to the greater stress, strain, and hurry of modern life; yet the days when a great civil war was raging can hardly have been times of ease and freedom from care; probably brains nourished on wholesome fare, when nearly everything was home-made, home-cured, or home-grown, were fitter to resist strain than ours. An anæmic race could never have survived the cuppings, caustics, setons, and emetics with which they were treated, nor have bequeathed to their posterity the traditional physique of a John Bull that exists nowadays in the pages of *Punch* alone.

CHAPTER VIII

TRAVELLING

IN the very opening of the century Stow plaintively remarked, ' Nowadays all the world goes upon wheels '— and this when hackney coaches were not yet introduced, and mail coaches were still a novelty! Truly in the matter of speed and cheapness, of ease and extent of locomotion, we have left our forefathers lagging far behind ; yet in some of the essential elements of travel we are, after all, not so much the gainers. Certainly they did not go abroad every year, many of them but once in a lifetime ; but then they took far longer over it, saw infinitely more, and found in foreign countries all those characteristic peculiarities which the railways and the universal bagman have gone far to obliterate. If they brought home wrought-iron from Nuremberg, goldsmith's work from Genoa, lace from Malines, glass from Venice, it was not to find the same patterns duplicated and reduplicated in the first London shop they entered when they got back, but to display to the admiring eyes of home-staying friends who had never beheld the like. They saw strange countries, each with its distinctive stamp of manners, customs, costumes ; and in truth there was more of travel in its real sense in those days between London and Penzance than in these between London and Peru.

Yet if the traveller was more a foreigner in one sense, he was less so in another, for his letters of introduction made him free of the best society in whatever town he made any stay, and all the great universities with their universal language of spoken Latin still made cultured Europe one. Nowadays the thing is reversed; the traveller with a Cook's circular ticket is sent express by rail to a selection of towns which he must get through in a month; he adheres to the railway since time presses, and sees little or nothing of his route. He goes the round of the stereotyped sights, puts up at hotels at which he eats the same food and is served in the same manner as at home, and talks to no one but other travelling English, for he is utterly an outsider; of the life of the people of his own class in France, Italy, Germany, Spain he sees no more than if he had never set foot out of England.

Our forefathers managed differently. A young man's education was not considered complete until he had gone abroad for a year or two to see the world—a world which is not to be seen from the windows of railway carriages nor at the tables of anglicised hotels. If he were a poor scholar he contrived to get a year or so at some foreign university—Leyden, Padua, Bologna, or perhaps Paris—but in the case of a wealthy man his father gave him a handsome outfit, a servant, perhaps a travelling tutor, a couple of good horses or a coach in which to travel post, letters of credit to bankers in each town of importance where he planned to stay, and what was almost as essential, introductions to various people of good position who could give him the entry into good society. Thus equipped, his year of travel very quickly made a man of the world of one who had started a raw youth.

As to hardships, well, are they not of the very essence of travel? Where else does the spice of adventure come in? Is it not *au fond* the craving for hardness that nowadays sends the true traveller mountaineering?—a thing which the seventeenth century man seldom cared for, having his desires in this respect sufficiently sated with duels, highwaymen, coach accidents, and snowdrifts. After all, a series of these unpleasant mishaps would not go far to outweigh the sweeping horror of a modern railway accident.

Even if we do not entirely endorse Ruskin's dictum that the dulness of travel is in exact proportion to its speed, since there is certainly an exhilaration in rapid motion, yet it is true enough that the traveller by train, tram, motor, or even bicycle, sees far less than the wayfarer who goes afoot, though he may cover ten times the extent of country. Even the swift phantasmagoria from the windows of a railway carriage, though it does not lack charm, rarely attracts the notice of the passenger who is always provided with his daily paper. For delight the two most ancient methods of travel, riding on horseback and sailing, have never been surpassed. That the former was appreciated in the days of which I speak, Mr. Peacham's description of a ride, quoted in the chapter on country pastimes, evidences, as well as many slight references scattered up and down the pages of letters and journals. The hardships of sailing vessels have been a good deal insisted on ; certainly the accommodation was often very rough, the boats ill-found, and tiresome delay incurred in waiting for wind and tide ; yet it is fair to remember that it was always disasters and delays that left a record ; the brief entry, a good passage, may cover untold charm of moonlight upon summer seas, or of the joy of scudding before a fresh breeze with all sail set. Then, as now, it was the complaints that found utterance.

The fullest and most detailed account of continental travel towards the middle of the century is of course to be found in John Evelyn's *Diary*. He was the ideal traveller of the Baedeker type, noting down carefully all the regulation sights, churches, picture galleries, show places of all sorts ; but he also had an eye for little characteristic touches, such as the 'goodly lime-planted 'quay or margent at Amsterdam, paved with clincars, a 'sunburnt white brick,' and such oddities as the wooden frame like a churn, which a woman who had two husbands was condemned to wear. He spent many years peram- bulating foreign lands ; not only did sight-seeing appeal to his refined and curious tastes, but he was thankful to absent himself for a time from his own country where the political troubles distressed him, while he felt in himself no power to meet or cope with them. To the royal cause he gave his sympathy and contributions in money, once for a very brief while his sword, but personal devotion, possibly courage, was lacking ; so while sedition ripened to rebellion, and war stalked through the land, he roamed across the picture galleries and museums of France and Italy, picking up curiosities and treasures of art to adorn his home when peace should be restored, and filling his diary with interesting trifles, from the mass of which I glean a sample here and there.

He visits two of the celebrated printing presses. At Leyden he says : ' Here was the famous Dan. Heinsius, ' whom I so longed to see, as well as the Elzevirian ' printing-house and shop, renown'd for the politeness of ' the character and editions of what he has publish'd ' through Europe.' His mention of the fascinating Maison Plantin is even slighter. After an enthusiastic description of the many sights of Antwerp, he says : ' Returning by ' the shop of Plantin, I bought some books for the ' namesake only of that famous printer.'

It is curious to find the *pension* already in full swing at Amsterdam : ' I changed my lodgings out of a desire ' to converse among the Sectaries that swarm in this city. ' It was at a Brownist's house where we had an extra- ' ordinary good table. There was in pension with us my ' L. Keeper Finch, and one Sir J. Fotherbee. Here I ' also found an English Carmelite with another Irish ' gentleman.'

Returning to England for a few months on business, while the battle of Edgehill was being fought, he was admiring the curiosities of Winchester, where he ' vissited

' the Castle, Schole, Church, and King Arthur's Round
' Table, but especially the Church, and its Saxon Kings'
' Monuments which I esteemed a worthy antiquity.'
Obtaining license to travel again, he crossed from Dover
to Calais in the snow, and proceeded on horseback to
Paris. Of all that excites his alert curiosity in that city
time would fail to tell, but it is worthy of remark that in
the Louvre it is the more recent painters who find most
favour in his eyes, Veronese, Titian, Michael Angelo,
Correggio; the pre-Raphaelites are unmentioned.

On his visit to Fontainebleau he passes through the
forest, which left a most unpleasant impression on his
mind: ' By the way we passed through a Forest so
' prodigiously encompassed with hideous rocks of whitish
' hard stone, heaped one on another in mountainous
' height, but I think the like is not to be found elsewhere.
' It abounds with staggs, wolves, boares, and not long
' after a lynx or ounce was killed among them which
' had devoured some passengers. On the summit of one
' of these gloomy precipices, intermingled with trees and
' shrubs, the stones hanging over, and menacing ruin, is
' built an hermitage. In these solitudes rogues frequently
' lurk and do mischiefe.' Nothing can be imagined in
greater contrast to our ideas of the picturesque than the
abhorrence of such men as Evelyn for ' horrid ' woods,
' hideous ' precipices, and the like, though possibly these
epithets may have been used in a sense slightly different
from ours, implying rather serried and jagged or awful
and stupendous. In crossing the mountains between
Siena and Rome he was wonderfully impressed by the
sight Ruskin has so frequently described of looking down
from above the clouds. ' As we ascended,' he says, ' we
' entered a very thick, solid, and dark body of cloudes
' which look'd like rocks at a little distance, which lasted
' near a mile in going up; they were dry misty vapours,
' hanging undissolv'd for a vast thicknesse, and obscuring
' both the sun and earth, so that we seemed to be in the

' sea rather than in the cloudes ; till, having pierced thro'
' it, we came into a most serene heaven, as if we had
' been above all human conversation, the mountaine
' appearing more like a greate island than joyn'd to
' any other hills, for we could perceive nothing but a sea
' of thick clowdes rowling under our feete like huge
' waves, every now and then suffering the top of some
' other mountaine to peepe thro', which we could discover
' many miles off ; and betweene some breaches of the
' clouds we could see landskips and villages of the
' subjacent country.   This was one of the most pleasant,
' new and altogether surprizing objects that I had ever
' beheld.'

But the kind of scenery he unaffectedly enjoyed is
described in another place when he is journeying from
Aix to Marseilles.   ' In this tract all the heathes or
' com'ons are cover'd with rosemary, lavender, lentiscs,
' and the like sweet scented shrubs for many miles
' together which to me was very pleasant. . . . We had
' a most delicious journey to Marseilles, thro' a country
' sweetly declining to the South and Mediterranean coasts,
' full of vineyards and olive-yards, orange trees, myrtils,
' pomegranads, and the like sweet plantations, to which
' belong pleasantly-situated villas to the number of above
' 1500 built all of freestone, and in prospect shewing as
' if they were so many heaps of snowe dropp'd out of
' the clouds among those perennial greens.'   He was a
sketcher, which must have enhanced his appreciation of
these lovely scenes.   On the road to ' Lions,' at a little
place called Tarrare, he records : ' Before I went to bed I
' took a landskip of this pleasant terrace,' and a little
later at Avignon : ' The prospect was so tempting that I
' designed it with my crayon.'   And when he was in
England again he went to Putney ' and other places on
' the Thames to take prospects to carry with me into
' ffrance where I thought to have them engraved.'

After his smooth and pleasant journey through the

south of France his visit to the galleys at Marseilles
reminds the reader with a shock of the harsh and dreadful
side of those days. At 'Canes,' a small port on the
Mediterranean, he took ship for Genoa, and sailing by
Nice and Monaco, 'Menton' and Ventimiglia, encountered
a severe storm before he got to port. His journey by
Pisa, 'Empoly,' Florence, and Siena to Rome is extremely
interesting to those who have covered the same ground;
indeed his description of the Tribune at Florence might
have been penned yesterday. On his arrival at Rome
it is pleasant to find him meeting our old friend, whose
escape with his little brother Placid was related in the
previous volume : 'Mr. Patrick Cary, an Abbot, brother
' to our learned Lord Falkland, a witty young priest who
' afterwards came over to our Church.' Another little
extract gives a picture of his pleasant idling : 'Hence
'(as was my usual custom) I spent an afternoone in Piazza
' Navona, as well to see what antiquities I could purchase
' among the people who hold mercat there for medaills,
' pictures and such curiosities, as to heare the montebanks
' prate and distribute their medicines.'

His stay in Rome lasted seven months—autumn,
winter, and spring—and his expenses there he considered
moderate. 'The Bills of Exchange I tooke up from my
' first entry into Italy till I went from Rome amounted
' but to 616 Ducati di Banco, though I purchased there
' many books, pictures and curiosities.' At Bologna he
invests in wash-balls, for which that city was famous, as
well as for its sausages and Parmesan cheese, and in
Venice, of course, the immortal treacle. 'Having packed
' up my purchases of books, pictures, casts, treacle, etc.
' (the making and extraordinary ceremonies whereof I
' had been curious to observe, for 'tis extremely pompous
' and worth seeing) I departed from Venice accompanied
' by Mr. Waller.'

But we must not let our traveller depart from Venice
without saying what impression the Queen of the Sea,

then in the zenith of her glory, made upon him. He
arrived there one night in June. 'The next morning,
' finding myself extremely weary and beaten with my
' journey, I went to one of their bagnios where you are
' treated after the Eastern manner, washing with hot and
' cold water, with oyles, and being rubbed with a kind of
' strigil of seal's skin, put on the operator's hand like a
' glove.' Thus refreshed he took a gondola, 'which is
' their water-coach,' and proceeded to explore the city.
The Merceria he was especially struck with. It is, he
says, 'one of the most delicious streets in the world for
' the sweetness of it, and is all the way on both sides
' tapistred as it were with cloth of gold, rich damasks and
' other silkes which the shops expose and hang before
' their houses from the first floor, and with that variety
' that for more than halfe the yeare spent chiefly in this
' citty, I hardly remember to have seen the same piece
' twice expos'd ; to this add the perfumers, apothecaries
' shops, and the innumerable cages of nightingales which
' they keepe that entertaine you with their melody from
' shop to shop, so that shutting your eyes you would
' imagine yourself in the country, when indeede you are
' in the middle of the sea. It is almost as silent as the
' middle of a field, there being neither rattling of coaches
' nor trampling of horses.'

He was much struck with the costume of the Venetian
ladies, which was in a style of their own, with the crisped
dyed hair, the transparent sleeves of tiffany showing their
arms through, and jewelled girdles of the Veronese
pictures, and quite unlike what was worn in other parts
of Italy.

On the road from Verona he is reminded of English
downs. 'The next morning we travelled over the downs
' where Marius fought, and fancied ourselves about
' Winchester and the country towards Dorchester.' The
fireflies, or, as he calls them, flying glow-worms, he found
quite a nuisance, but was amused to find that he could

read by their light when he caught a few and placed them
on the page.

For a while he returned to Paris, where there was for
him a great attraction, for a year after the king's death
he married the daughter of Sir Richard Browne, the
English Resident there. After his marriage he went
home to England and settled down to the care of his
estates, for though maintaining unostentatiously his royalist
and High Church principles, he escaped sequestration,
having taken little or no active part against the ruling
powers.

Sir Kenelm Digby, whom Evelyn occasionally encountered on his travels, and for whom he seems to have
had a great dislike, was another who could not easily
lay down his traveller's staff. He journeyed in Spain,
France, Germany, Morocco, to say nothing of his wonderful
buccaneering expedition to Scanderoon, and was always
meeting or imagining the maddest adventures. To follow
his wanderings would far exceed the scope of this chapter,
and we will turn to some who, travelling for business,
combined a good deal of pleasure and interest with it.
James Howell's *Letters* abound in touches of description,
less detailed than Evelyn's, but almost as graphic, of the
many towns in Holland, France, Spain, and Italy which
he visited in pursuance of his glass-blowing researches.
Like all travellers he comments on the cleanliness of the
Dutch towns and on the remarkable varieties of religion
to be found there. 'I believe in the street where I lodge,'
says he, 'there be near as many religions as there be
' houses ; for one neighbour knows not, nor cares not
' much what religion the other is of ; so that the number
' of conventicles exceeds the number of churches here.
' And let the country call itself as long as it will the
' United Provinces one way, I am persuaded in this point
' there is no place so disunited.'

Like a true Welshman, when he gets to Brittany the
thing he notes is the similarity of the language to his

own ; all the radical words, he observes, are no other than
Welsh.   Upon the Alps he is even more severe than Mr.
Evelyn.   'I am now got over the Alps, and returned to
' France ; I had crossed and clambered up the Pyreneans
' to Spain before ; they are not so high and hideous as
' the Alps ; but for our mountains in Wales as Eppint
' and Penwinmaur, which are so much cried up among us,
' they are molehills in comparison of these ; they are but
' pigmies compared to giants, but blisters compared to
' imposthumes, or pimples to warts.   Besides, our mountains
' in Wales bear always something useful to man or beast,
' some grass at least ; but these uncouth huge monstrous
' excrescences of nature bear nothing (most of them) but
' craggy stones ; the tops of some of them are blanched over
' all the year long with snow ; and tne people who dwell
' in the valleys drinking, for want of other, this snow-
' water, are subject to a strange swelling in the throat,
' called goytre, which is common among them.'

He is of course 'ravished with the high beauty' of
Venice, and admired 'her magnificent buildings, her mar-
' vellous situation, her dainty smooth neat streets, whereon
' you may walk most days in the year in a silk stocking
' and sattin slippers without soiling them.'   Naples he
' finds to be 'a gentle city, swelling with all delight,
' gallantry and wealth. . . . This is a delicate luxurious
' city, fuller of true bred cavaliers than any place I saw
' yet.'   In Rome he recognises in good sooth the capital
of the world.   'Rome, they say, is every man's country,
' she is called Communis Patria ; for every one that is
' within the compass of the Latin church, finds himself
' here, as it were, at home, and in his mother's house.'
The intense insularity which has been one of the consequences of the Reformation had evidently not yet grown
upon Englishmen.

We might linger endlessly with Mr. Howell on his
journeys, but must rather take now a more distant one in
company with Mr. Rawdon, who travelled for his uncle,

first in the wine-growing parts of France, and afterwards
went out to the Canaries, where he settled for some years.
In 1629, having already travelled for the business in
Holland and become a trusted agent, he was sent to France.
' About the middle of October he imbarkt at Rie, and soe
' for Deepe, and soe to the cittie of Roan and Parris, and
' from Parris he went away in company of the messenger
' for Bourdeaux, beinge about 300 miles. To this
' mesinger givinge a certaine summe of mony you are
' furnisht with a very good horse and exelent diet all the
' way, havinge noe care of anie thinge more than to risse
' when the mesinger calls you.' So the courier was already
an institution. ' In this journie Mr. Rawdon took he
' arrived saifly att Bourdeaux, and remained thir factor
' for his unckle and severall other marchants in that
' vintage, and in the springe about the beginninge of
' Aprill 1630, he went to see the ruines of Rochell, whosse
' walls and fortifications tow yeares before were the best
' in France ; but uppon thir rebellion, King Lewis the
' 13th, havinge taiken the towne, demolisht all save the
' walls towards the seaside, which he left standinge. From
' thence he went through Britanie, beinge desierous to see
' that country, and in the way tooke Nantes and St. Malos,
' tow of the principall cities of that country, wher he was
' most nobly entertained as he past, by the marchants
' ther resident. From St. Malos, after he had taiken a
' view of the country, and bene at Renes, where the Court
' of Parlement, or Chiefe Court of Justice for that province
' is kept, he imbarkt for England, and landed in the Ile of
' Waight. Here he staid about 3 dayes to take a view of
' the iland, went to Newport the chiefe towne, and havinge
' satisfied himselfe thir, he tooke passage for Southampton,
' where by Mr. Prescod, Mr. Priaulx, Mr. Hilliard, and Mr.
' Chambers, merchants of the towne, he was highly feasted.'
   After several business journies his uncle sent him out
to the Canary Islands. ' He set saile from Bastable
' (Barnstaple) about the end of April 1639, in the way he

I

'tucht at the Iland of the Maderas, sold part of his goods
'thir for redie mony, which he carried with him to the
'Canary Ilands, beinge a pretious commoditie in thosse
'parts.   Towards the latter end of May he arived in
'Santa Crux, a port towne of the Iland of Tenerife, one
'of the chiefest ilands of the Canaria, from whence the
'best Canary wine comes.   After he had bene thir some
'small time, he setled himselfe at Lalaguna, the chiefe
'cittie of that iland, where he hired a faire howse in which
'he lived nere seaven yeares, in which time he had large
'cargaisons of goods sent him booth from his unckle Sir
'Marmaduke and other marchants of London, and from
'other parts of England, France, and Ireland, his com-
'missions beinge worth then above a thousand pownds
'per annum, with which he lived very nobly, in great
'creditt, and gott a good estate.'

While at Lalaguna he made several exploring journies,
one to the Peak of Teneriffe, which he describes :—' He
'had likewisse a desier, whilst he staid on that iland, to
'goe uppon a high mountaine called the Pike of Tenerife,
'which hath snow and ice uppon itt all the yeare longe.
'Itt is by Sir Walter Raighley and other learned men
'held to be the highest land in the world ; soe, in company
'with severall English, Dutch, and German gentlemen, to
'the number of sixteene, besides sarvants, about the
'middle of August, havinge horses and mules laden with
'wine and provisions, they set forward from the towne of
'Orotava, and travelled all that day on horsebacke till
'they came to the bottome of the mountaine, where they
'remained that night, where thir came a most bitter coald
'aire from the top of the mountaine, soe cold as if they
'had been in Frizland, soe that some of thir company
'found themselves in the morninge, after they had slept,
'soe stiffe that they were nott able to perform thir journie
'up ; but to preventt that Mr. Rawdon, and one Mr.
'Cowlinge, a Yorkshire gentleman, would not sleepe, but
'spent most of that night in makinge great fires of

' Spanish brome and other combustible stuffe that grew
' thirabouts, with which they kept thir limbes stirringe
' and plyant, soe in the morninge about fower of the
' clocke thir guide called uppon them to be marchinge ;
' soe they went on foote, having brood single soold shoes,
' made on purposse, accordinge to the custome of the
' country, such as the goat-keepers that climbe up the rocks
' were, beinge they are not soe subject to slip as other shoes
' are. Soe they all endeavored to follow thir guide, but
' some remained a quarter part of the way, some halfe the
' way, and could get no further ; but Mr. Rawdon got up
' very well, and was the seacond person uppon the pick, thir
' beinge only one German gentleman before him. They
' gott to the top of this Picke about seaven of the clocke ;
' the top is a brood place of about three or fower akers of
' ground, hollow, like to a shallow coper kettle that they
' commonly boil fish in ; the reason is that formerly it
' brooke out and was blowne up with fire, as appears by
' pummice stones and other burnt stones that yett remaine
' thir, and abundance flew from thence to severall places
' of the ilande. Thir is within the earth a fire continues
' thir still, and thir comes out of severall crannies smooke
' wher, if you hold your hand a little while, itt wil be
' covered with a sulphurous matter like brimstone, and
' thir is a quantitie of brimstone found thir which they
' sell in the shops. Itt is thought att some time or other
' this greate mountaine will have a fitt of the chollicke and
' send out a blast of fire, brimstone, and stones, to the great
' prejudice of the places nere adjacent. Uppon the tope
' of this picke they staid about an hower, havinge cleere
' sun shininge morninge, by the benefitt of which they saw
' six of the seven Canary Ilands, one of them beinge 150
' miles distant from that place which they see, and thosse
' that were twenty, thirty, and fifty miles distant they
' shewed closse by ; but of that Iland of Teneriffe on
' which they were, though itt is threescore mile longe and
' fifteene mile brood, they see not one bitt more then part

' of that pick whereon they stood, thir beinge an inter-
' position of clowdes betwixt them and the earthe. They
' seemed to be in the middle region, the clowdes lyinge
' like fleeces of woole under them. Whilst they staid here
' Mr. Rawdon called their guide, beinge a lusty proper
' fellow, the tallest of all in the company, gave him a pece
' of mony, and told him that he would have him taike
' him uppon his shoulders, and that after that he should
' taike upp none els, which he promised him to doe ; soe,
' when he was set uppon his shoulders lookinge about him,
' he said to the company, " I am now the highest man in
' " the world, and the nearest heaven of anie man livinge."
' After they had satisfied themselves with lookinge about,
' and refresht themselves with the wine and provisions that
' was brought up for them, after an hower or an hower
' and a halfe stay, they went down to thir station where
' thir horses were, where they had a very good dinner ;
' and havinge dinde, they took horse and returned the
' same way they came to the town of Orotava, from
' whence they sett forthe.

 ' Whilst he staid uppon this iland of Teneriffe he did
' sometimes vizit some of the other ilands, as the iland of
' the Gomera, where there is some store of red deare ; the
' iland of the Palma, which produceth store of sugar
' and some good red wines ; and he went often to the
' iland of the Grand Canaries, a pleasant iland, affording
' good store of game for birdinge and fowlinge, as quailes,
' partridges of a larger sies, much bigger then the English
' partridge, and of a bewtiful couller ; also thir is store
' of turtle-doves and your ordinary wild piggeons, stocke-
' doves and ring-doves, and an infinite number of wild
' rabbitts all the iland over.'

 Mr. Rawdon, being a rich man, put up with no hardships that he could avoid, and was accustomed to travel
in great state and luxury. This was his provision for a
voyage on one occasion : 'Tow pipes of Canary wine.
' Tow dozens of gamons of bacon and neats' tongues.

'Tow firkins of severall sorts of fish boild and sousd or
'pickled after a most exelent way.   Fowerteene live
'sheepe.   Thirtie turkies.   One hundreth and twentie
'hens.   Two live hoggs.   Fortie small jars of olives and
'capers of severall sortes.   Six smale barills of fine
'white bisket.   Fower smale barills full of boxes of
'mermelade of severall sorts.   Severall sortes of dried
'sweetmeats.   His provisions were soe greate that the
'ilanders reported that he went for England to be made
'a bishop, thinking thosse provisions could belonge only
'to some greate churchman.'

It is impossible to take leave of him without touching
on his English journeys.   Upon his return home he
'went to see the Bathe in the Bath coach, his man
'Tosta on horseback, in which coach went one Mrs.
'Penelope Wells, waitinge gentlewoman to Sir Thomas
'Kemish his lady of whom they did enjoy very good
'company. . . . Att Bathe they staid about twenty daies
'and from thence went to Bristoll, and soe from thence
'back to Bathe where they took coach for London.'
They slept at Marlborough, stopping for lunch at a place
halfway called Sandie-lane.   He remained in town till
the latter end of June, 'att which time for some small
'distemper he found in himselfe he went to drinke the
'watters at Tunbridge, accompanied only with his
'Spaniard Tosta, which waters did him much good,
'and he was very happy thir in meeting with exelent
'company, which did much divert him, and I think did
'him as much good as the waters.   In the afternones
'he would ride out with some gentlemen to see the
'places adjacent, as the Earle of Licester's howse at
'Penshurst, a gallant seate ;   my lord of Abergany's
'howse ;   alsoe a towne where thir is a chappell where
'the Earls of Dorset are buried, where thir are many
'fine monuments worth the seeinge.   Sometimes in the
'afternones he would goe a fishinge, thir beinge exelent
'pondes well stord with fish thir abouts.'

He seems to have been continually encountering distressed damsels travelling by coach or otherwise, and
with great gallantry giving up his seat or helping them
in any way he could ; for though nothing would induce
him to marry, he appreciated the company of ladies, and
was not without chivalry towards them. As might be
expected with so wealthy a merchant, several young
ladies were offered to him by their friends, but he
excused himself as being not settled, and likely to go
abroad again. 'And the trewth is though he naturally
' loved the company of woemen yett he was allwayes
' naturally averse to marriage, and sometimes, dreaming
' he was married, hath wept in his sleep very much.'
While in York he was much pressed to choose between
' tow very gentlewomen booth for parts and fortune,
' booth widdows, but this pill of marriage seemed soe
' bitter to him that he durst not ventur to swallow itt.'
One of the widows was Lady Key or Kaye, sister to
Sir Henry St. Quintin ; in spite of Mr. Rawdon's
insensibility to her charms, this lady had four husbands.

One great disadvantage those days had from a
woman's point of view, namely, that women rarely
travelled at all, and if they did, it was under considerable
difficulty. Sometimes a fortunate wife, like Lady
Fanshawe, accompanied her husband in his journeys,
and encountered all kinds of hardships and perils with
unfailing pluck and good humour ; or one like poor
Mary Verney was obliged to struggle alone with the
difficulties of travelling in war time for necessity, not
pleasure. More often they stayed at home, their longest
journeys to the county town for a ball, or to visit a
neighbour a score of miles distant ; but we may console
ourselves for what they missed with the reflection that,
surrounded with beauty as they were, they needed it far
less than we do. It had not always been so ; in an
earlier day pilgrimages to some shrine had drawn women
as well as men from their own fire-sides, and still the

Catholic ladies made journeys to pay their devotions to some special saint. These pilgrimages were usually made in large parties. Lady Falkland on one occasion visited St. Winefride's Holy Well in Flintshire, in company with about 1400 persons and 150 priests. Details of that journey would have been most welcome, but we do not even learn how they travelled; most likely they went on horseback. There were, of course, stage-coaches for long journeys; but most women could ride, and for those who were old, delicate, or nervous, there was always the pillion—a broad cushion firmly strapped on behind the saddle, on which the lady sat as on a chair, and held on by a strap round the waist of husband or manservant who rode the horse.

Of another kind of travelling, and that the most fascinating of all, we learn little or nothing : of the lonely rambles up and down the country-side in fair weather or foul, by high-road or by-path of the chapman, the travelling tinker, the wandering fiddler who haunted the road in the days when towns were sparse and railways were not. Some faint hints of this kind of journeying may be gleaned from *The Pennyles Pilgrimage* of that queer character, John Taylor the sculler, called the Water-Poet, since part of his pilgrimage was performed on foot, and he often slept out in the open, taking no money with him, and depending on chance hospitality the whole way from London to Edinburgh and back. The adventure seems to have been undertaken in some kind of wager with Ben Jonson, or at any rate was suggested by the incredulity of Ben as to whether it could be done at all. The title-page of the book in which he records his experiences is a preface in itself, and sets forth the contents at great length.

THE
PENNYLES PILGRIMAGE
OR
THE MONEY-LESSE PERAMBULATION
Of JOHN TAYLOR, Alias
The King's Majesties
Water-Poet

How he travailed on foote
from London to Edenborough in
Scotland, not carrying any
Money to or fro, neither Begging,
Borrowing, or asking Meate, Drinke
or Lodging
With his Description of his Entertain-
ment in all places of his Journey, & a
true Report of the unmatchable Hunting
in the Brea of Marre and Badenoch in
Scotland.
    With other observations, some
serious and worthy of Memory,
& some merry & and not hurtful to be
Remembred
Lastly that (which is rare in a
Travailer) All is true.

LONDON
Printed by Edw: Allde at the charges
Of the Author 1618.
Dedicated to the Duke of Buckingham.

He begins his tale with an address 'To all my loving
' Adventurers by what name or title soever, my general
' Salutation . . . and now, reader, if you expect—'

That I should write of Cities, scituations,
Or that of Countries I should make relations:
Of brooks, crooks, nooks; of rivers, boorns and rills
Of mountaines, fountaines, Castles Towers & hills;
Of Shieres, & Pieres, & memorable things,
Of lives and deaths of great commanding Kings:
I touch not those, they not belong to mee,
But if such things as these you long to see,
Lay downe my Booke, and but vouchsafe to reade
The learned Camden, or laborious Speede.

He proceeds to relate in verse, with occasional lapses
into prose, how he set forth on foot from Aldersgate on
the evening of July the 14th: 'My legges I made my
' oares and row'd by land.' That night he only got as
far as Islington, his friends treating him as he went. He
did not, like a genuine tramp, carry his baggage on his
back, but had a packhorse, and in his knapsack was—

> Good Bacon, Bisket, Neates-tongue, cheese,
> With Roses, Barberries, of each conserves
> And Mithridate that vig'rous health preserves.

So he was well fortified at the outset against want. St.
Swithun's day was fair and he reached St. Albans, and
the next day, plodding towards Dunstable, and finding
none to treat him, he bewails—

> My very hart with drought methought did shrink.
> I went twelve miles & no one bad me drinke
>
> When Puddle-hill I footed downe & past
> A mile from thence I found a hedge at last
> There stroke we sayle, our Bacon, Cheese and Bread
> We drew like Fidlers, & like Farmers fed.
> And whilst 2 hours we there did take our ease,
> My Nagge made shift to mump green Pulse & Pease.
> Thus we our hungry stomachs did supply,
> And dranke the water of a Brooke hard by.

Passing through Stony Stratford he thinks to gain the
fields and make his bed in the hay, but from the window
of an inn a friendly voice hails him.

> But at the Queene's Arms from the window there
> A comfortable voyce I chanced to heare
> Call Taylor, Taylor, & be hang'd come hither!
> I looked for small intreaty & went thither.

Next day, in spite of the fair promise of St. Swithun,

> In blustring weather, both for wind and raine
> Through Tocetter I trotted with much paine.
> Two miles from thence, we sat us downe & dynde
> Well bulwarked by a hedge from Raine & Winde.

At Daventry his reception excites his ire, as the folk came out to stare but offered no hospitality, so he pursued his way to Dunchurch, and on Dunsmore Heath they cut down rushes and green fern—

> Of which we made a fieldbed in the field
> Which sleep and rest & much content did yield.
> My bed was curtained with good wholesome ayres,
> And being weary, I went up no stayres :
> The skie my canopy, bright Phœbe shinde
> Sweet bawling Zephirus breathed gentle winde.
> In Heav'ns Starre Chamber I did lodge that night
> Tene thousand Starres me to my bed did light.
> There barracadoed with a bank lay wee
> Below the lofty branches of a tree,
> There my bed fellowes and companions were,
> My Man, my Horse, a Bull, foure cows, two Steere :
> But yet for all this most confused rowt
> We had no bed-staves yet we fell not out.
> Thus Nature, like an ancient free upholster,
> Did furnish us with bedstead, bed & bolster ;
> And the kinde skies, (for which high Heaven be thanked,)
> Allowed us a large covering & a Blanket :
> Aurora's face gan light our lodging dark,
> We rose and mounted with the mounting larke.
> Through plashes, puddles, thick, thinne, wet & dry,
> I travailed to the Citie Coventry.

From Coventry he went on his way to Lichfield where, his horse needing shoes, they were supplied by 'a mad smuggy smith' who obligingly 'referred the 'payment unto God.' Rainy weather seems to have pursued the wayfarers. One wet night they spent very snug in a hayfield, where with green broom and hay they made a dry shelter ; and thus through wet and fine they make their way to Newcastle. Tired of verse, the narrator occasionally drops into prose for a page or so, but nothing but verse could convey his enthusiasm for Manchester, where he was right nobly entertained at the Eagle and Child.

> Whereas my hostesse a good auncient woman
> Did entertain me with respect not common.

> She caused my Linnen, Shirts & Bands be washt,
> And on my way she caused me be refresht.

So he passes on his way from inn to inn, paying no
score, till he reaches the Border and crosses the Esk,
there so narrow that

> Without Horse, Bridge or Boat I o're did get
> On foote I went, yet scarce my shooes did wet.

After a little dissertation on the history of the Border,
he once more descends to prose, and complains that the
Scots miles were very long measure.

'I found that daye's journey the weariest that ever I
'footed; & at night being come to the Towne, I found
'good ordinary Countrey entertainment, my fare and my
'lodging was sweete and goode, & might have served a
'far better man than my selfe, although my selfe have
'had many times better.' Next night indeed he fared
considerably worse; but at length after all hardships,
'about two of the Clocke in the afternoone of Wednesday,
'being the thirteenth of August, & the day of Clare the
'Virgin (the Signe being in Virgo), the Moone four dayes
'olde, the Winde at the West, I came to take rest at the
'wished, long expected Auncient famous Citty of Eden-
'bourough, which I entred like Pierce Penilesse, altogether
'moneyles, but I thanke God not friendlesse; for being
'there for the time of my stay I might borrow, (if any
'man would lend) spend if I could get, begge if I had
'the impudence & steale if I durst adventure the price of
'hanging. . . . But here all my acquaintance was—Non
'est inventus.' A stranger, however, as usual took him
in, and housed him and his horse. He gives brief
description of the town, of the 'Neatherbow,' of Holyrood
House, of the lanes and closes wherein were the houses
of the gentry, and the High Street where the merchants
and tradesmen dwelt. From thence he went to Leith,
where dining with some acquaintance at Burnt Island he
recognised an old friend Sir Henry Withrington, on which

he remarks sententiously, 'Men have more privilege than 'mountains in meeting.' From Dunfermline he visits Sir George Bruce's 'cole-mines,' recently discovered at the Cooras, and vividly describes his delight and amazement. It had one entrance by land and another by the sea at low tide, so well fenced that the sea could not break in. The bed of coal was found forty feet below sea-level, and 'following the veine of the mine they did 'digge forward still: so that in the space of eight and 'twentie, or nine and twentie yeares, they have digged 'more then an English mile under the sea.' His enthusiasm rises to verse, in which he calls it 'A darke, light, 'pleasant, profitable hell.'

Through 'Glaneske' he rides up the mountains by a bridle path, 'not above a yard broad in places, so fearfull '& horrid it was to looke down into the bottome for if 'either horse or man had slipt he had fallen (without 'recovery) a good mile downright.' In an 'Irish' hovel where he lodged the night he made acquaintance with what he calls 'Irish musketoes, a Creature that hath six 'legs and lives like a monster altogether upon man's 'flesh. But they were the first and last he encountered on all his travels, which shows that English inns were clean even if rough.

He describes the Highlanders as 'Red shankes,' speaking nothing but Irish, and their attire struck him as very strange and barbarous, although he himself on one occasion went hunting with 'my Lord of Marre' 'in that 'shape.' The height of the mountains impressed him greatly; compared to them, he says, Shooter's Hill, Gad's Hill, Highgate, Hampstead, Birdlip or the Malverns are but mole-hills, or as the gizzard upon a capon's wing. He does not forget to comment upon a Scotch mist, 'which wets an Englishman to the skin.' He returned from his pilgrimage by a slightly different route to London, where the day after his arrival he was entertained 'with much good Cheere, and after Supper we had a

' Play of the Life and Death of Guy of Warwicke, plaied
' by the Right Honourable the Earle of Darbie his men.
' And so on the Thursday morning being the fifteenth of
' October, I came home to my house in London.'

Shall we leave the joys of the road and say nothing
of the wayside inn? numbered now alas amongst the
vanished joys of life. As a recent writer has said:
' Unless we are greatly deceived by the old writers, an
' English inn used to be a delightful resort, abounding in
' comfort, and supplied with the best of food ; a place,
' too, where one was sure of a welcome at once hearty
' and courteous. The inns of to-day, in country towns
' and villages, are not in that good old sense inns at all ;
' they are merely public-houses.' In Professor Elze's
Life of Shakespeare we read that in his day 'inns had
' become a well organised institution'; indeed, it is
probable that they were so from a much earlier period,
at any rate on the well travelled pilgrimage routes.
Harrison in describing them says : 'each comer is sure to
' lie in clean sheets, wherein no man hath been lodged
' since they came from the laundress, or out of the water
' wherein they were last washed. If the traveller have a
' horse, his bed doth cost him nothing, but if he go on
' foot he is sure to pay a penny for the same. But
' whether he be horseman or footman, if his chamber
' be once appointed, he may carry the key with him, as
' of his own house so long as he lodgeth there. If he
' lose aught while he abideth in the inn, the host is bound
' by a general custom to restore the damage, so that there
' is no greater security for travellers than in the greatest
' inns of England.' It was also a pleasant life there,
according to Elze, for there was music in the morning
and at dinner, and the host and hostess vied with each
other in entertaining the guests at meal times, though
they did not eat with them.

We may easily picture the comfort of the arrival,
either for the footsore pedestrian who had tramped since

daybreak, or the horseman who had battled through wind and rain, or ridden smartly to escape nightfall on the open heath. With what delight would he hail the ruddy glow that greeted him from afar, and the warmth of hospitable greeting while the ostler ran out to take round his horse, and the hostess came beaming to the door to know what he would have. And then he might sit by a roaring fire in good company, and relate the perils of the way. Mayhap he felt the crowning pleasure of the day's journey was the journey's end.

CHAPTER IX

WHAT PEOPLE READ

NOT the least among the joys of a quiet country life was the possession of a well stocked library. ' I pity unlearned ' gentlemen upon a rainy day,' was Lord Falkland's characteristic remark ; and his library at Great Tew was one of the many attractions of that charming abode, where scholars loved to foregather. Abraham Cowley, to that modest wish of his for a small house and large garden in the country, added a desire for

> ——a few friends and many books, both true
> Both wise and both delightful too !

The typical country squire of a later day, whose ideas were bounded by his stable and his kennels, if not absolutely non-existent, was far less common than he became after the Revolution and during the Hanoverian regîme. In Stuart days libraries were matters of pride and some ostentation, and considerable sums of money were spent on books by the fashionable and well-to-do.

The opening of this century saw the institution of the Bodleian Library. There had been a public library in Oxford earlier, founded by Duke Humphrey of Gloucester, and enriched by many subsequent donors, but this the greed and fanaticism of the Reformers of Edward VI.'s time had utterly destroyed. Anthony Wood says that ' some of the books so taken out by the Reformers were ' burnt, some sold for Robin Hood's pennyworths, either

' to Booksellers, or to Glovers to press their gloves, or
' Taylors to make measures, or Bookbinders to cover
' books bound by them, and some also kept by the
' Reformers for their own use.' This he learned from old
inhabitants who were living at the time of the pillage.
By the end of the sixteenth century the literary spirit
was fully awake again, and Sir Thomas Bodley was
moved to restore the old library, of which the room still
remained, and to ' make it fit and handsome with seates
' and shelfes and desks and all that may be needfull
' to stir up other benevolence to help furnish it with
' bookes.' In 1602 the Library was opened, already
containing more than two thousand volumes, and two
years later Royal Letters Patent were granted.

James I., who was a very bookish if not a very learned
man, took great interest in the scheme, and when on a
visit to Oxford he saw the statue of the founder, remarked,
' He should have been called Sir Thomas Godley.' Soon
after an advantageous agreement was entered into with
Stationers' Hall that one perfect copy of every new book
published should be presented to the Bodleian. Other
men's benevolence was soon stirred up, and valuable gifts
flowed in. The learned Alleyne bequeathed his precious
store of ancient MSS. and books to his favourite pupil
Sir Kenelm Digby in these words : ' I give to Sir Kenelm
' Digbie Knight, my noble friend, all my manuscripts and
' what other of my books he shall or may take a liking
' unto.' This bequest Sir Kenelm, at the instigation of his
earlier tutor Archbishop Laud, made over to the new library.
The MSS. were to the number of two hundred and thirty-
eight, uniformly bound and stamped with the Digby arms.

Raleigh, Cotton, Bacon, Butler, all appear among the
donors of this period, as well as Selden a little later, who
bequeathed a very valuable collection of oriental and
Greek MSS. and Rabbinical and Talmudic literature ;
Cromwell too gave some Greek MSS. The Puritans do
not seem to have inherited the iconoclastic zeal of their

predecessors as regards books, for Fairfax placed a guard round the library when Oxford fell into the hands of the rebels.   The statutes were rightly very rigid in the matter of allowing books to be taken out, and both Charles I. and the Protector were refused a loan ; a refusal which each took in good part.[1]

This is in some sense a digression, except as showing the general estimation in which books were held, but our concern is rather with the private reading of private men, and amongst them the taste for books was a growing one. We hear a good deal of Sir Kenelm Digby while in Paris busying himself in obtaining rare and curious volumes for his friends, chiefly from M. Cottard, the principal book-seller there, who had a world-wide reputation and had correspondents in Italy, Germany, Spain, or wherever rare and precious works were to be picked up.   Sir Kenelm offered to procure for Lord Conway through Cottard, *La Conqueste du Sang Real* and *The Legend of Sir Tristram*.   He could furnish also, as he informed his friend, an entire collection of all books known in that kind, ' in especiall a curious *Amadis* in XII. volumes ' in any bindings that might be wished.   In the same letter he mentions that Mr. Selden's book has been sent to M. Cottard, and is much esteemed.   This may have been the polemic against tithes that gave so much offence to the Archbishop, or possibly one of Selden's Socinian writings, which were just then attracting a good deal of attention.[2]

There must have been in those days a certain zest and freshness about books of necessity lacking to us now who are overwhelmed not only with a flood of trash, which no one is under any obligation to read, but with too much even of what is good and abundantly worth study, more than our limited capacity can grasp and hold fast. Though printing presses were increasing fast, a book was

[1] From an article on the Tercentenary of the Bodleian Library, *Church Times*, Oct. 24, 1902.

[2] *Sir Kenelm Digby*, by one of his descendants.

K

still a thing to be prized, to be read and re-read till it became part of the mind's furniture. When the circulating library was not, books must needs be bought or borrowed from a friend, who perhaps lent somewhat grudgingly, not knowing when he might see his treasure again, and they were valued accordingly. There was then no stream of light literature through the house, half of which is barely dipped into; but a book was taken down from its shelf by the aid of a step-ladder, and kept at hand for long leisurely perusal.

Yet there was ephemeral literature of a sort; it was not all hard study or solid reading for improvement. To say nothing of the weekly news-letter, which most well-to-do people would have the opportunity of seeing, or the Diurnals and Correntes that gave the public news, there was an enormous output in pamphlets during the years immediately preceding the war, and these would be eagerly bought and read by the townsfolk, and despatched by carrier into the country to friends, who even in sylvan solitudes were keenly interested in what was doing in the great world.

Besides this journalistic literature there was a large amount of light reading of another kind, much lighter indeed than romances, which in those days were apt to be both long and ponderous. Pope speaks of 'the mob of 'gentlemen who write with ease,' but these already flourished a century and more before his time. It had become the fashion for every man of culture, and a good many women too, to produce *vers d'occasion* on demand, often graceful and charming, not seldom laboured and so full of affected conceits as to be worthy of preservation as literary curiosities alone. Suckling in his *Session of Poets* enumerates not a few competitors for 'the bays' that are very minor poets indeed, and like the dense undergrowth in a coppice, crowd round the knees of the giants who lent lustre to that day.

Amongst the amateurs must be reckoned Lord

Falkland, though he now and then struck a very true and tender note ; Endymion Porter, who confessed that to him writing a poem was as bad as having a tooth drawn ; Margaret Duchess of Newcastle, that hare-brained poetess for whom Charles Lamb had so whimsical a devotion ; and Katharine Phillips 'the matchless Orinda.' Amongst these and many nameless ones there was a craze for anagrams, acrostics, and such spurious forms of art, which in a day of great literary activity will always amuse the frivolous and waste minds meant for better things by a pretence of wit. Passing over these we find a host whose exquisite lyrics, amatory, pastoral, religious, are among our best treasures. Among these we reckon Herrick, Edmund Waller, Davenant, Carew, Habington, Andrew Marvell, Henry Vaughan called the Silurist, Crashaw, and George Herbert, a galaxy which any other age would fail to match.   Most of the dramatists were lyrists also ; indeed, voluminous as are the plays of Ben Jonson or of the pair of friends Beaumont and Fletcher, it is by their exquisite lyrics they are best remembered.

It is odd to realise now, but there were men, critics rather than playgoers they must have been, who esteemed Jonson above Shakespeare. To a modern taste his comedies seem stiff and artificial, lacking in that broad, human appeal by which Shakespeare keeps an undying hold upon our sympathies.   But it must be borne in mind that the satire in which they deal is largely concerned with the jests and fashions of a passing day, which must to some extent lose their savour, while tragedy is for all time.   *Hamlet* and *King Lear* are as fresh as when they first were penned, but comedy carries date, and nothing evaporates so quickly as a jest.   Even with Shakespeare himself, except where the humour is blent with pathos or philosophy as in his matchless fools and clowns, the jokes do not ring in our ears in quite the same way, nor call forth quite such a quick response as those of our own day ; our laughter is a trifle forced.   The satire of Ben

Jonson is clever and biting, but we are conscious that we sometimes miss the point.   Perhaps this is the reason that *Drink to Me only* or *See the Chariot at Hand* linger in memories that have wholly let slip *The Alchemist* or *Every Man in his Humour*.

A special fashion of the day was for epitaphs and elegies ; where we should send a wreath on the death of a friend, they sent a copy of verses—a more abiding memorial.   An immense number were written on the death of Venetia Digby.   Her husband had so many friends among the poets, dabbling a little in poetry himself, and besides her great beauty, her romantic story, and her early death singled her out for this kind of homage.   The most touching among those preserved is the one written by Habington.   He addressed the lines to his own wife, Lucia Powys, under the name of Castara ; she had been an affectionate friend of the dead lady.

> She passed away
> So sweetly from the world, as if her clay
> Laid onely down to slumber.   Then forbeare
> To let on her blest ashes fall a teare.
> But if th'art too much woman, softly weepe,
> Lest griefe disturbe the silence of her sleepe.

Another beautiful specimen in the same kind was Lord Falkland's *Elegy on the Ladie Marquesse Hamilton*, who was one of the many victims to consumption.   It is unequal, but the following lines are very fine :—

> How sharpe a judge of all her home-bred thoughts !
> How weake a censurer of fforaigne faults !
> Who could such balm for different woundes prepare ?
> So temper insolence and calm despaire ?
> Who taught the simple like her, or who drew
> Like her the learn'd to practice what they knew ?
>
> .   .   .   .   .   .
>
> Eyes of soe modest yet soe bright a flame,
> To see her and to love her was the same.

That was indeed a golden age which, in its opening years, saw the production of some of Shakespeare's greatest

plays, and for which Spenser's *Faery Queen* had not yet
lost its first freshness, in its ripeness too was adorned by
Milton's great epics.   It was not, however, in poetry alone
that the age shone resplendent ; prose style attained
during the first half of the century its highest perfection.
Shaking itself free from the affected euphuisms of the
preceding reign, it stood forth graphic, nervous, not yet
overloaded with epithet as it shortly afterwards became,
and with a balanced symmetry of construction and music
of rhythm that make it stand in much the same relation
to modern prose as does the Gothic architecture of the
ancient cathedrals to the composite indeterminate style of
the buildings of to-day.   Shelley, no mean critic, thus
speaks of Bacon's style : ' His language has a sweet and
' majestic rhythm which satisfies the sense no less than
' the almost superhuman wisdom of his philosophy satisfies
' the intellect.'

The early years of the century saw the completion of
that grand achievement, the translation of the Holy Scripture, which was authorised by King James for use in the
Church of England, and has remained the standard
rendering ever since.   A careful comparison of it with the
version which the joint labours of three hundred revisors
have produced, will reveal how far our language has fallen,
not in beauty merely but in force and expressiveness from
that of an earlier day.   The scholarship of that day,
moreover, had not only attained a very high level, but
enjoyed certain special advantages.   For over a century
Oriental scholars had been swarming into all the universities of Europe, and it may well be supposed that men
who were in constant intercourse with Greeks, for whom
their language was still a living one, had better opportunities for appreciating the force and vividness of the tongue
than those for whom it had truly become a dead language.
The *Athenæ Oxonienses* has a brief notice of one Christopher
Angel, born in the Peloponnesus, thrust out by the Turks,
who, coming to Yarmouth in 1607, was helped by the

Bishop of Norwich. He spent three years at Trinity College, Cambridge; in 1610 went to Oxford and was 'exhibited' there also; studied at Balliol and did very good service there among the young scholars who were 'raw in the Greek tongue,' and continued there until his death in 1639. He published several books. His case is typical of many. The account books of Winchester College record many payments during this century to refugee Greeks, and it is probable they were employed to teach their own tongue as the French refugees did theirs at a later day.

The 'new way' of pronouncing Greek, though introduced into Cambridge nearly a hundred years earlier by Sir John Cheke, tutor to the young King Edward VI., had by no means yet won universal acceptance, as is shown in a very interesting passage in Adam Martindale's Memoirs; he is speaking of one of the masters at St. Helen's Free School about the year 1634, and says: 'He 'had beene brought up not only at a good schoole in 'Bolton, but after at the University a good season (I have 'heard five yeares), where having a great affection to the 'Greeke tongue, an opportunity to heare the public 'professor, and to converse with other men, he had 'attained to a marvellouse exactnesse in pronouncing it in 'the University manner, which till then I had not heard 'of.' Sir John Cheke, the first holder of the Greek Lectureship which Henry VIII. founded in Cambridge, had, together with his learned friend, Sir Thomas Smith, thought out what he considered to be the true and ancient method of pronunciation, 'partly by considering the power 'of the letters themselves, partly by consulting with Greek 'authors, Aristophanes and others; in some whereof they 'found footsteps to correct them how the ancient Greeks 'pronounced.'[1]

This involved him in a hot controversy with the Chancellor, Gardiner, Bishop of Winchester, who forbade

[1] *Life of Sir John Cheke*, by Strype.

that these new-fangled methods should be taught in the University.   Cheke appealed to the authority of Erasmus, who also considered the pronunciation in vogue corrupt ; and it is worthy of remark that it was the Reformers in religion who were most keen on reforming Greek, so that it became quite a party question.   It is, however, not a little singular that neither disputant should have referred to the practice of learned Greeks themselves, though to judge by the specimens cited by Cheke, the pronunciation then in use must have been almost identical with that of educated Greeks of to-day.   That Cheke was hardly a trustworthy guide in such matters we may guess by his extraordinary spelling of his mother-tongue, which was by no means the casual haphazard spelling of his day, but thought out on a system of his own, and which he constantly endeavoured to introduce.   In his system the final *e*, making a syllable long, was to be banished, and in its place all letters in a long syllable doubled, as *maad, straat, desiir, liif ; y* also he would banish, using instead a double *e*.   His new method with English never took hold of his contemporaries, but, supported by being considered the mark of a true Protestant, his Greek pronunciation won its way.

There is a remarkable passage in Gibbon bearing upon the survival of the true Greek tongue.   ' In their lowest ' servitude and depression, the subjects of the Byzantine ' Throne were still possessed of a golden key that could ' unlock the treasures of antiquity, of a musical and prolific ' language that gives a soul to the objects of sense, and ' a body to the abstractions of philosophy.   Since the ' barriers of the monarchy, and even of the capital, had ' been trampled under foot, the various barbarians had ' doubtless corrupted the form and substance of the ' national dialect ; and ample glossaries have been com- ' posed, to interpret a multitude of words, of Arabic, ' Turkish, Sclavonian, Latin, or French origin.   But a ' purer idiom was spoken in the court, and taught in the

' college, and the flourishing state of the language is
' described, and perhaps embellished, by a learned Italian,
' who, by a long residence and noble marriage, was
' naturalised at Constantinople about thirty years before
' the Turkish conquest. "The vulgar speech," says
' Philelphus, "has been depraved by the people, and
' " infected by the multitude of strangers and merchants,
' " who every day flock to the city and mingle with the
' " inhabitants. It is from the disciples of such a school
' " that the Latin language received the versions of Aris-
' " totle and Plato, so obscure in sense, and in spirit so
' " poor. But the Greeks who have escaped the contagion
' " are those whom we follow, and they alone are worthy
' " of our imitation. In familiar discourse they still speak
' " the tongue of Aristophanes and Euripides, of the
' " historians and philosophers of Athens, and the style of
' " their writings is still more elaborate and correct. The
' " persons who, by their birth and offices, are attached to
' " the Byzantine court, are those who maintain, with the
' " least alloy, the ancient standard of elegance and purity ;
' " and the native graces of language most conspicuously
' " shine among the noble matrons, who are excluded
' " from all intercourse with foreigners." ' It was this
pure-spoken Greek which, after the fall of Constantinople,
was dispersed among all centres of learning throughout
Europe, and formed a living link with the tongue of the
ancients.

On the scholarship of that day we may take the
testimony of the German critics who are allowed high
authority on the question ; they assert that ' Few of these
' recent Anglican scholars (except it be Bishop Lightfoot)
' would or could pretend to critical equality with Bishop
' Bryan Walton and his colleagues,' the men who, under
the direction of Archbishop Laud, produced the London
Polyglot Bible, of which Professor Nestlé, in the last
edition of his book on the *Textual Criticism of the New
Testament*, has said : ' Of the four great Polyglots that of

' the Anglican scholars is the most copious, convenient,
' and critically valuable, and still the most used.'   Elsewhere these scholars have been called 'a splendid galaxy
' of Archbishop Laud's disciples—men of eminent scholar-
' ship.'   Of one of them, Edmund Castle, who after the
Restoration was made chaplain to Charles II., it is
recorded that during the Puritan 'reign of terror' he
worked on the great Bible for seventeen or eighteen hours
a day.

This has led us far from the ordinary reading of ordinary
folk ; the Polyglot was written by the learned for the
learned ; but these men were the immediate successors of
those who had given the Authorised Version to the people,
and that was increasingly in the hands of every one, gentle
or simple.   The High Churchmen no less than the
Puritans delighted in the study of it, reading the daily
lessons appointed if unable to hear them read in church.
In our own day Ruskin has given his testimony to the
influence its pure and stately diction had on his own
writing, and it is not improbable that many seventeenth-
century writers more or less consciously formed their style
on the same model.   Undoubtedly, from his regular
attendance at daily matins and evensong, Clarendon's ear
would be familiar with its beautiful cadences, and not only
his vivid narrative, his graphic delineation, his simplicity,
but also the music of his rhythmical sentences owed as
much to that source as to his earlier study of Shakespeare.
The age of prose literature which began with Bacon may
be said to have culminated in Clarendon ; though he wrote
during the Restoration period, he belonged to the earlier
day which had formed his style, and was untouched by
the change in literary taste which then prevailed.   Some
might perhaps assign rather to Milton this culminating
place.   He indeed, though he wrote earlier, may be taken
as a turning-point, since he ushered in the new rather
than represented the old.   His prose, compared with that
of the masters of the first half of the seventeenth century,

is turgid, over-emphasised, and loaded with epithet; he needed the trammels of verse to do his best work.   Though his political writings have fine passages, he is lacking in restraint, and has more of the passion of the pamphleteer than the dignity of the historian.

History was at that time a very popular study; Camden's *Annals* and Baker's *Chronicle* were both new books and much read.   The first Lord Falkland, who was a distinguished man and of considerable literary taste, if less so than his son Lucius, was reputed to be the author of a *History of the most Unfortunate Prince, King Edward II.*, and Lord Herbert of Cherbury, in the midst of his travels and various adventures, found time to write a *Life of King Henry VIII.*   The Classics, either in the originals or in translations, were much in favour, especially Plutarch's *Lives*, Pliny, and Herodotus.   Translations from Italian and Spanish were also greatly in vogue; but Dante seems to have been familiar to English readers chiefly in the Latin translation.   French history, too, was a good deal read.   The Earl of Warwick, not the Lord High Admiral, but his son, found solace in his fits of the gout in having it read aloud to him by his devoted wife.   Her own tastes lay rather in the direction of theology, which was indeed popular with nearly every one at this period, and the lists of books for her own reading in her later life are composed of such serious writers as St. Bernard, George Herbert, Jeremy Taylor, Baxter, Samuel Rutherford, Clarke, The *Confessions* of St. Augustine, John Janeway's *Dying*, Foxe's *Book of Martyrs*, Cayley's *Glimpses of Eternity*, and hosts of sermons.   When she was a girl her favourite reading had been romances, which she and her young sister-in-law used to devour, and in 1637 her father's New Year's gift to her was Sir Philip Sidney's *Arcadia*.

Ladies were then, as ever, great readers of romances, though their day does not seem to have been as fortunate in that line as in the higher walks of literature.   To a modern taste the lengthy tales they read appear insipid

and tiresome to a degree ; indeed the charming Dorothy
Osborne, who found them a great resource in her quiet
country life, is often very caustic in her comments upon
them.   There do not appear to have been many written
in English ; most of those she criticises were translated
from the French.   In one letter she remarks : ' I have no
' patience neither for these translators of romances.   I
' met with *Polexander* and *L'illustre Bassa* both so disguised
' that I, who am their old acquaintance, hardly knew them ;
' besides that, they were still so much French in words and
' phrases that it was impossible for one that understands
' not French to make anything of them.   If poor *Prazi-*
' *mène* be in the same dress I would not see her for the
' world.'   To this is appended a note by the editor of the
Letters : ' *Prazimène* and *Polexander* are two romances
' translated from the French—the former a neat little
' duodecimo ; the latter a huge folio of more than three
' hundred and fifty closely printed pages.   The title-page
' of the first runs as follows :—" Two delightful Novels,
' " or the Unlucky Fair One ; being the Amours of
' " Milistrate and Prazimène, Illustrated with Variety of
' " Chance and Fortune.   Translated from the French by
' " a Person of Quality.   London.   Sold by Eben Tracy,
' " at the Three Bibles on London Bridge."   *Polexander*
' was done into English by William Browne, Gent., for the
' behoof of the Earl of Pembroke.'

Cleopâtre and *Le Grand Cyrus* Dorothy read in the
original.   The latter had been translated by Madame de
Scudéry in ten volumes of ten parts each.   One is disposed
to pity Sir William Temple when Dorothy proposes to
send him *Cleopâtre* in twenty-three volumes of twelve
parts ; one only hopes he had not to stand an examination
in them.   In return he lent her a translation by Robert
Codrington of *La Reine Marguerite*, Memoirs of Marguerite
de Valois.   Her criticism on it is interesting : ' If you
' will have my opinion of her, I think she had a good deal
' of wit and a great deal of patience for a woman of so high

' a spirit.   She speaks with too much indifference of her
' husband's several amours, and commends Bussy as if she
' were a little concerned in him.   I think her a better
' sister than wife, and believe she might have made a
' better wife to a better husband.'

Though her chief taste was for romances, Dorothy read
poetry with some discrimination, and quotes with much
appreciation Cowley's verses on David and Jonathan.   On
the *Poems and Fancies* of Margaret Duchess of Newcastle,
Charles Lamb's 'thrice noble, chaste, and virtuous, but
' again somewhat fantastical and original brained Margaret
' Newcastle,' Mistress Dorothy is somewhat severe ; she
says : 'And first let me ask you if you have seen a book
' newly come out, made by my Lady Newcastle?   For
' God's sake if you meet with it send it to me ; they say
' 'tis ten times more extravagant than her dress.   Sure
' the poor woman is a little distracted, she would never be
' so ridiculous else as to venture at writing books, and in
' verse too.'   Later she writes : 'You need not send me
' my Lady Newcastle's book at all, for I have seen it, and
' am persuaded there are many soberer people in Bedlam.'

She occasionally varied her reading by a book of travels.
In one letter she says : 'By the way, have you read the
' story of China written by a Portuguese Fernando Mendez
' Pinto, I think his name is?   If you have not, take it
' with you, 'tis as diverting a book of the kind as ever I
' read, and is as handsomely written.   You must allow
' him the privilege of a traveller, and he does not abuse it.
' His lies are as pleasant and harmless ones as lies can be,
' and no great number considering the scope he has for
' them.' [1]

Travels, from the days of Marco Polo through the
stirring times of Elizabeth, when almost year by year fresh
realms were being discovered, were always fascinating, and
the tales of explorers must have been followed with an even
keener zest in those days when so much of the round world

[1] *Letters of Dorothy Osborne*, Judge Parry.

From Account of the Embassy of Nieuhoff, by George Hornius.

WILD BEASTS OF TARTARY.

PLATE XI.

was still unknown, than that with which we greet the
narrative of a Stanley or a Nansen. Hakluyt's *Voyages*
were still fresh, having been published in 1600, and were
continually being followed by accounts of travels in the
New World or the Old. In 1625 appeared *Purchas His
Pilgrims*, giving an account of the experiences of various
travellers, and adorned with woodcuts and maps, and about
the same time Sir Kenelm Digby published a description
of his buccaneering adventures in the Bay of Scanderoon
and elsewhere, which was, to say the least, highly coloured.
Some time in this century a remarkable book of travels
in the interior of Thibet appeared, written by a Jesuit
missionary. A very curious book (which, however, was
not published till a little later) was written about this time
in Latin by one George Hornius, giving a full account of
the embassy of Nieuhoff from the Low Countries to the
great Khan of Tartary, describing his sojourn in that
region, with pictures of cities, streets, and temples, of
customs and costumes, of flora and fauna that are most
curious, and must have filled untravelled folk with amazement. The map, if less accurate than a modern Ordnance
Survey, is far more suggestive, giving not only mountains
and rivers in a pictorial style, but depicting the ships,
trees, and wild beasts that the traveller might expect to
encounter in the various localities he came to.

In the Diary of John Rous, incumbent of Stanton
Downham, Suffolk, there is a most interesting account of
a book which he appears to have read with great attention,
as he gives a complete *résumé* of it; it was printed in
1631, and was called 'God's Power and Providence in
' preserving 8 Englishmen, left by mischance in Greenland,
' 1630, 9 Months and 12 Days, reported by Edward
' Pelham.' 'The booke contayned a mappe of Greenland,
' lying from 77 N. L. to 80; with it a whale described
' (which is ordinarily 60 foote long); his fashion somewhat
' like a gogeon. Also the manner of taking, killing,
' cutting, and boiling of him; a description of a sea-morce,

' as big as an oxe, etc.' Mr. Rous gives at some length the description of the country and the adventures of the crew of the *Salutation*, who, by some accident, got left behind at Bell's Sound from August until May, and endured great hardships by the excessive cold.

The Essay was another form of writing which had a great vogue at this time; it was brought into fashion by Bacon, who found it an appropriate vehicle for his lighter thoughts, and suited to a variety of subjects, being capable of expansion to suit a discursive theme such as his most charming dissertation on Gardens, or of contraction to an almost epigrammatic brevity to convey some didactic reflections on Friendship, Religion, or the like. Dr. Earle made use of the same form for his clever satirical little character sketches in his *Microcosmography*, for which it was equally well suited. Sir Thomas Browne's *Religio Medici* is really a series of essays, though in the shape of numbered sections of a long treatise. His dissertation upon Urn Burial, called *Hydriotaphia*, appeared in pamphlet form, as did most antiquarian papers or articles on kindred subjects, for the day of the magazines was not yet.

The Verneys do not appear to have been great readers; Sir Ralph's anxious inquiries as to the welfare of Turkey-work cushions and armour which he fears might have fallen a prey to moth and rust, include but slight mention to books; a casual inquiry about '*The Booke of Martirs* and other bookes in the withdrawingroom' comprises his anxiety on that head; but in the unoccupied leisure and dulness of a French country town, he turned to reading as a resource and wrote to Dr. Denton to send him books. His taste leaned to politics and religion; he asks for no poetry and no romances, though Mary had a weakness for the latter for which Uncle Denton rebukes her. Ralph's request was for 'Milton's *Iconoclastes*; the *Levellers* ' *vindicated;* Prynne's *Historical Collection of ancient* ' *Parliaments;* an *Impeachment against Cromwell and* ' *Ireton;* Ascham; Bishop Andrews 2 manuals; Hooker

' his 6 and 8 books ; *History of Independency ;* 2 Sclaters.'
In answering Dr. Denton ' heartily recommends Sclater to
' landlady's reading.' This was one of his pet names for
Mary. ' It treats or rather indeed mencions AntiXt . . .
' tell her it is now time to leave her romanz ; to please
' me it is one of the best books I ever read ; he is
' strangely piquante and short and strangely convincing.'

Sir Ralph, though he never attained much fluency in
speaking French, had a competent knowledge of it for
reading and writing, and Dr. Denton, anxious no doubt
to suggest a wholesome occupation to him that should
keep him from brooding on his troubles, suggests, ' If
' you would do a good worke indeed you should translate
' Canterbury and Chillingworth their books into French,
' for certainly never any books gave a greater blow to
' papacy than those two.' ' Canterbury's ' book is probably
the one written by Laud in answer to Fisher the Jesuit :
a book which King Charles thought very highly of and
bequeathed to his little daughter Elizabeth ' to ground
' her against Popery.' After the execution of the Archbishop Henry Verney sent to his brother his last sermon
and prayer, ' it is, I assure you,' he wrote, ' a true book
' and a good one.'

The King was a great reader, and the list of his books
which he had with him in captivity, and which were in
Mr. Herbert's charge, show what were his tastes ; they
comprised ' a Bible, Bishop Andrews' Sermons, Hooker's
' *Ecclesiastical Polity*, Dr. Hammond's works, Villapandus
' upon Ezekiel, Sands's *Paraphrase upon King David's*
' *Psalms*, Herbert's *Divine Poems ;* and also *Godfrey of*
' *Bulloigne*, writ in Italian by Torquato Tasso, and done
' into English Heroick verse by Mr. Fairfax, a poem his
' Majesty much commended, as he did also *Ariosto* by
' Sir John Harrington, a facetious poet much esteemed
' by Prince Henry his master ; Spenser's *Fairy Queen*
' and the like for alleviating his spirits after serious studies.'
' In many of his books,' continues Mr. Herbert, ' he

' delighted himself with the motto *Dum spiro spero* which
' he wrote frequently. He understood authors in the
' original, whether Greek, Latin, French, Spanish, or
' Italian, which three last he spoke perfectly : and none
' better read in histories of all sorts, which rendered him
' accomplisht and also would discourse well in Arts and
' Sciences, and indeed not unfitted for any subject.' [1]

In these lists of books, whether of royal or private
readers fiction appears to take the lowest place, the
middle region is occupied by travels, essays, and history,
while the highest honours are accorded to Poetry and
Divinity. A classification which, it must be owned, has
much to recommend it.

[1] *Memorials of the Last Days of King Charles*, by Sir Thomas Herbert.

CHAPTER X

NEWS

WITH what eager interest must news have been looked for during the stirring years of the second quarter of the century. Long before the war actually broke out the ferment was working, and thoughtful men were looking anxiously for developments of a strained situation. Clarendon speaks of the opening years of the reign of Charles I. as a time of great peace and prosperity, but from the very beginning the fires of discontent were smouldering, and from the moment of the meeting of the Long Parliament no man could tell what a day might bring forth. And as yet there were no daily papers, no morning news of the debates overnight; men had to wait with what patience they might for the weekly newsletter, and perhaps for several days after it had arrived in the neighbourhood for their turn for a sight of it.

Though by the time the war began an immense number of Diurnalls and Correntes were in circulation, they did not for long supplant the private newsletter which was such a feature of the time, and upon which most country dwellers depended for reliable information of what was passing. And this for obvious reasons : the Censor was then a power beyond the privilege of the Press. Not Lord Kitchener himself could be more strict about war correspondents than were those in power on either side, and no news was permitted to pass which had not been authorised. But the news-letter was a private

matter. A gentleman living in the country, or two or
three neighbours combining to share the expense would
arrange to have news supplied regularly by some professional writer, of whom there were at that time many
in town, who sent copies to several patrons at a certain
fixed rate, and a cipher would be agreed upon to convey
dangerous matter in case of the letters being opened.
Impartiality, of course, was no more to be expected than
in the public prints, and would not have been acceptable;
the writer knew what views were expected, and wrote
accordingly, but at least he was unmuzzled. A recent
book by Lady Newdigate, strangely called *Cavalier and
Puritan*, though dealing with post-Restoration times, gives
very interesting specimens of this kind of correspondence,
carefully preserved by the descendants of Sir Richard
Newdigate, to whom the letters were supplied, and though
they do not bear on the period under consideration, they
give a very fair idea of the kind of channel of communication that existed, when several days' journey over bad
roads lay between many a country home and the news
of the town.

For long the public newspapers were neither daily nor
even weekly ; the earliest were yearly. *Gallo Belgicus*,
which was supposed to be the first published in England,
was a kind of Annual Register or History of our own
Times. A note to Earle's *Microcosmography* says : ' It
' was writ in Latin and entitled *Mercurii Gallo-Belgici :
' sive, rerum in Gallia et Belgia potissimum : Hispania
' quoque, Italia, Anglia, Germanica, Poponia, Vicinisque locis
' ap anno 1588, ad Martium anni 1594, gestarum nuncii.
' Vol. I. printed in 8vo at Cologne, 1598, and published
' annually till 1605 ; then half-yearly.'* There was
certainly a great advantage in the use of a common
tongue, so that one newspaper could supply the nations
of Europe without translation.

Mercurius seems to have been the favourite title,
though the papers are sometimes mentioned as Corente

Christ Church Coll: Ox: Canterbury Minster Trinn: Colledge Camb:

MERCURIUS RUSTICUS

Countiss of Rivers plundered page 11

Sr John Lucas house plundered Page 3

THE COVNTRY COMPLAINT Recovnting the Sad Events of this vnparraleld WARR

Sr Rich Minshuls house plundered page 31

A Bonfire for the voting downe Episcopacy page 26

Mr Jones a Minr carried on a Beare, page 81

Warder Castle defended by a Lady page 4

Edge-hill Battle

Frontispiece to Mercurius Rusticus for 1646.

or Curante (Courant). Lady Brilliana Harley says in one letter, 'The Curantes are lisenced againe,' and in another, 'If the venter (vendor) of the Corrantes be in prison.' *Mercurius Rusticus* appears to have been an annual publication, and in the year 1646 a republication of it appeared, or possibly merely selections from it, giving a brief *résumé* of the course of the war in a small duodecimo. In a copy of this belonging to J. C. Palmer, Esq., some hand has written under the title in faded ink, 'by John Cleveland ye Poet.' The frontispiece with which it is adorned is prefixed to this chapter. My reason for thinking this to be rather an epitome than the original publication is that the account of the siege of Corfe Castle is more briefly given than in the one quoted in Hutchins's *History of Dorsetshire*, no mention appearing of the inventory of goods, and also that the despoiling of cathedrals and the complaint of the universities appear in separate parts at the end. It is full of interesting matter, but would lead us too far into the domain of politics. It was of strictly Royalist principles, and gives many harrowing details of the rough usage of the clergy and their families at the hands of the Puritans. *Mercurius Brittanicus*, the popular organ, would enlarge rather on the licence of the Cavaliers; no doubt both sides found abundant matter for complaint. *Mercurius Aulicus* was the official Royalist paper published at Oxford, and on the other side were *Mercurius Politicus* and *Mercurius Pragmaticus*. Needham's newspaper, which appeared in 1643, had the reputation of being a turncoat.

There is a large collection of these newspapers bound up with the pamphlets of the day in the British Museum; most of them seem to have appeared at erratic intervals in pamphlet form; they did not assume their modern shape of a large sheet printed in columns till much later. The *Moderate Intelligencer* for the week, from Thursday, July 15, to July 22, 1647, is a very fair specimen of the Government organ of that day. It gives fairly full parliamentary reports with the news that Fairfax was appointed Generalissimo of the Forces. Eleven members ask for six months' leave to go beyond the sea. This was a good deal later than the compulsory signing of the Covenant, which sent so many into voluntary exile, but it is highly probable they wished to be out of the way if, as was feared, the imprisoned king should be brought to trial. There is plenty of foreign intelligence, most of it of fighting; from Hamburg, from 'Frankfurd,' from 'Cullein,' from the Hague and Ratisbon comes news of some sort or another. At Naples, we learn, two galleys had arrived bringing news of the French fleet. From Rome comes a full account of the ceremony of the Pope, attended by the Cardinals, going on Whit Sunday to the Vatican, and thence in procession with the blessed Sacrament to St. Peter's. Venice at this time was fighting with the Turks, and a battle is reported.

Parliament had its private newsletters supplied by special correspondents, and published them or not as seemed fit. One of April 28, 1642, gives an account of a political meeting at Blackheath, and another of the same month sends from Ireland news of victories there. These two were published.

The dates of these papers are often perplexing on account of the variations of the calendar; the Roman calendar had been rectified by Pope Gregory XIII. in 1527; his alterations were accepted on the Continent by Catholics but refused by Protestants, and while England followed the old style till 1752, Scotland adopted the new in 1600, to the utter confusion of dates in the records of the time. In the earlier calendar, the year was held to begin with Lady Day, a much more appropriate season than the dead of winter, and this custom was followed till long after the other points of the changed calendar had been accepted.

Of gossip there was plenty in these papers, especially when just before the war the king was at York, and exaggerated or distorted reports of his sayings and doings flew about. Clarendon has a quaint little story of this :—

'Mr. Hyde had been absent four or five days from the
'Court; and came into the Presence when the King was
'washing his Hands before Dinner; and as soon as the
'King saw him He asked him aloud, "Ned Hyde, when
'"did you play with my Bandstrings last?" Upon
'which He was exceedingly out of Countenance, not
'imagining the Cause of the Question, and the Room
'being full of Gentlemen, who appeared to be Merry
'with what the King had asked. But his Majesty
'observing him to be in Disorder, and to blush very
'much, said pleasantly, "Be not troubled at it, for I have
'"worn no Bandstrings these twenty Years": and then
'asked him whether He had not seen the Diurnal, of
'which He had not heard till then; but shortly after,
'some of the standers-by shewed him a Diurnal, in which
'there was a Letter of Intelligence printed, where it was
'said that Ned Hyde was grown so familiar with the
'King that He used to play with his Band-strings, Which
'was a Method of Calumniating They began then, and
'shortly after prosecuted and exercised upon much
'greater Persons.'

A gossiping report from the refugee Court in Paris in 1645 is quoted in the Verney Letters. In a Diurnal from London appeared 'A Letter from a Gentleman of 'quality out of ffrance, giving some account of the 'English Queen at the Louvre and the English refugees 'who were with her.' These, it appeared, gave great offence to the ultra-Protestant section by attending Catholic churches, rather than the schismatical worship of the Huguenots. The writer says :—

'I have now been 15 days at Paris where our
'queene of England is with her court at the Louvre, at
'the resident's sir Richard Brown we have sermons, the
'common prayer, the booke of execration against the

' Parliament and their faction, as they term them, duly
' and devoutly read, by the Bishop of Londonderry, Dr.
' Cousins, who came hither disguised in a Miller's habit
' and others of these worthy instruments of superstition,
' keeps a constant preachment of railing against the
' roundheads, just as the capuchins do against the
' Protestants.   The ladyes of honour to the queen and
' the rest of the royalists are constantly there.   The
' queene goes on Tuesday to St. Germains.   Dr. Verne,
' chaplain lately to our King, is turned Papist, and
' writes against the Protestants.   They hate the French
' Protestants, and seldom or never come to Church but
' with the Papists.'   The grammar of this is rather wild,
and very likely some of the statements were equally so,
as there seems no trace anywhere else of the ' booke of
' execration.'

Except these Letters of Intelligence there was no
correspondence in the papers of those days ; if people
wanted to air their views they wrote pamphlets ; indeed
the pamphlet entirely took the place of the leading
article of our own times.   So great a man as Milton did
not disdain the pamphlet as a vehicle for his opinions,
and while he was Cromwell's secretary he poured forth
a stream of articles on the topics of the day.   Fine as
are certain passages on the freedom of the Press and
kindred subjects, his admirers cannot but regret that he
should rather have lowered his powers to the level of
journalism than have raised the pamphlet to a style
worthy of him ; he seems to have had as great a
command of abusive language for his adversaries as he
had of noble diction for his high poetic themes ; and
worse, at Cromwell's bidding he could not only write against
the book he had already acknowledged to be the king's,
endeavouring to fasten the authorship on Hammond and
Harris, but could stoop to insult the memory of the fallen
monarch.   In his *Iconoclastes* or *The Image-breaker* he
' follows the King's meditations with refutation, mockery,

'and ridicule . . . savagely vindictive in his antipathy,
'he revives the malignant calumny that Charles had
'poisoned his own father.' In a previous tract against
another opponent, 'his luckless adversary is mauled,
'tumbled, rolled in the dust through pages of angry
'vituperation—he is a pork, a clod, an idiot by breeding
'and a solicitor by presumption . . . basest and hungriest
'inditer . . . a boar in the vineyard, a snout in this
'pickle, an unswilled hogshead, a brazen ass.'[1]

Innumerable writers, great and small, known and
unknown, poured forth pamphlets day after day, more
or less angry and incoherent. Not many of these had
or deserved the immortality of Milton's masterpieces of
vituperation which are still read and quoted; most repose
in dusty obscurity upon the shelves of the British Museum,
although from a historical point of view the most worthless of them has its value for the sidelight it throws on
the motives and points of view of the average man of
the day. There is much in them that reminds the reader
✗ quaintly of some of the pro-Boer, anti-vaccination, or
Liberationist literature of our own day. If one sometimes
marvels where people get their strange opinions it is well
to read what they read, and gain some idea of the mental
atmosphere they live in. Of literary criticism the journals
contained none. In fact the critic of that day was rather
a commentator and, as Bishop Earle says, 'sells books
'dearer by swelling them into folios by his comments.'

An odd writer of the day, whose travels we had in
a former chapter, John Taylor, called the Water-Poet,
should be reckoned rather with the journalists than with
serious writers. Originally a Thames waterman by trade,
he developed a surprising facility with the pen either in
prose or verse, sometimes publishing in a Broadsheet an
account of a murder, or a description of a naval sham-
fight, or a display of fireworks on the occasion of a royal
wedding, or inditing a copy of verses for the Ballad-

[1] *Life of Milton*, Masson.

✗ "Pro-Boer" literature is tame compared with
that of the anti-Boer-; the Liberationist literature
is tame compared with that of the clerical claims
& vituperations against nonconformists.

mongers in the penny-a-liner vein. Clever and versatile, he attracted the notice of King James, and was a great ally of Archie Armstrong, one of the last of the royal jesters, to whom he inscribed his *Very Merrie Wherrie Ferry Voyage.* More in the nature of a book was his *Pennilesse Pilgrimage* already described. He also published a brief *Chronicle of the English Sovereigns*, adorned with little woodcuts. He begins very early with Brute, Locrine, Leire, etc., coming down through Constantine to Uther Pendragon and Arthur; it extends to King Charles. A rather fuller one with bigger woodcuts began only at the Conquest.

It is difficult to realise a time when news travelled so slowly as it must have done then, when the speed of a horse was the maximum attainable; yet with all the advantages the telegraph has brought, which our fathers could not miss, never having known, it may be doubted whether it has not inflicted more sorrow and anxiety than it has saved. In the old days of war when news came, it came complete, by personal messenger more often than by post, so that questions could be asked and details learned at once. Now the bare fact of dead, wounded, or missing is flashed over the wires, and followed by agonising weeks of waiting to learn particulars; and very often letters come in the meanwhile penned in full health and strength, unknowing of the doom which the recipient has already learned.

It was remarkable, however, what could be accomplished in the way of speed when there was necessity, as Clarendon remarks, alluding to the time when the king was at York, Lord Falkland with him, and he himself, Mr. Hyde as he then was, remained in London to send despatches of everything that transpired in Parliament. He says: 'It was a wonderful Expedition that was then used ' between York and London, when Gentlemen undertook ' the Service, as enough were willing to do: insomuch as ' when they dispatched a Letter on Saturday Night, at

' that Time of the Year (April) about twelve at Night,
' they received always the King's Answer Monday by ten
' of the Clock in the Morning.'[1]

A propos of these letters, it is worth recording, since
Charles I. is so often accused of unfaithfulness to those
who served him, that lest Mr. Hyde might receive some
prejudice with the Parliament if any report should get
about, the king always copied those lengthy despatches
with his own hand before any one else should see them.
' Mr. Hyde told him that he writ a very ill Hand, which
' would give his Majesty too much Trouble to transcribe
' himself, and that He had so much Friendship with
' Secretary Nicholas, that He was well contented He
' should be trusted : to which the King said, Nicholas
' was a very honest Man ; and He would trust him in
' anything that concerned himself; but that in this
' Particular, which would be so penal to the other, if it
' should be known, it was not necessary ; for He would
' quickly learn to read that Hand, if it were writ at first
' with a little the more Care ; and no Body should see it
' but himself. And his Majesty continued so firm to this
' Resolution, that though the Declarations from the
' Houses shortly after grew so voluminous, that the
' Answers frequently contained five or six Sheets of
' Paper very closely writ ; his Majesty always transcribed
' them with his own Hand ; which sometimes took him
' up two or three Days, and a good Part of the Night,
' before He produced them to the Council ; where they
' were first read, and then He burned the Originals.
' And He gave himself no Ease in this Particular till Mr.
' Hyde left the Parliament, and by his Majesty's Command
' attended upon him at York.'[2]

Letters were not always so speedily transmitted as by
the royal express. The Postmastership, which conferred
the sole right of forwarding letters and keeping post-
horses upon the king's highway was a much-coveted

[1] *Clarendon's Life.*   [2] *Ibid.*

monopoly, and any infringement was much resented. At one time it was granted to Endymion Porter with reversion to his son George. It was, however, so little to be relied on that we usually find people preferring to send their letters by carrier. Lady Brilliana Harley nearly always despatched her letters to her son at Oxford by carrier as well as the hampers which she sent from time to time with apples, mead, or violet cakes. Sir William Temple and his charming Dorothy made use of the same means of communication, as the carrier is occasionally bitterly reproached if a letter goes astray, though, to do them justice, it seems to have happened much seldomer than with the legitimate post.

The carrier was a great institution, and it may not be generally known that the Cambridge carrier of this date, one Hobson,[1] is supposed to have been the origin of the phrase 'Hobson's choice,' as he kept post-horses as well, and insisted on his customers taking the horse that stood nearest the stable door. As a purveyor of news the carrier must have been slow, but no doubt in many a country village he was the sole link with the outer world, and was looked for in those days of war with as much anxiety as the mail coach in the days of Waterloo, as he made his leisurely journey by the deep-rutted lanes or through the snow.

[1] Hobson, as we learn from Milton's sonnet, died of being stopped in his work. When the plague was raging in London he was forbidden to go thither, and the cessation in his accustomed habits killed the old man.

CHAPTER XI

THE LITERARY COTERIE

DURING the halcyon time, as Clarendon calls it, between the accession of Charles I. and the outbreak of the Great Rebellion, the literary coterie blossomed abundantly. Ever since the Renaissance literature had been in fashion amongst men of the world, and the patron had been for long, and still was, an institution. In the previous reign the Earl of Southampton who was Shakespeare's friend, the great Duke of Buckingham, and the Earl of Arundel, had all shone in this capacity, as did also both King James and King Charles, but in the latter reign something a little different in character came to the front. The fact was, literary men had gradually obtained a much higher social standing than had formerly been theirs; the men of fashion themselves now took up the pen; and in place of a crowd of pensioners waiting on the favour of the patron, we find a party of guests, entertained at his table by a man of culture and high position, in many cases forming a brilliant galaxy of talent.

Clarendon compares this time with the much-vaunted Elizabethan era somewhat to the advantage of his own day. Undisturbed by wars, unthreatened by any foreign foe, it was yet a stirring time; the ideals of the Renaissance and of the Reformation were still seething in men's brains; the political ferment of the future was already working, seeds which were almost immediately to bring forth the temporary overthrow of Monarchy amongst ourselves, and later to issue in the French Revolution, were already germinating : for the moment it was Peace, but not 'the long, long canker of Peace' which the nineteenth-century poet thought so fatal to the national character.

The Coffee House as a meeting-place for wits and poets was as yet undeveloped ; the earliest was started in Oxford in 1649, and though the club at the Mermaid drew the actors and dramatists together, there were some who did not care for the high play or noisy company of the tavern, and they generally found a resort at some great man's table. Sir Thomas Gresham's new College in the City was the chief centre for the men of science who already formed the nucleus of what was to be the Royal Society, and among them were numbered not only such scientific students as Sir Thomas Browne, Robert Boyle, or the versatile Sir Kenelm Digby, but even some of the poets, as Cowley, Waller, and later Dryden ; the purely literary element of society, however, met more often in private houses. Endymion Porter, who had learned some-thing of the duties of the patron under the roof of his wife's kinsman the Duke of Buckingham, kept open house in the Strand, and thither resorted not only the fashionable world but a concourse of poets, artists, and musicians. The pencil of Vandyck and the pen of Suckling help us to picture these gatherings, for one of the painter's best portraits of himself, already referred to, includes Mr. Porter in the same canvas, and likenesses of Suckling, Carew, Killigrew, and many another, set them before us as they looked and dressed.

We can fancy the host, handsome, stout, and kindly, with a gay good-humour that would set every one at his ease ; the hostess, dark-haired and sparkling, exquisitely dressed, with something of Villiers' pride to temper her husband's easy bonhomie ; sometimes perhaps the gentle, aged grandmother with the pretty little boys would have come up from the country—but I forget ; in the days we have come to, just before the war, the grandmother was at rest, and the boys had shot up into tall slender lads

ready to serve the king.   The painter himself would be
often there with his pretty wife, Mary Ruthven, for he was
a near neighbour, and she would be able to take part in
the music that formed a feature of the entertainment, since
she was a performer on the king's favourite instrument, the
viol da gamba.   Then there would be Nicholas Laniere
and Wilson the lute player, and many another of the Royal
Band, or 'the King's Music,' as it was called.   Henry
Lawes, too, whose charming melodies, 'wedded to immortal
' verse,' are better known in these days than most of those
of his contemporaries.   Madrigals and Catches would be
sung, and chamber music played, such as drew tears from
the eyes of Wilson.

As to the poets, their name was legion, for in those
days every person of quality wrote verse more or less ; and
doubtless many of these social gatherings were devoted to
the reading of some new play or copy of verses, or perhaps
to the manufacture of the anagrams, acrostics, and quaint
metrical conceits which were so greatly in fashion.   Ben
Jonson would no doubt be a frequent visitor, and Dekker,
Davenant, May, and a swarm of others, who owed a good
deal to their host's generous helpfulness, were always
welcome guests at his table.   Davenant was an intimate
friend of the Porter family, and Endymion with his Court
influence had been able to come to his aid when his play
The Wits was censured by Lord Herbert, Master of the
Revels.   The portions which the Censor had Bowdlerised
were such expressions as Faith ! Sdeath ! and Sleight !
singular, when plots so offensive to good taste if not to
morality, as were many of the plays of that day, were
allowed to pass unquestioned.   Porter, to whom the play
was dedicated, took the poet's part, and showed it to the
king, who decided that the exclamations condemned were
asseverations, not oaths, and allowed them to stand.[1]

Porter also wrote a prelude to Davenant's poem on
Madagascar, which was an ode addressed to Prince Rupert

[1] *Letters of Mr. Endymion Porter.*

at a time when there was a scheme on foot for setting him up as a kind of Rajah over that island. On the title-page of the book is written, 'If these poems live may 'their memory by whom they were cherished, Endymion 'Porter and Henry Jermyn live with them.' Jermyn, who was a Catholic and the Queen's favourite, would be on friendly terms with Mrs. Porter, who was one of the Queen's converts; and Davenant was a great admirer of Olivia's, and addressed to her some charming lines, 'To 'Endymion's Love.' Herrick, too, was a very old friend, and no doubt it was the charm of the literary society he found gathered at their house on his infrequent visits to town that drew from him his sigh for London, and his momentary self-pity for his 'irksome banishment.'

Edmund Bolton's grand scheme for a Literary Academy on the same lines as the French Academy probably took its rise, or at any rate was discussed in all its details round Mr. Porter's table. Bolton was a critic of eminence, and a distant cousin to the Duke of Buckingham, which latter fact threw him a good deal into Porter's society, whom in the dedication of his *Historical Parallel, shewing the difference between Epitomes and Just Histories,* he calls, 'his good and noble friend.' The idea of this Academy was that it should review and superintend all English secular writings and translations from foreign languages, and publish an *Index Expurgatorius* for the benefit of the vulgar. It was to be under royal patronage, and to hold its meetings at Windsor Castle. A paper read before the Society of Antiquaries by the Rev. Joseph Hunter, F.S.A., gives the following particulars. 'The Academy Royal of 'King James, as originated by Edmund Bolton, encouraged 'by the Duke of Buckingham, and finally planned in 1624, 'was to consist of three classes of persons: Essentials, or 'working members (of whom Bolton drew up a pre- 'liminary list of eighty-four); Tutelaries, who were to be 'the Knights of the Garter, with the Chancellors of the 'two Universities and the Lord Chancellor; and Auxili-

' aries, who were to consist of lords and others, selected
' out of the flower of the nobility, and councils of war
' and of the new plantations.' [1]

'Bolton's list of eighty-four Essentials included the
' following names among others : John Cotton, Michael
' Drayton, Sir John Beaumont (author of *Bosworth Field*),
' Sir William Alexander, George Chapman (poet and
' translator of Homer), Ben Jonson, Sir Henry Spelman,
' Sir Thomas Hawkins (translator of Horace), Edmund
' Bolton (founder), Inigo Jones, Sir Henry Wotton, James
' Clayton (friend of Sir J. Beaumont), Sir Robert Ayton,
' Le Neve (Clarenceux), Bradshaw (Windsor), and Sir
' James Burrowes (Norroy, afterwards Garter).'

This scheme greatly pleased King James, who loved
to pose as a patron of learning, but its incorporation was
too long delayed.   The mutterings of the war - cloud
soon to burst caused it, like the Royal Society, to be
shelved, but, unlike that, it never was revived.

A story was told by Nicholas Rowe, and also by
Suckling in his *Session of Poets*, of a discussion held,
according to Rowe, at Porter's house, to decide who best
deserved the Laurel.   Suckling, who was himself one of
the company, enumerates them all in halting verse, with
a good many quaint touches of character :—

> Then Selden, and he sat hard by the chair ;
> Weniman not far off, which was very fair,
> Sands with Townsend, for they kept no order :
> Digby and Shillingworth a little further
>
> .   .   .   .   .
>
> Jack Vaughan and Porter and divers others.
>
> .   .   .   .   .
>
> The first that broke silence was good old Ben
> Prepared before with canary wine,
> And he told them plainly he deserved the Bayes,
> For his were called Workes, where the others were Playes.

Apollo reminds him that it must go by merit, not

[1] *Athenæum*, Sept. 6, 1902.

presumption, whereupon he 'in great choler' offers to go
out. Then—

> Tobie Mathews—how came he there?—
> Was whispering nothing in somebody's ear.

Suckling brings himself in as one who—

> Loved not the Muses so well as his sport,
> And prized black eyes, or a lucky hit
> At bowls, above all trophies of wit :
> But Apollo was angry and publiquely said
> 'Twere fit that a fine were set upon's head.
>
> Wat Montague now stood forth to his tryal
> And did not so much as suspect a denial ;
> But witty Apollo asked him first of all
> If he understood his own Pastoral.
> For if he could do it, 'twould plainly appear
> He understood more than any man there.
>
>   .   .   .   .
> Hales set by himself most gravely did smile
> To see them about nothing keep such a coil ;
> Apollo had spied him, but knowing his mind
> Past by, and called Faulkland that sate just behind
>   .   .   .   .   But
> He was of late so gone with Divinity
> That he had almost forgot his Poetry
> Though to say truth (and Apollo did know it)
> He might have been both his priest and his poet.

According to these satirical verses, the Laurel was at
last placed on the head of a wealthy alderman, Apollo
having openly declared that

>   the best signe
> Of good store of wit's to have good store of coyn.

But according to Rowe the debate had a better ending.
Suckling himself was upholding the claims of Shakespeare
and defending him with some warmth against the criti-
cisms of Ben Jonson, who did not consider him sufficiently
classical, when Mr. Hales roused himself from his ab-
straction and told them 'That if Mr. Shakespeare had
' not read the ancients, he had likewise not stolen any-

'thing from them: and that if his opponents would
'produce any one topic finely treated by any one of
'them, he would undertake to show something on the
'same subject at least as well written by Shakespeare.'
A similar story is told of a certain symposium at Great
Tew, and it seems very probable that it may be the
same incident, the narrator having forgotten at which
house the discussion took place.

For Lord Falkland at his country home near Oxford
kept open house for all the scholars and literary men
who chose to foregather there. The discussion on
Shakespeare is thus related by his biographer:[1] 'Hales
'once got up a disquisition whether the poets of antiquity
'were superior to Shakespeare, before a jury composed
'of Falkland, Suckling, and all the persons of quality
'that had wit and learning, and the decision was
'unanimous in favour of Shakespeare. Ben Jonson,'
he adds, 'was occasionally apt to decry him,' moved
possibly by a jealousy not uncommon in the highly
educated man of talent of the untaught genius who
carries all before him.

Is it credible, one may ask, amazed by the ever fresh
claims of Baconian authorship for Shakespeare's plays,
that such a gathering as this of men of taste and dis-
cernment, as well as of keen intellect, familiar with the
writings, if not with the personality of both men, should
have had no suspicion of the fraud which the Baconites
pretend was being practised, or guessing it, should have
entered into a conspiracy of silence to delude posterity?
They were astonished, as every one invariably is
astonished, at the achievements of transcendent genius;
they could hardly understand how a man whose learning
was of the slightest (the learning of the schools, that is,
having little Latin and less Greek) should have sprung
into fame at a bound, hence their arguments about his
due place; but that the plays had really been written

---

[1] *Falklands*, by the author of *Sir Kenelm Digby*.

M

by the great lawyer and natural philosopher, whose writings on lighter subjects, both essays and romance, proved him to have as little insight into the dramatic possibilities of human nature as he had of the practical requirements of the stage, should have turned playwright secretly and bribed Shakespeare to lend his name to a fraud that could profit no one, for the amusement of a remote posterity, would have seemed to them a thesis worthy of Bedlam.

Very probably the discussion on Shakespeare's merits and position among the poets was one that often took place, for he had but lately passed from among them, and it takes time before the final verdict is pronounced which sets a writer among the immortals; or it is not unlikely that this particular argument may have been held at old Lady Falkland's, she having taken a house in town for a time to make a home for her second son Lorenzo, where she delighted in entertaining his friends. ' Many of their friends, Oxford scholars and others, came ' much to her house, and were exceedingly welcome to ' her, who always loved good company so much that the ' contrary was insupportable to her.' She was a woman of very keen intelligence and a good talker, and one can well believe that the wits and poets resorted freely to her hospitable and easy entertainments. She and her son Lucius had the same idea of true hospitality: to let their friends come and go as they would, always secure of a dinner or a bed, but expected to observe no formalities; just the kind of thing appreciated by literary men.

It would be likely there would be a good deal of intercourse between her house and that of the Porters in the Strand, as both she and Mrs. Porter were converts to the Roman Catholic Church, and both consequently in high favour with Henry Jermyn, with Con the Papal Envoy, and with the Queen's party generally. Such debates may well have been begun in one house and carried on in the other, and, the company being so much

G. Pitcher, photo.   Walker & Boutall ph. sc.

Lucius Cary, 11ᵈ Viscount Falkland

from the portrait by Vandyck at Wardour Castle.

in the possession of Lord Arundell of Wardour.

the same, the *habitués* may not always have remembered
at which any particular talk took place. Before 1634
Lucius, who was constant in his attendance at Parliament,
was a good deal at his mother's house, but that year or
the next he retired to his country home at Great Tew,
although only too much interested in politics, for he felt
too deeply the pain and disappointment which attended
his vain effort to make his own moderate and conciliatory
views avail before it should be too late.

Here he spent five peaceful and happy years, far
from the strife which had vexed his soul, absorbed in his
books and in intercourse with his chosen friends. Of
this time and of the delightful circle he had gathered
about him a charming picture has been drawn by the
hand of his most intimate friend, Lord Clarendon, who
had a singular gift for delineating character.[1]

'His House was like the University itself for the
' Company that resorted there. No troublesome Ceremony
' or Constraint, his Library supplying all the Books his
' Guests could desire. He himself during this Time
' studied all the Classical Authors and the Greek and
' Latin Fathers, and his great Delight was in Discussions
' of debateable Points of Theology or Poetry. He was
' very indulgent to Differences of Opinion ; very rigid in
' all Points of personal Honour, Truth, or Chastity. In
' his Conversation, which was the most chearful and
' pleasant that can be imagined, though he was young
' (for all that I have yet spoken of him doth not exceed
' his Age of twenty-five or twenty-six years) and of great
' Gaiety in his Humour, with a flowing Delightfulness of
' Language, He had so chaste a Tongue and Ear, that
' there was never known a profane or loose Word to fall
' from him, nor in Truth in his Company ; the Integrity
' and Cleanliness of the Wit of that Time not exercising
' itself in that Licence before Persons for whom they had
' any Esteem.'

[1] *Clarendon's Life.*

We may remember that, according to gossiping
Aubrey, in his college days Lucius Cary was a wild lad,
but ''twas not long before he took up to be serious and
' than grew to be an extraordinary hard student.'   When
he came to England at the age of eighteen, to quote
again from Clarendon, ' He was not only Master of the
' Latin Tongue, and had read all the Poets, and other of
' the best Authors with notable Judgment for that Age,
' but He understood and spake and writ French as if He
' had spent many Years in France.'   He resolved he
would not go to London until he had mastered Greek,
and in a very few years he had read not only all the
Greek historians but ' Homer likewise' and such of the
' Poets as were worthy to be perused.'

Anthony Wood refers to his reputation in an article
on his father, who was an Oxford man, which the son was
not.[1]   ''Tis said that during his stay at Oxford (he was
' at Exeter College), his chamber was the *rendezvous* of
' all the eminent wits, divines, philosophers, lawyers,
' historians, and politicans of that time, but how true it is,
' seeing that Henry was then a young man not graduated,
' I cannot in the least perceive.   Had those things been
' spoken of Lucius Cary his son, who retired to, and
' several times took commons in Exeter College while his
' brother Lorenzo studied there in 1628 and after, I
' should have rather believed it——   But let the matter
' rest as 'tis.'

' With these advantages,' pursues Clarendon, ' he had
' one great Disadvantage (which at the first Entrance
' into the World is attended with too much Prejudice) in
' his Person and Presence, which was in no Degree
' attractive or promising: his Stature was low, and
' smaller than most Men ; his Motion not graceful ; and
' his Aspect so far from inviting that it had in it some-
' thing of Simplicity ; and his Voice the worst of the
' three, so untuned, that instead of reconciling it offended

[1] *Athenæ Oxonienses.*

' the Ear, so that no Body would have expected Musick
' from that Tongue: and sure no Man was less beholden
' to Nature for its Recommendation into the World ; but
' then no Man sooner or more disappointed the general or
' customary Prejudice ; that little Person and small Stature
' was quickly found to contain a great Heart, a Courage
' so keen, and a Nature so fearless, that no Composition
' of the strongest Limbs, and most harmonious and pro-
' portioned Presence and Strength, ever more disposed any
' Man to the greatest Enterprize ; it being his greatest
' Weakness to be too solicitous for such Adventures : and
' that untuned Tongue and Voice easily discovered itself
' to be supplied and governed by a Mind and Under-
' standing so excellent, that the Wit and Weight of all
' He said, carried another Kind of Lustre and Admiration
' in it, and even another Kind of Acceptation from the
' Persons present, than any Ornament of Delivery could
' reasonably promise itself, or is usually attended with ;
' and his Disposition and Nature was so gentle and obliging,
' so much delighted in Courtesy, Kindness, and Generosity,
' that all Mankind could not but admire and love him.'

To this we may add Anthony Wood's testimony :
' His answers were quick and sudden, and though he had
' a great deal of true worth treasured up in him, yet he
' had much of modesty withal.'

Round this remarkable host gathered an intimate
circle of friends not unworthy of him, and one of them
has described them all. There was Sidney Godolphin,
younger son of an old Cornish family, who also owed
little to outward charm of person ; of him Clarendon
says : ' There was never so great a Mind and Spirit con-
' tained in so little Room ; so large an Understanding
' and so unrestrained a Fancy in so very small a Body ;
' so that the Lord Falkland was used to say merrily, that
' He thought it was a great Ingredient to his Friendship
' for Mr. Godolphin, that He was pleased to be found in
' his Company where He was the properer Man ; and it

' may be the very Remarkableness of his little Person
' made the Sharpness of his Wit, and the composed
' Quickness of his Judgment and Understanding the more
' notable.   He had spent some years in France and in
' the Low Countries; and accompanied the Earl of
' Leicester in his Ambassage into Denmark before He
' resolved to be quiet, and attend some Promotion in the
' Court; where his excellent Disposition and Manners
' and extraordinary Qualifications, made him very accept-
' able.   Though everybody loved his Company very well,
' yet He loved very much to be alone, being in his Con-
' stitution somewhat inclined to Melancholy, and to
' Retirement among his Books; and was so far from
' being active that He was contented to be reproached by
' his Friends with Lasiness; and was of so nice and
' tender a Composition that a little Rain or Wind would
' disorder him, and divert him from any short Journey
' He had most willingly proposed to himself; insomuch
' that when He rid abroad with those in whose Company
' He most delighted, if the Wind chanced to be in his
' Face, he would (after a little pleasant Murmuring)
' suddenly turn his Horse and go Home: yet the Civil
' War no sooner began (the first Approaches to which He
' discovered as soon as any Man, by the Proceedings in
' Parliament, where He was a Member, and opposed with
' great Indignation) than He put himself into the first
' Troops which were raised in the West for the King;
' and bore the Uneasiness and Fatigue of Winter Marches
' with an exemplar Courage and Alacrity; until by too
' brave a Pursuit of the Enemy, into an obscure Village
' in Devonshire, he was shot by a Musket; with which
' (without saying anything more than Oh God, I am hurt)
' He fell dead from his Horse; to the excessive Grief of
' his Friends, who were all that knew him; and the
' irreparable Damage of the Public.'

Happier fate than that of the young poet, Sir John
Suckling, gallant and graceful, handsome and tall, with

his golden locks and short curled beard; he raised a troop
for the king, but regarded it rather as a part in a pageant
than as serious warfare, for his troopers were chosen for
their good looks and gallant bearing, and, clad in doublets
of snow-white with breeches of scarlet, drew the eyes of
all the maidens in the towns they passed through.   How
would they have met Cromwell's Ironsides? we wonder.
Their deeds are not recorded; in the fierce fire of that
death-struggle they melted away; their commander fled
to the Continent and died by his own hand in Paris.

The poets did not come out so well as the musicians.
Edmund Waller, who sided with the King and later joined
in a plot to restore him, when it failed, panic-struck, turned
traitor to his friends.   Clarendon has a somewhat sarcastic
mention of him among the guests at Great Tew.   He was
too intent, he says, on improving his fortune, which he
endeavoured to do by marrying a very rich wife in the
City.   Truly the lover of Sacharissa was not worthy of
her; she did well to choose her young soldier in preference.   'He was befriended by Dr. Morley: the Doctor
' at that time brought him into that Company which was
' most celebrated for good Conversation; where He was
' received and esteemed with great Applause and Respect.
' He was a very pleasant Discourser, in Earnest and in
' Jest, and therefore very grateful to all Kind of Company,
' where He was not the less esteemed for being very rich.
' He had a graceful Way of Speaking, and by much
' Thinking upon severall Arguments (which his Temper
' and Complexion that had much of Melancholic inclined
' him to) He seemed often to speak upon the sudden,
' when the Occasion had only administered the Oppor-
' tunity of saying what He had thoroughly considered,
' which gave a great Lustre to all He said; which yet
' was rather of Delight than Weight.   There needs be no
' more said to extol the Excellence and Power of his Wit
' and Pleasantness of his Conversation, than that it was
' of Magnitude enough to cover a World of very great

' Faults ; that is so to cover them that they were not
' taken Notice of to his Reproach ; viz. a Narrowness of
' his Nature to the lowest Degree ; an Abjectness and
' Want of Courage to support him in any virtuous Under-
' taking ; an Insinuation and servile Flattery to the
' Height the vainest and most imperious Nature could be
' contented with ; that it preserved and won his Life from
' those who were most resolved to take it ; and in an
' Occasion when He ought to have been ambitious to have
' lost it ; and then preserved him again from the Contempt
' and Reproach that was due to him for so preserving it
' and for vindicating it at such a Price ; that it had Power
' to reconcile him to those whom He had most offended
' and provoked, and continued to his Age with that rare
' Felicity that his Company was acceptable where his
' Spirit was odious ; and He was at least pitied where He
' was most detested.'

Another poet, Thomas May, who began well on the
loyal side, turned out unworthy, and on the refusal of a
pension to which he was in no way entitled, turned his
pen against the king, and subsequently died mad.   Carew
remained loyal, but no especial service is recorded of him ;
he was, unlike most of the frequenters of Falkland's house,
a man of unworthy life, but he died, says Clarendon, in
Christian penitence.

Mr. Chillingworth, ' another of small stature and great
' powers of mind,' was for some time resident under Lord
Falkland's roof as tutor to his young brothers and sisters,
and between him and his host existed a kind of intellectual
friendship which expressed itself in continual argument,
for Falkland loved to sharpen his wits in contest with a
friendly antagonist.   The elder Lady Falkland had a great
repugnance to his sceptical temper, and took, as was related
in a former volume, a great deal of trouble to get her
boys away from his influence.   Clarendon sums him up
as ' A Man of a keen and restless Mind, which ever
' inquiring carried his Inquisitiveness into the Church of

' Rome and brought him back again.'   He was possessed
of sincerity and candour, and was ' of so rare a temper in
' Debate that as it was impossible to provoke him into
' any Passion, so it was very difficult to keep a Man's self
' from being a little discomposed by his Sharpness and
' Quickness of Argument and Instances, in which He had
' a great Facility, and a great Advantage over all the Men
' I ever knew.'

Behind these brilliant talkers was to be discerned a
more silent group of men of worth and learning.   Sir
Francis Wenman, a near neighbour, of whose sound
judgment the host had the highest opinion, saying of him,
' No man better understood the affections and temper of
' the kingdom.'   Then there was Mr. Hales, Professor of
Greek at Oxford, who sat silently by while the discussion
on Shakespeare's merits was going forward, interposing
presently with a decisive word ; the learned Selden ; Dr.
Earle, whose sharp observation of men and things
crystallised into the epigrammatic little character sketches
of the *Microcosmography ;* Dr. Morley, afterwards Bishop
of Winchester ; Dr. Sheldon, chaplain to the Lord Keeper
Coventry ; and Hugh Cressy, Lord Falkland's own private
chaplain, of whom more anon.

For five happy years this group of kindred spirits
continued to gather round the hospitable board at Great
Tew, discussing all manner of problems in art or literature,
politics or religion, till the storm burst upon them and
shattered for all time a society, the like of which the world
will hardly see again.

CHAPTER XII

FRIENDSHIP

IT was indeed the Golden Age of friendship. From the coteries of intimates bound together by congruity of tastes and pursuits, by political or intellectual sympathy, stand out many pairs of friends united by a strong and life-long affection. I think no time of which we read has more instances to show than this of friendships which have become immortal. Whether men's hearts were really warmer, their affections quickened perhaps by a sense of coming danger and disaster, whether the friendships which were in so many cases cut short by death were by that very severance preserved in fadeless bloom from the slow decay which often saps them, it is hard to say. The expression of affection was certainly much warmer and more unaffected; the 'deare Harte' of Ralph Verney's letters from his college chum, the 'deare Sweetheart' which was Falkland's name for Edward Hyde, sound exaggerated in our colder and more sophisticated ears, which have grown ashamed of anything more expressive than 'old man' or 'old chappie.'

The men of that day had a high ideal of all that friendship implied: Fulke Greville, Lord Brooke, desired to be remembered on his tombstone as 'The Friend of Philip Sidney.'

In a letter addressed to his friend Margaret Blagge, John Evelyn sums up his conception of it. True, the actual words were penned some years later than the time

of which I speak, but he was himself the child of the
first half of the century, looking back rather than forward,
and the friendship which he describes is more characteristic of the days when he was young than of the
frivolity of the Restoration.

' This Altar (the Altar of Friendship) is the Marriage
' of souls, and the Golden Thread that tyes the hearts of
' all the world ; I tell you, Madam, Freindshipp is beyond
' all relations of flesh and blood, because it is less
' materiall ; there is nature in that of parents and kindred,
' butt Freindshipp is of course and without election, for
' which the Conjugall state itselfe is not alwayes the most
' happy ; and therefore those who have had best experi-
' ence chuse their friend out of all these circumstances,
' and have found him more lasting, and more effectuall.'
As to its duties and claims he thus proceeds : ' The
' privileges I claim (in virtue of that character) are that
' I may visitt you without being thought importunate ;
' that I may now and then write to you to cultivate my
' stile ; discourse with you to improve my understanding ;
' read to you to receive your Reflections ; and that you
' freely command me upon all occasions without any
' reserve whatsoever : you are to write to me when I am
' absent ; mention me in your prayers to God, to admonish
' me of my failings, to visitt me in sickness, to take care
' of me when I am in distresse, and never to forsake me,
' change or lessen your particular esteeme, till I prove
' unconstant or perfidious, and noe man's freind ; in a
' word, there is in Freindshipp something of all relations,
' and something above them all. These, Madam, are the
' Laws, and they are reciprocall and eternall.'

This age saw the production of the first of the three
most celebrated laments of modern poetry on the death
of a friend : *Lycidas*, which was more than a mere elegy
or epitaph, a threnody rather, led the way to *Adonais*
and *In Memoriam*. And yet with all its beauty, its
richness of imagery and illustration, its harmonious flow,

it is not *Lycidas* that gives the measure of the friendship
of that day ; that we seek rather in the tender simplicity
of ' A sweet Assurance given by looks,' or

> She passed away
> So sweetly from the world as if her clay
> Laid only down to slumber.

For, after all, there was no broken heart beneath the
pastoral lament ; it was a poetic exercise inspired by the
pathos of a sad event, the early death by drowning of a
young man full of promise with whom the poet's acquaintance was of the slightest.   It was not only a subject on
which to hang a wealth of classical allusion and poetic
conceit, but also an occasion for a cheap sneer at the
popular preacher of the day and for complaint of many
another grievance.   These nymphs and shepherds with
their melodious oaten pipes utter no such passionate cry
as rings through *Adonais*, no such deep longings as in *In
Memoriam* strive to pierce the clouds which wrap the
dead.   It is all very beautiful, very interesting ; we admire
but our eyes are dry.

A very beautiful elegiac poem was that written by
Ben Jonson on the death of Sir Henry Morrison, whose
friendship with Sir Lucius Cary, as he then was, was a
notable one.   They were brothers-in-law as well as friends,
for Lettice Morrison was the sister of Sir Henry.   Falkland was a man of many friends and greatly beloved, but
there were one or two who were specially dear to him.
This early friendship of his has been thus immortalised :—

PINDARIC ODE

TO THE IMMORTAL MEMORY AND FRIENDSHIP OF THAT NOBLE
PAIR, SIR LUCIUS CARY AND SIR HENRY MORRISON

The Strophe or Turn

> It is not growing like a tree
> In bulk, doth make man better be ;
> Or standing long an oak, three hundred year,
> To fall a log at last, dry, bald, and sere.

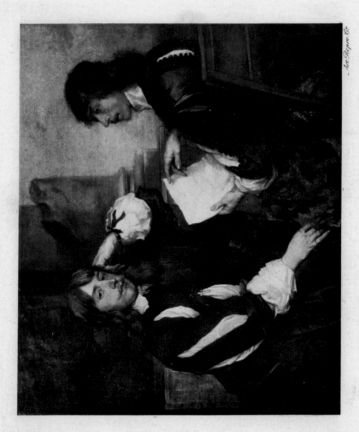

Sir John Killigrew & Thomas Carew.

From the portrait by Vandyck at Windsor.

Art Repro C°

A lily of a day
Is fairer far, in May,
Although it fall and die that night;
It was the plant and flower of light.
In small proportions we just beauties see;
And in short measures life may perfect be.

And shine as you exalted are;
Two names of friendship, but one star:
Of hearts the union, and those not by chance
Made, or indenture, or leas'd out t'advance
The profits for a time.
No pleasures vain did chime,
Of rhymes or riots at your feasts,
Orgies of drink, or feigned protests:
But simple love of greatness and of good,
That knits brave minds and manners, more than blood.

The Epode or Stand

And such a force that fair example had,
As they that saw
The good, and durst not practise it, were glad
That such a law was yet left to mankind;
Where they might read and find
Friendship indeed was written not in words;
And with the heart, not pen,
Of two so early men
Whose lines her rolls were, and records:
Who, e'er the first down bloomed on the chin,
Had sow'd these fruits and got the harvest in.

Many historic pairs of attached friends rise up before us as we glance over the records of the time. Beaumont and Fletcher, who lived together and wrote together, and whose work is so closely intertwined that their very names seem to have grown together and become but one; Sir John Killigrew and Thomas Carew, another pair of poets, West country men both, whose friendship has been immortalised in one of Van Dyck's most charming canvases; and the musicians Lawes and Cooper, or Coperario as he chose to be called, are all notable instances.

The friendship of Falkland's which is best remembered is that which grew up between him and Edward Hyde, with whom, says the latter, ' He had a most entire Friend-' ship without Reserve, from his Age of twenty Years, to ' the Hour of his Death, near twenty Years after.' For this friendship had great influence not only on their own lives and characters, but on English history. These two, associated together as they were not only by common tastes and personal affection, but by their work in Parliament, and by the growing interest they felt in the burning questions of the day, influenced each other strongly even when, as occasionally happened, they took opposite sides in debate ; and when the threatening storm-cloud burst, when Strafford had fallen, the archbishop was in prison, the throne itself in jeopardy, they resolved to stand shoulder to shoulder and do their utmost to support the king and avert disaster. What they were able to accomplish in this respect, and how in the end they failed, belongs rather to political history, but must be referred to here, as it was owing to their constant and unshaken mutual confidence in those days of treachery and doubtfulness they owed it that they were able to do as much as they did. Clarendon's description of his friend, quoted in the preceding chapter, could only have been written by one who knew and loved him well.

While on this subject it is impossible to ignore the current charge so undeservedly brought against Charles of being a faithless friend. It rests, of course, mainly and derives all its force from the solitary instance of the abandonment of Strafford. Deplorable as that was, a blunder as well as a sin, and expiated by bitter penitence and by disaster in which Charles himself saw the judgment of God, it was not a sin against friendship in that closer sense in which we are now considering it, for Strafford was never the king's personal friend. He was his adherent, his loyal and devoted servant, but there was never any such tie as united Charles to Buckingham, the friend of his youth, nor to five or six who stood nearest him in later days. The crime was in the betrayal of a faithful servant who had adventured himself into peril trusting in the king's power and will to protect him, and the only thing which might be pleaded in extenuation was that at the time Charles was talked into signing the warrant he believed he would have the power to reverse it. None of the king's enemies could reproach him more bitterly with it than he reproached himself, as may be read in the pages of his private meditations. Apart from this I do not recall a single proved instance of ingratitude to those who served him. A man struggling with his enemies is in no position to reward his adherents with anything but promises, and when the fortunes of war go against him, how shall those promises be redeemed?

That the king's reserved manner sometimes led to misunderstanding of his feelings is shown by Clarendon's account of his reception of the news of the assassination of the Duke of Buckingham. The intelligence was brought him while he was at prayers in the private chapel at Windsor, and with his characteristic reserve and self-control he said nothing, but desired the service to proceed. The rumour of his indifference and coldness was at once bruited about; but matins being ended, he retired to his chamber, flung himself on his bed and wept for hours. Moreover he gave to his friend's memory something more practical than tears, for he paid his debts, which were considerable, and adopted his children, not merely officially as wards of the crown, but bringing them up in his own nursery, and treating them with fatherly affection.

For Falkland and Hyde, who stood by him in perplexity and defeat, he had always regard and confidence, for Hyde indeed a warm affection. Falkland he admired and trusted, but the latter's over-eager, impulsive manner sometimes annoyed him and made him less willing to be convinced than a more deferential address would have done. For Sir Richard and Lady Fanshawe he had an affectionate regard, and for those who were in personal attendance on him, Endymion Porter in the days of his prosperity, and Sir Thomas Herbert in adversity and imprisonment, he showed always a true affection. He was always attached to Jack Ashburnham too, though Clarendon never liked him, and suspected him of worse than folly in the disastrous attempted escape from Hampton Court which ended in Carisbrooke. Beyond the exclamation, 'Oh, Jack, thou hast undone me!' he never reproached Ashburnham for that most deplorable blunder. But it is in friendships in private stations that we have most concern.

The *Verney Letters* are full of friendships ; Sir Edmund was a most loyal and warm-hearted man, and both he and his eldest son were full of that helpful kindness on which others feel they may securely count. The former kept up an affectionate correspondence with his brother-in-law, Sir John Leake, in Ireland, and with his wife's brother, Sir Alexander Denton of Hillesdon, he lived in equal amity, though they were such near neighbours as to have little occasion for letters. Ralph's early affectionate intimacy with his college friend, James Dillon, did not stand the test of years, but it seems there was a cause for that ; a coldness ensued after Dillon's ambitious marriage with Henrietta Wentworth, sister of the Lord Deputy, and as there was some early attachment between Dorothy Leake and the young Irishman, Ralph may well have thought his kinswoman had been slighted. With the uncle who was so nearly his own contemporary, William Denton, he kept up an unbroken friendship from boyhood to old age, which was not even disturbed by their taking opposite sides in the war. Indeed when he was so utterly cast down and morbid with sorrow as to contemplate self-destruction, Dr. Denton's cheering and sustaining letters did more than anything else to restore his fortitude.

One would have expected the friendships of women for each other to have left abundant record in those days of voluminous correspondence, but for some unexplained reason letters between women friends are very much to seek. Perhaps when boarding-schools were few, such intimate friendships as existed between boys were not formed between girls ; or perhaps the letters of girl friends were not deemed worth keeping, for there are certainly instances of lasting intimacies, but no letters. Dorothy Osborne had the unfortunate habit of destroying her letters, for there is hardly one even from Sir William Temple. Perhaps she did not wish posterity to be taken into confidence, but she must have had letters, and letters she valued too, from Lady Diana Rich, whom she so frequently speaks of as 'my Lady,' and between whom and her lover she was so anxious to promote a good understanding. We read of Diana's pretty looks, her charming manners, and the weakness of the eyes from which she suffered ; but of her opinions, her interests, or the subjects the two friends discussed together, there is not a trace.

That very delightful woman, Anne Murray, had a girl friendship with Anne Howard, whose brother was her first lover in her youthful and romantic days, as has already been related at length, and who no doubt shared in those independent expeditions to the play or to Spring Gardens which she and her sisters used to make under the escort of the footman. It is satisfactory to know that the brother's faithless behaviour did not lessen this friendship at all, but during her later and more unhappy engagement this attached friend stood by her with sustaining sympathy. Anne Murray expresses herself so graphically in her memoirs that it is much to be regretted none of her intimate letters are extant.

In a few lines Edmund Waller has sketched Dorothy Sidney and her chief friend, Anne Cavendish, reproaching the fair Saccharissa with using her girl companions as a defence against the attentions to which she was cold :—

N

> Tell me, lovely, loving pair,
> Why so kind and so severe,
> Why so careless of our care?
> Only to yourselves so dear?

Of friendships between men and women the times afford many and worthy instances. The example was set in high places by the daughter of James and sister of Charles, the ever-popular and admired ' Queen of Hearts,' whose misfortunes as well as personal charms drew round her all her life an enthusiastic devotion both of sword and pen from many quarters. One of her earliest friends was the accomplished and learned courtier Sir Henry Wotton, whose exquisite lines on her, beginning ' You meaner beauties of the night,' are familiar to all lovers of seventeenth-century verse. In his eyes she was—

> In form and beauty of her mind,
> By virtue first, then choice a Queen.

Intercourse with so charming and cultivated a man must have done much to polish and refine her quick, bright intelligence. In her later, sadder days there was Lord Craven, who joyfully spent his whole fortune in her cause; and during the hopeless struggle for the crown of Bohemia, into which her ambition, as well as the enthusiasm for the Protestant cause on the Continent which she had imbibed from her favourite brother Henry, induced her husband to plunge, the young Duke Christian of Brunswick devoted his sword and all his service to her with a zeal worthy of a knight-errant. There was a touch of the Don Quixote about his eager championship; he used to be called, ' the ' mad Halbertstadter,' but it is very evident from a letter of his to his mother, as well as from the whole tenor of his intercourse with Elizabeth, that his feeling for her was of the purest — friendship touched with romance and heightened by devotion to a failing cause, reverence to the woman and service to the princess, entirely self-sacrificing and without alloy. Indeed, about the Queen of Bohemia and these loyal servants of hers there never arose the faintest breath of scandal ; her devotion to her husband, with whom she corresponded daily whenever they were separated, was notorious, and made such a thing out of the question ; they worshipped her as Dante worshipped his Beatrice or Petrarch his Laura, and served her without any idea of personal reward.

A friendship of a similar character was that between Dr. John Donne and Magdalen Herbert, mother of George Herbert, who, being early left a widow, devoted herself to the education of her children, and removed from Wales to Oxford, where she lived for some years that her sons might enjoy the advantages of the University without missing her care. Her acquaintance with Dr. Donne must be described in Walton's words. Speaking of her sojourn at Oxford, he says, ' in which time her great and harmless wit, her ' cheerful gravity, and her obliging behaviour, gained her ' an acquaintance and friendship with most of any eminent ' worth or learning that were at that time in or near that ' University ; and particularly with Mr. John Donne, who ' was after Dr. Donne, and Dean of St. Paul's, London ; ' and he, at his leaving Oxford, writ, and left there in verse, ' a character of the beauties of her body and mind. Of the ' first he says :—

> No Spring nor Summer beauty has such grace
> As I have seen in an Autumnal face.

' Of the latter he says :—

> In all her words to every hearer fit,
> You may at revels or at council sit.

' The rest of her character may be read in his printed ' poems, in that elegy which bears the name of " The ' " Autumnal Beauty." For both he and she were then ' past the meridian of man's life.

' This amity, begun at this time and place, was not an ' amity that polluted their souls ; but an amity made up ' of a chain of suitable inclinations and virtues ; an amity ' like that of St. Chrysostom's to his dear and virtuous

'Olympias, whom in his letters he calls his saint: or an
'amity, indeed, more like that of St. Hierome to his Paula;
'whose affection to her was such that he turned poet in
'his old age, and then made her epitaph, wishing all his
'body were turned into tongues, that he might declare
'her just praises to posterity.' A letter of his to her is
quoted, and a sonnet, with which were enclosed some
hymns now lost, of which Mr. Walton says: 'Doubtless
'they were such as they two now sing in heaven.'

Abundant evidence has already been given, in the
many letters quoted which were exchanged between Lady
Sussex and Ralph Verney, of the terms of affectionate
intimacy that for many years subsisted between them,
undisturbed, so far as we learn, by any breath of gossip or
unpleasantness. Her first husband was Sir Henry Lee of
Ditchley, and the Lees and Verneys had been intimate
for generations, so she married into the friendship, so to
say. She was extremely fond of Ralph's wife, and was
godmother to his boy, but it was Ralph himself who was
her especial friend, and with him she exchanged long,
chatty, confidential letters. She and he were at one in
their political sympathies, and during the years that she
was nursing her old second husband in dull seclusion at
Gorhambury, Ralph, from his place in Parliament, kept
her well informed of all the exciting events that were
taking place, and gave her a glimpse behind the scenes.
We can imagine what a relief those letters must have been
to the tedium of the sick-room, where she patiently sat,
her eager spirit burning to mix once more in the world
where such important things were happening. We have
seen already how carefully he executed her innumerable
commissions, and she rewarded him with occasional gifts
of 'gely of pipins' or 'perly-cakes.' Her third marriage,
to the Earl of Warwick, slackened the correspondence a
little; not that the friends ceased to have the same regard
for each other, but the Earl was Lord High Admiral, and
great in the confidence of the Parliament, and it would

hardly do for his wife to be in correspondence with one
who was in exile and in bad odour, for his refusal to take
the Covenant, and his deep disapproval of the murder of
the king. She, however, exerted herself *sub rosa* to get
the attainder taken off his estate, and received his wife
kindly when once she had made it clear that the old
intimate relations could not be publicly renewed.

Another example of such friendship—one which, however, did not escape calumny—was that which Falkland
formed with Mistress Moray, who was staying at Oxford
during the war, at the time the Court was there. She was
a woman of much intellectual charm, and he no doubt
found great solace in those sad and troubled days in her
conversation and sympathy, and in opening out his
perplexities to her, especially when his 'deare sweetheart'
Hyde was absent in attendance on the Prince of Wales
in the West. Everything said or done at the Court was
commented on, and that in no charitable spirit; it was
perhaps inevitable that stones should be thrown, and if
they were, Aubrey would not be behind with his little
pebble. Heedless, inquisitive, gossipy, and wildly in-
accurate, he is so demonstrably wrong in innumerable
matters of names, dates, and events, he need not be taken
seriously when character is at stake. His prime object
was to render his book amusing by every bit of scandal
he could adorn it with ; he was not likely to take much
pains to verify its source. This is his version of Lord
Falkland's death :—

'At the fight at Newbury, my Lord Falkland being
' there, and having nothing to doe, to chardge as the 2
' armies were engaging, rode in like a mad-man (as he
' was) between them, and was (as he needs must be)
' shott. Some that were your superfine discoursing
' politicians, and fine gent. would needs have the reason
' of this mad action of throwing away his life so to be
' his discontent for the unfortunate advice given to his
' master as aforesaid (That of besieging Gloucester after

' the victory of Roundway Down, whereby much advantage
' was lost) ; but I have been well informed, by those who
' best knew him, and knew intrigues behind the curtain
' (as they say), that it was grief for the death of Mrs.
' Moray, a handsome lady at Court who was his mistresse,
' and whom he loved above all creatures, was the true
' cause of his being so madly guilty of his own death as
' aforementioned.   (Nullum magnum ingentium sine
' mixtura dementias.) '

As to his being guilty of his own death, an uncon-
sidered rashness is surely not to be confounded with a
deliberate intention of suicide.   For the other matter, let
him speak who knew him best.

' He died as much of the Times as of the Bullet : for
' from the very Beginning of the War, He contracted so
' deep a Sadness and Melancholy, that his Life was not
' pleasant to him ; and sure He was too weary of it.
' Those who did not know him very well, imputed, very
' unjustly, much of it to a violent Passion He had for a
' noble Lady : and it was the more spoken of because
' She died the same Day, and as some computed it, the
' same Hour that He was killed ; but they who knew
' either the Lord or the Lady, knew well that neither of
' them was capable of an ill Imagination.   She was of
' the most unspotted, unblemished Virtue, never married,
' of an extraordinary Talent of Mind, but of no alluring
' Beauty, nor of a Constitution of tolerable Health, being
' in a deep Consumption, and not like to have lived so
' long by many Months.   It is very true that Lord
' Falkland had an extraordinary Esteem for her, and
' exceedingly loved her Conversation, as most of the
' Persons of eminent Parts of that Time did ; for She
' was in her Understanding, and Discretion, and Wit, and
' Modesty, above most Women ; the best of whom had
' always a Friendship with her.   But he was withal so
' kind to his Wife, whom He knew to be an excellent
' Person, that though He loved his Children with more

' Affection and Fondness than most Fathers do, He left
' by Will all He had to his Wife, and committed his
' three Sons, who were all the Children He had, to her
' sole Care and Bounty.' And yet another account describes him ' riding to his death as gaily as most men to
' a wedding.'

So we may leave him ; for the testimony of the one
who knew may far outweigh the irresponsible hearsay
judgments of the man whose only care was to write an
amusing book.

CHAPTER XIII

RELIGION

THROUGHOUT the records of this time, whether public or private, whether historical or personal, one subject is continually prominent, and that is Religion. When we read of the discussions of theological topics, the exchange of views that were so much in favour in certain circles ; when we note the heresies which were in the air, or the cleavage in religious opinion which ran through the Church itself, we see a remarkable parallel between those times and our own. But here the likeness ends ; the contrast is quite as strong ; for with the men of those days religion as a motive power was all pervading, all prevailing. It was something more than a decent fashion; if they were intolerant it was because they really cared, and the newspapers and pamphlets, quite as much as the sermons of the day, show that it was the religious far more than the political ideal for which they did not scruple to plunge their country into civil war. With the contest in its public aspects we have here no concern, but in the ordering of men's daily lives it comes continually to the front.

Religious observance had not yet become, as it did under the Puritan rule, a matter for Sundays only. The Court attended daily matins and evensong, and so did all who were sufficiently near a church or were of consequence enough to have a private chapel. Family prayers, though already introduced, had not yet superseded public

worship. As to education, that was religious as a matter
of course without question; it is not too much to say
that such an idea as secular education had never been
heard of. Religion was the very foundation of the
training of children. In all public schools daily worship
in chapel and observance of the red-letter holy days was
the rule until the Prayer-book was forbidden under the
Commonwealth, and these practices came back at the
Restoration. Boys were brought up in habits of worship
quite as much as girls, and daily service had not come to
be regarded as chiefly the affair of women of leisure.

Besides this daily unquestioning observance of the
forms of religion, it was a matter of profound and
absorbing interest. There was little or none of that easy
tolerance of other people's views, springing more from
indifference than charity, which characterises ourselves,
and the differences were the more acute in that they
existed in the very bosom of the Church itself. It was
not so much strife between Church and dissent, which
developed later, nor the absolute incompatibility between
Catholic and Protestant, as on the Continent, as a struggle
between the two rival factions for supremacy within the
Church, which followed from the fact that in England
the Reformation had proceeded on two distinct and
divergent lines, producing a situation which was bound
to issue in tearing Church and nation into two opposing
camps. Puritan and Laudian alike considered himself a
loyal son of the Church, and each was bent on remodelling
her according to his own conception, so soon as Elizabeth's
strong hand was withdrawn from the compromise she had
kept working so long. Then, as now, the cleavage between
the two wings of the Church was deeper and more
fundamental than either that between the orthodox party
and the Church of Rome or between the Puritan faction
and Protestant heresy. The aims of the two were
absolutely incompatible, and had Englishmen been
possessed of the logical consistency of other people,

hostilities must have broken out sooner than they did. For one may note a certain peculiarity of national character then quite as much as now, whereby Englishmen seem to have the power of assimilating diverse and mutually exclusive dogmas.   An Englishman rarely drives his convictions to their legitimate conclusions, and is not seldom better than his creed.   Another factor in the situation was the characteristic insularity of Englishmen, which made them in their hatred of foreign interference actually prefer separation from the great body of Christendom, and which from the earliest times had inclined them to adhere obstinately to their own customs in various questions of observance, even in an indifferent matter like the new Calendar.   This feeling strongly influenced many who, though in their hearts attached to the old faith, could not forget that they were Englishmen, and whom the political situation under Elizabeth had alienated from Rome.   The accession of James I., who in his person extinguished the rivalry between the legitimate and illegitimate line, promised a peaceful solution of many problems, when the misguided and disavowed Gunpowder Plot terrified both king and nation into a renewed policy of severity, and sent many moderate men much further in the direction of Protestantism than they would otherwise have been inclined to. For in many minds patriotism and Protestantism had become synonymous.

The varying shades of opinion which existed between the two extremes tend to make the time harder to be understood, and so too does the lax and inconsistent use of the term Puritan.   In one sense it was applied to the many who, whatever their political leanings, were endeavouring to lead a life of good works and strict religious observance, and the word was fastened on all such by the worldly as a reproach, though there were as many of them among the Royalists as in the popular party.   Of these, notable examples were Lord Cork,

Lord Sunderland, the second Lady Falkland, and Anne
Murray, not to mention the king himself, who were no
less religious than Algernon Sidney, Colonel Hutchinson,
Lady Warwick, or Lady Brilliana Harley.   Later the
word came to have a political significance, and was
applied distinctively to those who despised forms and
sacraments, and distrusted all means of grace except
preaching.

The position of Roman Catholics was peculiar.   Very
intolerant laws against them were on the Statute-book,
but were seldom put in force except when quickened by
the outbreak of some plot against the throne.   James
was himself inclined to toleration towards those of his
mother's religion until his personal fears were aroused,
but at that day tolerance was a most unpopular quality.
Large portions of the country, especially in the north,
were still so full of recusants, as they were called,
that to attempt to put in force the laws against them
would have been both futile and dangerous.   One very
hard measure was only applied to those families who
were powerful enough to be dangerous, namely, the taking
away of their children at an early age to be brought up
as Protestants, as we have seen in the case of the younger
Carys and of Sir Kenelm Digby.   The religious position
of the latter is interesting, as being in many ways typical
of those who, belonging to old Catholic families, were
brought up in the State religion, and at times conformed
to it without ever really becoming converts.   The im-
pressible years of early childhood he passed with his
mother.   Most likely he grew up regarding his father as
a martyr to the Catholic cause ; then, as his intelligence
was unfolding, he passed under the influence of a man
whose keen logic must have impressed his mind, and
whose saintly character cannot but have influenced his
heart—one who aimed at dignity and beauty in worship,
and whose sacramental teaching was to a very great
extent in harmony with that to which he was already

accustomed.   Although Laud was as strong against the
Pope and the Jesuits as any Protestant of them all, and
had written that book in refutation of Fisher which the
king held in such high esteem, yet the faith taught was
one.   The young Kenelm does not seem to have felt that
it was a different religion to which his adherence was
asked ; he would not abjure either the one nor the other,
and attended the services of each with impartiality,
according as he was in England or abroad—a course
which has bewildered those who have written about him
of late years more than it did his contemporaries, to
whom the class known as Church Papists was familiar.
One of Bishop Earle's shrewd studies is concerned with
this character, who was a feature of the times which
Catholic emancipation has entirely done away with.

' A Church Papist is one that parts his religion
' betwixt his conscience and his purse, and comes to
' Church not to serve God but the King. . . . His main
' policy is to shift off the Communion for which he is
' never unfurnished with a quarrel, and will be sure to be
' out of charity at Easter. . . . He would make a bad
' martyr and a good traveller. . . . His wife is more
' zealous and therefore more costly, and he bates her in
' tires what she stands him in religion.'   It must be
remembered that all subjects were bound to attend
worship at their parish church, and to receive the Holy
Sacrament three times a year, of which Easter was to be
one, and that failure to do so theoretically involved fine
and imprisonment, though many contrived to evade the
law.   The fines and disabilities with which recusants
were loaded made more Church Papists than it did
converts ; a good many, like Kenelm Digby, were not
of the stuff of which martyrs are made.

The term ' lax Catholic ' was applied also to those
who, though loyal Catholics, could not forget that they
were loyal Englishmen, and the position of these must
often have been one of intense difficulty.   They, at any

rate, must have longed for the reunion which, when
Charles came to the throne and married a Catholic wife,
did not seem a quite impossible dream. For Charles
himself, devoted son of the Church of England as he
proved himself, could not but look with an indulgent eye
on those who professed the same religion as his adored
wife, and was always reluctant to put in force the laws
against them, though sometimes for State reasons compelled to do so. The frequent conversions to Rome
must have been a serious embarrassment to him in those
very critical times, as they certainly were to Con, the
Papal Envoy, who appears to have been a man of
extreme discretion, who walked warily and made himself
very acceptable to the king. His especial mission, as
well as that of his predecessor Panzani, was to endeavour
to obtain some mitigation of the laws against recusants,
and also to inquire into the foundation of hopes from
time to time entertained of the return of the English in
a body to the Roman Catholic obedience. Mr. Secretary
Windebank, who was always a friend of the queen and
subsequently went over to Rome, favoured the notion,
and entered into a discussion of its possibility with
the envoy.

Inevitably the Roman Catholic *entourage* of the queen
gained several adherents : many, no doubt, from sincere
conviction ; others because it was the fashion in the
Court, and not unnaturally won favour from the queen.
It is impossible to say in which class to count Endymion
Porter's wife, that quick-tempered, impulsive lady, whose
very faults seemed to have rendered her more attractive.
She was at any rate a zealous convert, more zealous than
discreet, and the wary Con frequently had to counsel
wisdom and moderation, for he was well aware that
headlong proceedings were certain in the then temper of
the country to end in disaster. Olivia's husband strongly
deprecated her change of religion, no doubt afraid it
would be a vexation to his royal master, and possibly

that it might bring himself into suspicion, as it undoubtedly did.   However, she was neither to hold nor
to bind, and having converted her old father, Lord
Boteler, carried him off in her coach to Woodhall, lest
her work should be undone by her sister, Lady Newport,
at that time an ardent Puritan.   She also brought all
her influence to bear on her cousin, the lovely young
Marchioness of Hamilton, who was dying of consumption,
the same on whom Falkland wrote his touching lines.
Con visited her, and her probable conversion was talked
of but never announced.   These frequent conversions
stirred up slumbering statutes, and the Middlesex Sessions
Rolls contain the names of no less than 1430 persons
proceeded against for recusancy.

There was a good deal of excitement about the
publication of Cosins's *Protestant Hours*, drawn up, it was
understood, at the express wish of the king.   Lady
Denbigh, sister of the Duke of Buckingham and a great
friend of Lady Falkland, was much concerned that the
devotions of the Catholic ladies in attendance on the
queen should put those of Anglicans to the blush, and it
was decided that Dr. Cosins should draw up such an
adaptation of the Breviary as should meet the need.
This book, hailed by some as showing that the Church of
England could supply all her children needed, was by
others denounced as a return to Popery, and dubbed
'Cozens's cozening devotions.'   They were, after all, far
more Protestant in tone than many later adaptations of
the Breviary, having been taken not directly from that,
but from a previous compilation issued by authority in the
reign of Elizabeth.

The Hours to be observed were matins and lauds
taken together, with psalms of praise and canticles ; terce,
called the golden hour of the Holy Spirit ; sext, in memory
of the Passion ; none, the end of the Crucifixion ; vespers
for evening ; and compline to be said at bed-time.   The
psalms and hymns selected are quite different to those

Walker & Boutall, ph.sc.

Elizabeth Wife of Henry 1ˢᵗ Viscount Falkland.

from a portrait by Vansomer.

in the possession of Viscount Falkland.

in the Breviary. Other devotions are added, and the
book opens with instructions in the principles of religion
and the precepts of the Church, which latter are especially
valuable as showing precisely what was taught by the
High Churchman of that day. Briefly they are these :—

' 1 To observe the Festivals & Holy-daies appointed.
' 2 To keep the Fasting daies with devotion & abstinence.
' 3 To observe the Ecclesiastical Customs & Ceremonies
' established & that without frowardness or contradiction.
' 4 To repair unto the publick Service of the Church for
' Mattens & Evensong with other holy offices at times
' appointed, unless there be a just and unfeigned cause to
' the contrary. 5 To receive the Blessed Sacrament of
' the Body and Blood of Christ with frequent devotion, &
' three times a year at least, of which times Easter to be
' alwaies one. And for the better preparation thereunto
' as occasion is to disburthen and quiet our conscience of
' those sins that may grieve us, or scruples that may
' trouble us to a learned and discreet Priest, & from him
' to receive advice & the benefit of Absolution.'

It seems remarkable that a book so moderate in tone
should have excited such wrathful indignation ; probably
one reason may have been that at this inopportune moment
Lady Falkland, who was known to have been much under
the influence of Dr. Cosins, gave her allegiance to the
Church of Rome. Far from this having been in any way
his desire, it was a source of deepest distress to him, not
the less because the proximate cause was his unwillingness
to receive her confession. While he doubted, questioned,
delayed, having retired into the country to consider the
matter, she, discouraged and perplexed by his uncertain
attitude, was received into the Church of Rome by Lord
Ormonde's chaplain in the stable ; it being a capital
offence for a convert to be received in the house of a
recusant.

The leaven had been working for a long while—almost
from her childish days when her father had put Calvin's

Institutions into her hands and bid her read it; 'against
' which she made so many objections, and found so many
' contradictions, that he said, "This girl hath a spirit
' "averse from Calvin!"' Her acute, logical mind slowly
worked out its own convictions. The reading of Hooker's
Ecclesiastical Polity, by many deemed a bulwark of the
Church of England, still further unsettled her adhesion to
the reformed Church, and discussions with her brother-in-
law, who had been much abroad, and the study of St.
Augustine in *De Civitate Dei*, brought her mind to its
final resolve. For awhile the arguments of the Bishop of
Durham had persuaded her that though acknowledging
the Roman Catholic to be the true Church she might yet
lawfully remain in the Church of her country as a true
branch of it, but the divided counsels and uncertain voice
of the Anglicans dismayed her. At least, she acted from
absolutely disinterested motives : she gave the deepest
offence to her husband, whom she adored, and to whom
she gave unquestioning submission in all but what
concerned her religion ; she suffered actual persecution,
poverty, amounting at one time to almost starvation,
obscurity, loss of friends, and, what she felt more than all,
separation from her children. All this she cheerfully
submitted to, refusing to take any advantage offered her
which might prejudice or vex her husband, and happy at
the last in his pardon and assured affection.

The king was placed in a most embarrassing situation
by these conversions. On the one hand were the laws
which he was bound to observe so long as they remained
unrepealed, the clamours of the Protestant party, becoming
more and more menacing, the indignant demands of the
lady's husband and mother that she should be reduced to
submission, his own desire to strengthen the Church of
England ; on the other, his aversion to harsh measures,
especially against the Catholics, many of whom were the
most loyal of his subjects, and his regard for his wife's
form of faith. No wonder Lady Falkland's biographers

complain of the king's alternate indulgence and severity, moved as he was now by his kindness of heart and sympathy, now by political necessity. So long as there was any hope of reunion the wiser heads on both sides deprecated the flaunting of individual conversions ; but it was impossible to restrain the indiscretion of the Queen, who insisted on parading her converts at a Christmas Eve service, when her chapel was kept open and brilliantly illuminated in order to outdo the private chapel at the Spanish Ambassador's. Nothing could have been more mischievous at such a moment or more calculated to stir up the smouldering hostility of an important section of the country, ever ready to flame forth against ' the Papists.'

It was becoming more and more evident that the Church itself was hopelessly divided. On the one hand stood the High Churchmen, who took their stand on the unbroken tradition from the fathers, who desired to restore, where intemperate zeal had destroyed them, all those matters of doctrine and ritual which had come down from the primitive Church, freed only from abuses of recent introduction ; who cherished no hostility to the religion of Rome, holding with her, ' one Lord, one faith, one baptism,' yet repudiating allegiance to the Pope and energetically refusing the recent decisions of the Council of Trent. The archbishop and the king both stood in the fore-front of this party, but behind them were arrayed the great body of the English clergy, who believed that they held their priesthood by direct succession from the apostles and offered a true sacrifice. Such men were George Herbert, Dr. Donne, Henry Vaughan, Dr. Hammond, and a host of others whose names rise to our recollection, and who were supported by such laymen as Izaak Walton, John Evelyn, Sir Richard Fanshawe, young Lord Sutherland, and many more whose names are forgotten, but whose spirit saved the Church from becoming one of the sects.

The other wing was composed of men no less earnest

O

and devoted, men in many cases of unblemished lives and unquestioned piety, but who looked at Reformation from a wholly different standpoint; in whose eyes it was the discovery of a new religion superseding and wholly antagonistic to the old, who did not wish to reform but to destroy. To these men forms were an evil, and every man his own priest; preaching was everything, because the individualistic conception of the conversion of each separate soul had come to obscure the vision of the kingdom of God on earth. They would abolish priesthood and sacraments, that is in any sense the Church had ever held, using the latter as mere symbols or acts of remembrance, and in their place would set up a religion of preaching and extempore prayer, holding these things more spiritual.

One of the chief methods by which they sought to spread their opinions was by the creation of lectureships by which licensed preachers, usually of extreme Protestant views, were intruded into many parishes, preaching on Sunday evenings or sometimes on Wednesdays. These lectures were still popular in the last century, and still exist in some places. These men were responsible only to those who appointed them, and owned or paid very little obedience to the bishop in whose diocese they worked, and the endeavour to introduce some control over them was one of Laud's most unpopular measures. In Cosins' *Visitation of the Archdeaconry of York* for the year 1627 an inquiry was put by whose authority the lecturer in any parish was appointed. Some other points in this *Visitation* are worthy of notice, showing what customs had crept in :—

'Is the Communion Table at any time abused by 'sitting or leaning upon it?

'Doth he (the parson) in regard of his own long 'prayer diminish the Divine Service? omit using the 'surplice? Doth he catechise? exhort the people fre-'quently to resort to Holy Communion? Doth he

' reveal confessions? marry without ring in unauthorised
' forms? Marry those who cannot say the Catechism?
' Read the Commination at the beginning of Lent? Go
' in the perambulations on Rogation Days?'

One query concerns the behaviour of the people: 'Is
' there any striving or contention for sitting in pews, and
' by whom?'

It was evident that the design of the Puritans was
nothing short of the destruction of all that was distinctive
of the Church of England, and the substitution of what
was then called Independency, and is now known as
Congregationalism; and that two such utterly incompatible
conceptions of what that Church meant could have existed
together so long, was due partly to that spirit of compromise which is so characteristic of Englishmen, partly
to the large body of conservative sentiment that lay
between. Men like Lord Leicester, the Earl of Warwick,
or Sir Edmund Verney, who had inherited the religion
of Elizabethan days, who were Protestants partly from
patriotism, partly from a love of simplicity, were attached
to the forms to which they were accustomed, and hated
change, whether Laud's attempt to restore the old, or
the Puritan desire to abolish what forms remained, and
resisted extremists on either hand. Amongst these there
was a great deal of very genuine piety, as indeed there
was amongst the schismatics, though with these latter one
cannot but observe their conception of religious freedom
was not only liberty to worship God their own way, but
also to compel others to do the like. The Sunday
question was a burning one; they had views of their
own concerning the obligations of the Jewish Sabbath,
and were determined to coerce those who differed from
them. Nothing gave more dire offence than the republication by King Charles of his father's declaration
on Sunday sports, in spite of its clear enunciation of the
primary obligation of the worship of God on that day.

Having thus sketched the position of the religious, a

word must be said of the irreligious, and it is here that
the contrast between those days and our own comes out
most strongly.   Between every party in the Church then
and now there is a parallel, but the immense body of
indifference and practical atheism, as well as the militant
atheism of a smaller section in our own day, is without a
counterpart.   There was a certain measure of indifference
without doubt ; there were always scoffers, worldly-minded
men and women without an interest beyond the pleasure
and amusement of the moment, but they were dis-
countenanced, out of fashion, so to speak ; they had
the grace of shame, and more often than not, like poor
Carew, they repented and made a good end.   A certain
amount of atheism and materialism were to be found.
Sir Thomas Browne quotes, not without an implication
of its truth, the saying current in Italy, *Ubi tres medici duo
athei*, but the sceptic of that age shrugged his shoulders
and went his way ; he did not attack the Church ; that
was left to the religious enthusiast who thought his own
doctrine the more spiritual.

Bishop Earle's notion of a ' Skeptic ' comes very near
an actual description of Chillingworth, whom he must
have had opportunity of knowing well in frequent meetings
at Great Tew, and who certainly was not an unbeliever according to modern ideas, but would rather be described as a
man of unsettled opinions. ' He is,' says the satirical bishop,
' toss'd to and fro, putting his foot in ' heresies as tenderly
as a cat into water, overthrown by ' Bellarmin, swayed
by Socinus and Vorstius.' [1]   This reads like a tolerably
accurate diagnosis of Chillingworth's religious history.

There was a great deal of free discussion, and in such
a house as Falkland's, an open unreserved expression of
convictions or of half-formed views, which must have
been dangerous in times when conformity was a thing to
be legally insisted on under pains and penalties.   However,
probably all the guests knew and could trust each other,

[1] Earle's *Microcosmography.*

though they might hold the most divergent opinions. Misunderstandings and false reports of what was said or held did notwithstanding get about, and it is not surprising to find that old gossip Aubrey asserting that Falkland was himself a Socinian. It is true that he was one of the first in England to procure and read the writings of Socinus, but he it was who, when Chillingworth was bitten, as he was with every fresh heresy, completely worsted him in argument, as Sunderland testified. Falkland's sisters, on the other hand, were persuaded that he was at heart a Catholic, and only withheld from joining his mother's church by a resolution he had made of not changing his religion till he was forty, an age he did not live to see. So open was his mind, so winning the beauty of his character, that men of every shade of opinion have always desired to claim him for their own. Macaulay would see in him a Puritan at heart, while to Matthew Arnold he is the martyr of sweetness and light. He was wide-minded in an intolerant age, with imagination enough to put himself in the place of others and see things from their point of view ; he liked to make himself acquainted with opinions before he condemned them, but he certainly died in full communion with the Church of England, since his last act before going into the battle, in which he laid down his life, was to receive the Blessed Sacrament at the hands of an English priest.

The religious influences brought to bear on him were diverse : there was first his mother, whose self-sacrificing devotion to the Church of her adoption cannot but have touched his warm heart ; there was his wife, no less saintlike in her piety, of a somewhat rigid and narrow Protestantism ; while among his inner circle of friends every shade of opinion might be found. One member of his household, whose name is never prominent, since his silent and melancholy temper kept him always in the background, was his chaplain Hugh Cressy, who later became a Roman Catholic and a Benedictine monk, under

the name of Serenus. He wrote many books, amongst
them a History of the Church in Brittany, and from all
we glean of him was a man with whom Falkland was
likely to have much intimate converse. Two members
of the old circle, Hyde and Dr. Earle, were much grieved
at the alteration they found in him after his conversion,
and deplored it to each other. 'Methinks apostacy too
' cholerick a word towards so a friend,' writes Hyde, but
wishes that he had remained a layman. His friends, says
Wood, 'find great mutations in him as to parts and
' vivacitie, and he seemed to some to be possessed with
' strange notions, and to others a reserved person, little
' better than a melancholic.' Perhaps these 'strange
' notions' were the ideas of the Quietists which he imbibed
from intercourse with Molinos.

Two strong influences there were to keep Falkland
loyal to the church of his baptism ; they were his friendship with Edward Hyde, who was a churchman of the
simple old-fashioned sort, and for whose opinions he had
the highest respect, and the example of the king. It
cannot but have had a marked effect on a mind so open
to religious influences as was his, in his daily intercourse
with Charles, to see him maintaining, whether in the
dissipations of the court or the distractions of the camp,
the same strict rule of prayer and meditation, to find that
neither the threats of foes nor the advice of well-meaning
friends could shake the constancy of his resolve to maintain intact the church whose appointed guardian he was ;
and although Falkland was frequently provoked with him
for not following what he considered the wisest and most
statesmanlike course, the serenity and fortitude with which
the king met adverse fortune showed that his religion was
not a mere form. 'He was,' said Hyde, who had equal
opportunities for intimate knowledge, 'the best Christian
' I have ever known.'

CHAPTER XIV

THE RELIGIOUS LIFE

AFTER the dissolution of the religious houses throughout the country, the life devoted exclusively to the service of God must be sought chiefly in the parsonage, and there were to be found holy lives not unworthy to be set beside those of a St. Francis d'Assisi or a St. Vincent de Paul. The ideal to which such lives should conform is very beautifully pictured by George Herbert in his *Country Parson*, and the more convincingly inasmuch as his own portrait, drawn by the hand of Izaak Walton, corresponds closely with it.

It was marked by a strictness in strong contrast with the easy-going laxity of the century which preceded and the one which followed, a strictness which the Evangelical revival of Wesley and Whitfield endeavoured to restore, and which the Tractarian Movement more successfully brought back, at the least as an ideal to be aimed at. The Country Parson was to wed Holy Poverty ; 'knowing ' that country folk live hardly, he must not be greedy to ' get, nor niggardly to keep . . . he avoids all luxury, ' especially drinking, because it is the most popular vice.' The rule of his life as regards money is to simplicity in living, and charity to the poor. His fare plain but wholesome, the plenishing of his house simple, ' but clean, ' whole and sweet ; his apparel plain, but reverend and ' clean, without spots or dust or smell ; the purity of his ' mind breaking out and dilating itself even in his body,

' clothes, and habitation.' We may perceive here the niceness of the man whose only fault, while he lived in the world, was said by his tutor to have been 'that he ' kept himself too much retired, and at too great a distance ' from all his inferiors ; and his clothes seemed to prove ' that he put too great a value on his parts and parentage.'

The country parson's character for uprightness must be unblemished ; 'because country people do much esteem ' their word, it being the Life of Buying and Selling, the ' Parson must be strict in keeping his ; his yea is yea, ' and nay, nay.' He should have a knowledge of tilling and pasturage and all farming operations, not only in order that he may manage his own glebe with discretion, but also that he may enter intelligently into the anxieties and troubles of his parishioners. But his chief study is that of Holy Scripture, comparing passage with passage, aided by commentaries and the writings of the Fathers. 'From them, the Schoolmen, and later writers he hath ' composed a body of Divinity which is the store house ' of his sermons. . . . This body he made by way of ' expounding the Church Catechism ; to which all divinity ' may easily be reduced. For it being indifferent in itself ' to choose any method, that is best to be chosen of ' which there is likeliest to be most use. Now catechising ' being a work of singular and admirable benefit to the ' church of God, and a thing required under canonical ' obedience, the expounding of our catechism must needs ' be the most useful form.' He must also be versed in cases of conscience, that he may be able to direct souls.

The conception of the priestly office is very striking. The priest appears before God 'not as himself alone, but ' as presenting with himself the whole congregation ; ' whose sins he then bears, and brings with his own to ' the heavenly Altar to be bathed and washed in the ' Sacred Laver of Christ's Blood.' Not only is his own manner reverent and grave, but he instructs his people in reverent behaviour ; 'by no means enduring either talking,

' or sleeping, or gazing, or leaning, or half-kneeling, or
' any undutiful behaviour in them ; but causing them,
' when they sit, or stand, or kneel, to do all in a straight
' and steady posture, as attending to what is done in the
' Church, and every one, man and child, answering aloud,
' both Amen, and all other answers which are on the
' clerk's and people's part to answer.   Which answers
' also are to be done, not in a huddling or slubbering
' fashion—gaping, or scratching the head, or spitting,
' even in the midst of their answer—but gently and
' pausably, thinking what they say. . . . If there be any
' of the gentry or nobility of the parish, who sometimes
' make it a piece of state not to come at the beginning
' of service with their poor neighbours, but at mid-prayers,
' both to their own loss, and of theirs also who gaze at
' them when they come in, and neglect the present service
' of God ; he by no means suffers it, but after divers
' gentle admonitions, if they persevere, he causes them
' to be presented.   Or if the poor churchwardens be
' affrighted with their greatness, (notwithstanding his
' instruction that they ought not to be so, but even to let
' the world sink, so they do their duty), he presents them
' himself; only protesting to them, that not any ill-will
' draws him to it, but the debt and obligation of his call-
' ing, being to obey God rather than men.'

His preaching does not exceed an hour.   Divine
service is read fully twice on Sundays, with preaching in
the morning, catechising in the afternoon ; a late evening
service was at that time unknown.   The rest of the day
he visits the sick, or exhorts those whom his sermons do
not or cannot reach.   ' At night he thinks it a very fit
' time, both suitable to the joy of the day, and without
' hindrance in public duties, either to entertain some of
' his neighbours or be entertained by them.'   As regards
his views on the vexed question of Sabbath keeping,
which in his day was so greatly exercising men's minds,
it is interesting to compare this passage with one in

Walton's *Life :* ' He made them to understand how happy
' they be that are freed from the incumbrance of that
' law which our forefathers groaned under : namely, from
' the legal sacrifices, and from the many ceremonies of
' the Levitical law ; freed from the Circumcision, and
' from the strict observance of the Jewish Sabbath, and
' the like.' He had no sour distaste to recreation ; his
own favourite amusement was music, ' in which heavenly
' art he was a most excellent master, and did himself
' compose many divine Hymns and Anthems, which he
' set and sung to his lute or viol : and though he was a
' lover of retiredness, yet his love to music was such, that
' he went usually twice every week, on certain appointed
' days, to the Cathedral Church in Salisbury ; and at his
' return would say, " That his time spent in prayer and
' " Cathedral-music, elevated his soul, and was his Heaven
' " upon earth." But before his return to Bemerton, he
' would usually sing and play his part at an appointed
' private Music-meeting ; and to justify this practice he
' would often say, " Religion does not banish mirth, but
' " only moderates and sets rules to it." '

Izaak Walton's account of his preaching tells how he
based it on the Church's teaching for the year, in the
collect, epistle, and gospel, and incidentally notes that
' the year is appointed to begin on the 25th day of
' March ; a day on which we commemorate the Angel's
' appearing to the Blessed Virgin, with the joyful tidings
' that she should conceive and bear a Son that should be
' the Redeemer of mankind.' The practice of daily
worship is thus described by Walton : ' And by this
' account of his diligence to make his parishioners under-
' stand what they prayed, and why they praised and
' adored their Creator, I hope I shall the more easily
' obtain the Reader's belief to the following account of
' Mr. Herbert's own practice ; which was to appear con-
' stantly with his wife and three nieces—the daughters of
' a deceased sister—and his whole family (*i.e.* servants),

' twice every day at Church-prayers in the Chapel, which
' does almost adjoin to his parsonage house. And for
' the time of his appearing, it was strictly at the canonical
' hours of ten and four : and then he lifted up his pure
' and charitable hands to God in the midst of the con-
' gregation . . . and there, by that inward devotion which
' he testified constantly by an humble behaviour and
' visible adoration, he, like Joshua, brought not only his
' own household thus to serve the Lord ; but brought
' most of his parishioners, and many gentlemen in the
' neighbourhood, constantly to make part of his congrega-
' tion twice a day : and some of the meaner sort of his
' parish did so love and reverence Mr. Herbert, that they
' would let their plough rest when Mr. Herbert's Saint's-
' bell rung to prayers, that they might also offer their
' devotions to God with him ; and would then return
' back to their plough.'

His gentleness with the poor comes out in the following
little story[1]: ' At which time of Mr. Herbert's coming alone
' to Bemerton (on his first appointment, when he went to
' see the Church and Parsonage), there came to him a
' poor old woman, with an intent to acquaint him with
' her necessitous condition, as also with some troubles of
' her mind : but after she had spoken some few words to
' him, she was surprised with a fear, and that begot a
' shortness of breath, so that her spirits and her speech
' failed her ; which he perceiving did so compassionate
' her, and was so humble, that he took her by the hand,
' and said, " Speak, good mother ; be not afraid to speak
' " to me, for I am a man that will hear you with patience ;
' " and will relieve your necessities too if I be able : and
' " this I will do willingly ; and therefore, mother, be not
' " afraid to acquaint me with your desire." After which
' comfortable speech, he again took her by the hand,
' made her sit down by him, and understanding she was
' of his parish, he told her, " He would be acquainted with

[1] Walton's *Lives*.

' " her, and take her into his care." And having with
' patience heard and understood her wants,—and it is some
' relief for a poor body to be heard with patience,—he, like
' a Christian Clergyman, comforted her by his meek be-
' haviour and counsel ; but because that cost him nothing, he
' relieved her with money too, and so sent her home with
' a cheerful heart, praising God and praying for him.

'At his return that night to his wife at Bainton, he
' gave her an account of the passages betwixt him and the
' poor woman ; with which she was so affected, that she
' went the next day to Salisbury, and there bought a pair
' of blankets, and sent them as a token of her love to the
' poor woman, and with them a message, " That she would
' " see and be acquainted with her when her house was built
' " at Bemerton." '

For although so saint-like in his own life, and so
absolutely aloof from the world, George Herbert was himself a married man ; yet his advice on the choice of a wife
shows in what light he regarded the question of a married
priesthood. 'The Country Parson,' he says, 'considering
' that virginity is a higher state than matrimony, and that
' the Ministry requires the best and highest things, is
' rather unmarried than married.' Yet he admits, having
regard to the times, that matrimony might be not only
lawful but expedient. His rule for the celibate priest was
higher and stricter, and if married 'the choice of his wife
' was made rather by his ear, than by his eye ; his judgment,
' not his affection, found out a fit wife for him.' That the
parson should make such a match as should unite him to
the world instead of helping him to be detached from it,
or that his usefulness should be curtailed by the necessity
of giving his sons a good education or so introducing and
dressing his daughters that they should be able to take
their place in fashionable society did not even present
itself for condemnation. His children may be bound
apprentice, 'but not to any vain calling, as taverns, lace-
' making and the like ; the eldest son may be brought up

' to follow his father, and all should be taught early to
' visit and tend other sick children.'

One of the parson's duties was to see that his church
was kept in good repair, and at festivals strewn and stuck
with boughs and perfumed with incense.   His own practice
here outran his principle, for he not only restored and
beautified both church and chapel at Bemerton, but, with
the aid of his friends Nicholas Ferrar and Mr. Woodnot,
a goldsmith, entirely rebuilt the church at Layton Ecclesia
in Huntingdon, which was fallen down.

Rules for fasting take the practice as a matter of course ;
the parson will keep all the fasts prescribed by the Prayer-
book, and will observe Fridays not only by abstinence of
diet but also of company, recreation, and all outward
contentments.   The methods of fasting are three—first,
eating less ; secondly, eating no over-nourishing or pleasant
things ; thirdly, eating no meat.   Of these he considers
the first two to be the most important, and he remarks
that the practice should not be carried to an extent that
would endanger health.   It may be noticed that at this
time the custom of fasting was strictly observed even
among the Puritans.   Lady Brilliana Harley, in her letters
to her son, often refers to the obligation, and is anxious
he should not eat too much fish in Lent, as it does not
agree with him.   The parson's rules of charity are equally
wise ; he gives his money to the poor, his hospitality to
those above alms.   True charity sees that all are set in
the way to earn their own livelihood, and no set pension
should be given to any that can do so.   Especial liberality
is enjoined at festivals and communions.

The Holy Sacrament is to be celebrated, if not once a
month, at least five times a year.   This is the only thing
in his rules that reminds us how widely the reformers had
departed from primitive customs.   In another point his
practice was more in accordance with Catholic rule and
primitive usage than is that of our own day : ' Children are to
' be admitted to the Holy Communion so soon as they can

' distinguish Sacramental from common bread.' It is noticeable that Bishop Cosins, in his Visitation, finding the usual
custom was to confirm children at seven years old, desired
that it should be deferred to the age of fourteen or fifteen ;
singular when we remember that girls were frequently
married as early as twelve or thirteen.

Rules are given for every portion of the parson's life.
In travelling he mixes with the company, gives thanks for
their safe arrival, and says grace.   He gives the host notice
that he will read prayers in the hall, ' wishing him to inform
' the guests thereof, that if any wish to partake, they may
' resort thither. Prayer and provender never hinder journey.'

This was quite a usual custom at that day ; Mr.
Rawdon, on one of his journeys, mentions how they met
with a clergyman who joined them on his invitation and
acted chaplain to the party.

Walton charmingly describes the pleasant manner in
which Mr. Herbert would enter into conversation with
those he met on the road to and from Salisbury on music-
meeting days : casual encounters which not seldom grew
into lasting friendships.   After telling of some, he relates
how, ' in another walk to Salisbury, he saw a poor man
' with a poorer horse, that was fallen under his load : they
' were both in distress, and needed present help ; which
' Mr. Herbert perceiving, put off his canonical coat
' (cassock ?) and helped the poor man to unload, and after
' to load his horse. The poor man blessed him for it, and
' he blessed the poor man ; and was so like the good
' Samaritan, that he gave him money to refresh both
' himself and his horse, and told him, " That if he loved
' " himself, he should be merciful to his beast."   Thus he
' left the poor man ; and at his coming to his musical
' friends in Salisbury, they began to wonder that Mr.
' George Herbert, which used to be so trim and clean,
' came into that company so soiled and discomposed : but
' he told them the occasion.   And when one of the
' company told him, " He had disparaged himself by so

' " dirty an employment," his answer was, " That the
' " thought of what he had done would prove music to him
' " at midnight ; and that the omission of it would have
' " upbraided and made discord in his conscience, whensoever
' " he should pass by that place : for if I be bound to pray
' " for all that be in distress, I am sure that I am bound,
' " so far as it is in my power, to practice what I pray for.
' " And though I do not wish for the like occasion every
' " day, yet let me tell you, I would not willingly pass one
' " day of my life without comforting a sad soul, or
' " shewing mercy ; and I praise God for this occasion.
' " And now let's tune our instruments." '

This picture of the life of a country parson is no mere
fancy sketch, nor was it fulfilled only in the life of him who
drew it; in many parishes, both in town and country, though
perhaps more frequently in the latter, were to be found
men who might have sat for the portrait, men of scholarly
attainments but of simplicity of life, who had set aside
ambition and wedded poverty and obscurity for love of
Christ and His poor. Such was Hammond, rector of
Penshurst, whose eloquence might have raised him to high
preferment, but who was content to work in his quiet
country parish. ' He was zealous in the discharge of his
' priestly office : read prayers daily morning and evening
' in the church ; celebrated the Holy Communion on
' Sundays and holidays, and catechised the school-children
' regularly in the church before Evensong. His charity to
' the poor was unbounded. He sold corn at a low price in
' time of scarcity, and when one summer the crops of a
' farmer were ruined by a bad flood, he remitted the tithe
' due to him, saying he could not take a tenth from a
' neighbour since he had lost the other nine parts.' This
reminds the reader of Dr. Earle's Grave Divine : ' He is
' no base grater of his tythes and will not wrangle for the
' odd egg.' Dr. Hammond, the story goes on, ' rebuilt
' the rectory which had been allowed to fall into ruins,
' and planted the garden and orchards which still surround

' the charming old house. Here he spent ten happy years
' with his old mother to keep house for him, and the books
' which were the favourite companions of his leisure
' hours until the Civil War began.'[1] Then his home was
plundered, his books burnt, and he himself driven out,
for such as these were the men who were deprived of
their livings and turned out of their homes for no crime
but their adherence to the Prayer-book and faithful
observation of the canons of the Church to which their
ordination vows bound them.

Another type of man, such as the Young Raw Preacher
of Dr. Earle's satirical sketch, found little difficulty in
accommodating himself to the new ways, in fact inclined
to them already. ' He takes on against the Pope without
' mercy, and has still a jest in lavender for Bellarmine ; yet
' he preaches heresy if it comes in his way. He will not
' draw his handkercher out of its place nor blow his nose
' without discretion. His commendation is that he never
' looks upon a book ; and indeed he was never used to
' it. . . . He has more tricks with a sermon than a Taylor
' with an old cloke, to turn it and piece it, and at last
' quite disguise it with a new preface. . . . His fashion
' and demure habit gets him in with some town precisian
' and makes him a guest on Friday nights. You shall
' know him by his narrow velvet cape and serge facing ;
' and his ruff next his hair the shortest thing about him.'[2]
This is no unfair sketch of the men who easily turned their
coats under Cromwell and back again at the Restoration,
keeping their preferment through all changes like the
immortal Vicar of Bray. It does not of course apply,
and was not intended by its author to apply to the graver
sort of Puritan divine ; many of these were not only
eloquent preachers, but men of high character and unblemished lives, though their zeal was often as one-sided
as their conception of the Christian character.

It is fair to set over against this the satirical comments

[1] *Sacharissa*. Mrs. Ady.   [2] Earle's *Microcosmography*.

of a Puritan, John Rous, incumbent of Holkham, on the customs of the Laudian clergy. He attends service at some church which we should now describe as 'High,' and is much exercised because the Psalms are read verse about. 'He staied for Mr. Peeke and some others to ' mutter eche other verse of the Psalmes ; & omitting a ' first lesson, he read a second lesson, wherein he mouthed ' it Je—sus with a low congie ; & in his sermon upon ' Matt. iii. 10, among those whom he made liable to God's ' fearful judgment, he named adulterers, oppressors, atheists, ' those that bowed not at the name of Jesus, & (I think ' also) those that were covered at divine service.'[1]

Sarcastic rhymes and pasquinades about 'the new ' Churchman' as he was called, were many. In one he ' swears by the half foot-ball on his pate '—'drops, ducks ' and bowes as made all of joints,' or 'his Roman nose ' stands full East.' 'He will be no Protestant but a ' Christian, and comes out Catholic the next edition.'

In all ages and in all countries persons of a certain religious temper have felt the need of a complete withdrawal from the world, and this period saw an experiment in the religious life in many ways unique. The times were too near the dissolution of the monasteries, the 'no ' Popery' excitement too intense for any attempt to revive an institution with monastic vows, and although the community at Little Gidding was stigmatised as 'the ' Protestant Nunnery,' it was in truth no nunnery, but a private family, who chose, as they had every right to do, to devote their lives to religious observance in the strict following of a rule, and who gladly extended their hospitality to others who sought to join them ; but its members were bound by no vows, and were perfectly free to return to the world or form marriage engagements should they wish to do so. The beautiful picture of this little community which is so familiar in the pages of *John Inglesant*, follows with close accuracy that given in Walton's *Lives*.

[1] *Diary of John Rous.* Camden Society.

P

It was formed of the household of Mr. Nicholas Ferrar, a man of some property who, having travelled much in Italy and deeply considered the Roman Communion, found nothing to detach him from his loyalty to the Church of England, but much which might be imitated to edification ; so on his return he established himself at an estate which he had bought in Huntingdonshire—that home of Puritanism—about eighteen miles from Cambridge, and with his mother, his widowed sister and her son and daughters, set about framing a rule of life devoted to works of piety and continual worship, in complete seclusion from the world.   His rule is thus described :—

'He and his family, which were like a little College,
'and about thirty in number, did most of them keep Lent
'and all Ember weeks strictly, both in fasting and using
'all those mortifications and prayers that the Church hath
'appointed to be then used ; and he and they did the
'like constantly on Fridays, and on the Vigils or Eves
'appointed to be fasted before the Saint's days : and this
'frugality and abstinence turned to the relief of the poor :
'but this was but a part of his charity ; none but God
'and he knew the rest.

'This family, which I have said to be in number about
'thirty, were a part of them his kindred, and the rest
'chosen to be of a temper fit to be moulded into a devout
'life ; and all of them were for their disposition service-
'able, and quiet, and humble, and free from scandal.
'Having thus fitted himself for his family, he did, about
'the year 1630, betake himself to a constant and methodi-
'cal service of God ; and it was in this manner ;—He,
'being accompanied with most of his family, did himself
'use to read the common prayers—for he was a Deacon
'—every day, at the appointed hours of ten and four, in
'the parish Church, which was very near his house, and
'which he had both repaired and adorned ; for it was
'fallen into very great ruin, by reason of the depopulation
'of the village before Mr. Farrer bought the manor.

' And he did also constantly read the Matins every
' morning at the hour of six, either in the Church, or in
' an Oratory, which was within his own house. And
' many of the family did there continue with him after
' the prayers were ended, and there they spent some hours
' in singing hymns or anthems, sometimes in the Church,
' and often to an organ in the Oratory. And there they
' sometimes betook themselves to meditate, or to pray
' privately, or to read a part of the New Testament to
' themselves, or to continue their praying or reading the
' Psalms ; and in case the Psalms were not always read
' in the day, then Mr. Farrer, and others of the congrega-
' tion, did at night, at the ringing of a watch-bell, repair
' to the Church or Oratory, and there betake themselves
' to prayer and lauding God, and reading the Psalms that
' had not been read in the day : and when these, or any
' part of the congregation, grew weary or faint, the watch-
' bell was rung, sometimes before, sometimes after mid-
' night ; and then another part of the family rose and
' maintained the watch sometimes by praying or singing
' lauds to God, or reading the Psalms ; and when after
' some hours, they also grew weary or faint, they rung
' the watch-bell and were also relieved by some of the
' former, or by a new part of the society, which continued
' their devotions—as hath been mentioned—until morning.
' And it is to be noted, that in this continued serving of
' God, the Psalter, or whole Book of Psalms, was in every
' four and twenty hours sung or read over, from the first
' to the last verse ; and this was done as constantly as the
' sun runs his circle every day about the world, and then
' begins the same again the same instant that it ended.
    ' Thus did Mr. Farrer and his happy family serve
' God day and night : thus did they always behave
' themselves as in His presence. And they did always
' eat and drink by the strictest rule of temperance, so as
' to be ready to rise at midnight, or at the call of the
' watch-bell, and perform their devotions to God. And

' it is fit to tell the Reader, that many of the Clergy,
' that were more inclined to practical piety and devotion
' than to doubtful and needless disputations, did often
' come to Gidden Hall, and make themselves a part of
' that happy society, and stay a week or more, and then
' join with Mr. Farrer and the family in these devotions,
' and assist or ease him and them in their watch by night.
' And these various devotions had never less than two of
' the domestic family in the night ; and the watch was
' always kept in the Church or Oratory, unless in extreme
' cold winter nights, and then it was maintained in a
' parlour, which had a fire in it ; and the parlour was
' fitted for that purpose.   And this course of piety, and
' great liberality to his poor neighbours, Mr. Farrer
' maintained till his death, which was in the year 1639.'

Besides these practices of worship, the course of life at
Little Gidding included occupations which were pursued
with the utmost industry : some taught poor children,
some visited and tended the sick, but the greater part of
the family were busy with the arrangement of the
Scripture Harmonies or Concordances, as they called
them, for which they were so famous.   These were
planned by Nicholas himself or his nephew, but the
mechanical part of the work, the pasting in of the slips
of different print of which they were composed, the
embroidery of the covers, and the binding itself, were
executed by the young ladies of the family, the daughters
of Mrs. Collet.   These Harmonies were made by Comparison : the account given by the different evangelists
printed in parallel columns—Composition : the narrative
woven together, and distinguished by small letters placed
against each passage—Collection : where all agree printed
in black letter, other portions in small type.   All the
slips used had to be pasted on a large folio page.

Another task on which the younger Nicholas Ferrar
was engaged was the making of a Polyglot Testament
in twenty-four languages, which was very highly thought

of by those to whom it was shown. This, it may be observed, was done some years before Laud's Polyglot Bible.

Among the visitors attracted by the fame of these works was the King, who was greatly delighted especially with the industry of the Misses Collet, and presented them with a beautiful work-case with little drawers, in memory of his visit. He desired also that a Harmony should be made for him, and also one for Prince Charles. On one that he borrowed he made marginal notes in his own hand, and used to study it every day for an hour ' in the midst of his progress and sports.' In one place he had written a correction, but afterwards crossed it out neatly with his pen, adding, ' I confess my error, it was ' well before, I was mistaken.' Another frequent visitor was Crashaw, the poet, with whose mystical temper the seclusion and constant round of worship was in harmony. Later, when all such religious practices in England were trodden underfoot, he went abroad and joined the Church of Rome.

A note to Walton's *Lives* gives the end of the story. ' The extraordinary course of life pursued at Gidding, the ' strictness of their rules, their prayers, literally without ' ceasing, their abstinence, mortifications, nightly watch- ' ings, and various other peculiarities, gave birth to ' censure in some, and inflamed the malevolence of others, ' but excited the wonder and curiosity of all. So that ' they were frequently visited with different views by ' persons of all denominations, and of opposite opinions. ' They received all who came with courteous civility, and ' from those who were inquisitive they concealed nothing, ' as indeed there was not anything either in their opinions ' or in their practice, in the least necessary to be con- ' cealed. Notwithstanding this, they were by some ' abused as Papists, by others as Puritans. Mr. Ferrar ' himself, though possessed of uncommon patience and ' resignation, yet in anguish of spirit complained to his

' friends, that the perpetual obloquy he endured was a
' sort of unceasing martyrdom.   Added to all this,
' violent invectives and inflammatory pamphlets were
' published against them.   Amongst others, not long
' after Mr. Ferrar's death, a treatise was addressed to the
' Parliament, entitled, *The Arminian Nunnery at Little*
' *Gidding in Huntingdonshire : humbly addressed to the*
' *wise consideration of the present Parliament.   The founda-*
' *tion is by a company of Ferrars at Gidding.   Printed by*
' *Thomas Underhill, 1641.*

' Soon after Mr. Ferrar's death, certain soldiers of the
' Parliament resolved to plunder the house at Gidding.
' The family being informed of their hasty approach,
' thought it prudent to fly ; while these military zealots,
' in the rage of what they called reformation, ransacked
' both the Church and the house ; in doing which they
' expressed a particular spite against the organ.   This
' they broke in pieces, of which they made a large fire,
' and at it roasted several of Mr. Ferrar's sheep, which
' they had killed in the grounds.   This done, they seized
' all the plate, furniture, and provision, which they could
' conveniently carry away.   And in the general devasta-
' tion perished the works which Mr. Ferrar had compiled
' for the use of his household, consisting chiefly of the
' Harmonies of the Old and New Testaments.'

It may well be supposed that two such devout souls
as George Herbert and Nicholas Ferrar, who had been at
Cambridge together, would maintain a warm friendship,
and this they did till the end of their days, though they
could not often meet.   'This holy friendship,' as Walton
says, 'was long maintained without any interview, but
' only by loving and endearing letters.'

This story of Little Gidding has been thus told at
length because it is in many respects unique and
characteristic of a phase of religion that belonged to that
time alone.   Whether such an experiment, had it gone
on without interference, could ever have taken root is

doubtful ; the attempt to combine family life with monastic rule, or to maintain observance of that rule without any vow of obedience or life-long dedication, had never been tried before, and has never been tried since. On the face of it, it does not appear that it could have had the elements of permanence ; it must either have dissolved of itself or been cast into another mould. One thing it seems to show—the desire that was in the hearts of the best men of that time to prove that the Church of England had not broken up the monastic system from the wish to adopt an easier standard, a desire which comes out very strongly in many saintly private lives.

Amongst the Puritan clergy, Adam Martindale is a very interesting example, as he tells his own story in much detail.[1] He was the son of a mason or carpenter, holding his own freehold in Lancashire, and he received an excellent education, partly in the free school at St. Helen's in the neighbourhood of Preston, partly at a school at Raisford where small fees were charged. At the age of twenty-three, having been for some years a schoolmaster, he was urged to offer himself for the ministry, the lack of suitable persons being in those days very great. He hesitated on the score of his want of university training, but his objections being over-ruled he set himself forthwith to study Hebrew, logic, ethics, and metaphysics, and being bent on taking his degree, through the interest of a friend he was allowed to be entered under-commoner at University College, Oxford, and the obligation of residence dispensed with, so that he merely had to go up for examination and took his degree.

With the body to which he belonged, the English Presbyterians, who had at this time, 1644, captured the Church, preaching seems to have been the only thing held of consequence, for having been tested in that capacity he officiated in three parishes before receiving Orders, and he himself was in no hurry to be ordained,

[1] *Memoirs of Adam Martindale.* Cheetham Society.

observing that 'Baptizings fell out so seldom in that
' small congregation, and neighbouring ministers were soe
' willing to doe that worke, that they felt little incon-
' venience that way ; and as for the Supper of the Lord,
' all that were in a capacity to have had it with us might
' be admitted to neighbour places neare enough.'

When after the lapse of four or five years he went to
London to receive Ordination from the Classis, it seems
to have been a very hasty and informal proceeding.
Arriving in town, he was told the Classis was then sitting
in St. Andrew's Undershaft, and hastening thither found
them, he says, 'just upon going home, and they had been
  gone ere I came, but that they were stayed by another
' young man that came as I did when they were upon
' the point of departing.   I acquainted Mr. Blackwell,
' minister of the place and scribe of the Classis, with my
' businesses, length of journey, and ignorance of the time
' and place.   He went in and pleaded my cause so that
' I was admitted, though Dr. Spurstowe, the moderator
' that day, was somewhat discontented at their late
' staying in that place.   In a word I was examined then
' and approved, and the next day, July 25, 1649 (as my
' testimonials show), ordained in the same church.'

His experiences amongst his parishioners throw a
good deal of light upon the strife and exasperated feeling
between the Presbyterians and Independents, each wishing
to remodel the Church on their own lines, neither willing
to tolerate the views of the other, and only at one in their
hostility to 'prelacy.'   He himself tried earnestly to find
a *modus vivendi*, and was by no means intolerant to
those who differed from him.   Though a strict Puritan,
he deeply disapproved of the usurpations of Cromwell
and the murder of the King ; he belonged to the party
who wished the Church brought into line with Geneva,
but by no means desired the overthrow of the government.

His memoirs, written by himself, depict a man of

sturdy independent character and kind heart, a good
scholar with a genuine love of learning, a zealous preacher,
holding preaching indeed as the main part of pastoral
office ; but of the spirituality of a George Herbert or a
Nicholas Ferrar there is not a trace.

CHAPTER XV

TYPES OF PIETY

NOT only in quiet country parsonages nor in homes set apart for the practice of religion was a high ideal of saintliness to be found, but also in lives lived in the great world. There is a very remarkable and quaint little book, rather rare inasmuch as it has not been republished in recent days, and indeed has very little literary attraction about it, which shows how the wife of an eminent statesman, the mother of a family, and mistress of a household noted for its hospitality, spent her days and ordered her home. It is especially curious as showing how the Protestantism of that day—for its subject was a thoroughgoing Protestant—entered into a wholesome rivalry with Rome in ' works,' fasting and almsgiving as well as prayer. The book is somewhat overweighted with title for its size, a small duodecimo, being called ' *The Returnes of Spiritual* ' *Comfort and Grief in a Devout Soul Represented* (*by* ' *entercourse of Letters*) *to the Right Honourable the Lady* ' *Letice Vi-Countess Falkland in her Life time and exempli-* ' *fied in the holy Life and Death of the said Honourable* ' *Lady. Published for the benefit and ease of all who labour* ' *under spiritual affliction.*'

The letters are those which passed between her and her chaplain who edits them, and they are followed by a brief memoir addressed to her mother, which probably served as model to the somewhat similar account of a court lady of a later day, which John Evelyn wrote in a

epistolary form addressed to a relative of his subject
Margaret Godolphin.   There is much that is akin in the
two lives, though led in such different surroundings,
Lettice Cary's in a Court so religious that her greatest
regret in being away from it was the loss of daily service
and weekly communion ; Margaret Godolphin's in the
midst of the frivolity of the Restoration, so that her
religious observances had to be all her own.   If Margaret
Blagge, as she was in her Court days, was tested by
prosperity, Lettice was tried in the furnace of affliction,
enduring the extreme of anxiety all through the early
years of the war while her husband was continually at
the King's side, then seeing him fall in the prime of his
years, and soon after losing her ' youngest and most dear
' son Lorenzo,' and through all her desolation obliged to
exert herself to manage her estate for her remaining son,
to care for her household and for the poor, to resist the
extortions of the Parliament, for she risked confiscation
sooner than pay contribution money against the King ;
and she had to struggle through all these difficulties with
failing health, for she died of consumption at the age of
thirty-five.

The story of her early years and careful education has
already been quoted in the volume on Home Life.   Very
soon she learnt to work for the poor.   Her biographer
writes, addressing her mother, 'You remember wel, I
' presume, the Purse her young fingers wrought for her own
' alms, and how importunately she would beg your single
' money to fill it ; and as greedy she was of imploying
' it too ; the poor seldome went from the house without
' the alms of the young daughter as wel as of the parents.'
She was most regular, too, in the observance of hours of
prayer, not only morning and evening but throughout the
day.   Living at a distance from the church, she does not
seem at this time to have been able to attend daily
service, but ' Every Lord's Day constantly forenoon and
' afternoon she would be with the earliest at them :

' somewhile (when she wanted convenience of riding) she
' walked cheerfully three or four miles a day, as young
' and weak as she was, to them.'　As often happens with
such religious souls the fault of her character was a
tendency to morbidness, which at thirteen years old
' tempted her to despair of God's mercy.'　Not improbably
she may have come across some of the Puritan preachers
whose ideas of the capricious mercies of God were
beginning to make themselves heard to the disturbance
of the quiet faith of timid introspective souls.　During
the years of her happy married life, under the bright and
wholesome influence of Lucius we hear of no such access
of religious melancholy, but when he was gone, in her
loneliness and weak health she often mistook her desolate-
ness and lowered spirit for a sign that God's favour was
withdrawn, as we gather from her letters.

Yet through the days of her prosperity, whether abroad
with her husband or at the Court, or during the halcyon
time, as Clarendon calls it, when she dispensed the easy
pleasant hospitalities of Great Tew and entertained her
husband's friends, she kept always the same seriousness
of disposition and the same regularity of religious
observance.　'Some years passed in which she was
' constant at Praiers and Sermons, and frequently received
' the Blessed Sacrament.'　She spent every day some
hours in private prayer ; then she would have her maids
to her chamber for an hour's prayer and catechising, and
if any missed attending she would devote an hour to her
later in the day.　There was public morning and evening
prayer in the church before dinner and supper, and family
prayer with reading the Bible and singing Psalms before
bedtime.　Every Saturday she fasted and sequestered
herself from company and from worldly employment.
She also observed the fasts of the Church the second
Friday in every month, and wished the last Wednesday
kept as well.　Keeping only the second Friday seems a
new and laxer rule ; George Herbert in his *Country*

× An ecclesiastical God that is placed only by
priestly sacramental intercession is anything
but merciful.

Parson implies that every Friday is to be observed. By what authority could this custom have been introduced? She also kept the holy days, and after church gave them as holidays to her servants.

Her charity was constant, and she was especially good to her own relations and her husband's, nursing her husband's mother wlth great devotion. It must have been good for these two women, the one a devout Catholic, the other an uncompromising Protestant, to have been brought so closely together as to see the true piety of each other's lives. There was considerable wisdom in the way she apportioned her alms, maintaining aged people or young children, but setting others to labour, and establishing schools. She would harbour strangers, clothe and feed beggars, answering to those that reproached her for their unworthiness: ' I know not ' their hearts; I had rather relieve unworthy vagrants ' than that one member of Christ should go empty away.' She visited the sick, provided physic and cordials for them and hired nurses to attend on them, though when- ever able she would go to them herself.' Like Margaret Godolphin of whom Evelyn says, ' Often would she ' herself walk out alone and on foote and fasting, and in ' the midst of winter, (when it was hardly fit to send a ' servant out) to minister to some poore creatures she ' had found out, and perhaps whom nobody knew of ' besides, soe far had her love to God and duty to others ' overcome nature and the delicate tenderness of her sex ' and constitution.'

Lady Falkland was a peacemaker among her neigh- bours, and herself most gentle and meek, though perhaps rather by grace than by nature, for she found it needful to make and renew resolutions against anger and evil- speaking; and her Director in one place remarks that she could ' reprove when needful with a good deal of ' power.' He also observes of her that she was ' after ' the manner of woemen too much governed by the 'nursery,' but she trained up her children to regular habits of prayer and learning Psalms by heart. When Parliament was in power, and church prayers forbidden, she continued to use them, encountering any risk of fine or sequestration sooner than give them up.

She was a very beautiful woman, and, to judge by her portrait, one who understood how to combine modesty and simplicity with a seemly richness of apparel. Her oval face, soft curling hair, and mild dark eyes suit the velvet, point-lace, and pearls in which she was painted, but after the death of her husband she always wore the long, black veil, shrouding the whole head and figure, which was the customary garb of widows at that day. In her portrait in it, prefixed to the little memoir, her fair face looks pathetically thin and worn for her less than thirty-five years.

One of her husband's latest biographers hints, rather gratuitously, that she may have been stupid, but this was not the view of her chaplain who, writing of her in her youth says, 'And within a short while by reading good 'authors, and by frequent converse with learned men, she 'improved her natural talents of understanding and reason 'to a great degree of wisdom and knowledge.' Incidentally, her letters show that she understood Latin, as did all educated women of her time. It would indeed have been hardly possible for a woman of ordinary intelligence to have lived in constant intercourse with such a mind as that of Lucius Cary, and to have listened to the discussions which went on at her table, and have retained any narrowness of understanding; that she was a woman of large views and alive to the importance of education was shown by the scheme which only the disturbed times prevented her from carrying out, for establishing colleges for young gentlewomen. She also was beforehand with Bishop Morley in planning a kind of College for widows in reduced circumstances; indeed, it seems not improbable, remembering how much he visited at Great Tew, that his

College for the Widows of Clergy in Winchester may have owed its first inception to conversations with her.

The letters exchanged between her and her private chaplain or director are interesting in their bearing on the subject of confession as practised at that day. So far as one may gather from them, she seems to have confided to him her sins even of thought, her difficulties and failures of faith, and to have received from him precisely the kind of direction a Catholic priest would have afforded to his penitent ; but there is no reference to any sacramental confession or absolution ; the consolations offered are those of a religious adviser. It may be observed that she was in intention, according to her upbringing, a decided Protestant, though she followed Catholic practices more closely than she knew. She keeps up as well as she can her regular observance of public and private worship, and laments the paucity of opportunity in the country : she misses the Court and cathedral services also, 'the country ' Village where the good Parson had Morning and Evening ' Prayer in the Church daily. Here there are only prayers ' Sundays, Holy days, and their evens, and Litany days, ' and Sacraments once a month.' She complains of spiritual dryness and ceasing to find the happiness in prayer which once she found, and her chaplain answers by advising devout postures and the aid of music. She still writes sadly and would fain abridge the pleasure she takes in history or philosophy (not a very stupid woman this) or the solace she seeks in her friends or her children ; but her director writes wisely, discouraging further self-mortification—poor soul, she had surely little enough outward solace then—but he urges her to distinguish between loss of grace and of sensible consolation, and illustrates his meaning by the instance of 'a Child from whom the Nurse is withdrawn that the Mother may gain ' its chiefest affections.' Thus the correspondence goes on till the clouds that overshadowed her soul are dispersed. In one letter her chaplain warns her both against the appeals

of Rome, and against the emotional preachers of the day.
It is not unlikely that while so cast down she may have remembered the always serene and happy faith of her mother-
in-law, sustained through so much difficulty and persecution.

Like Lady Warwick she had a fondness for walking
and meditating in the fields, and the calm beauty of the
country may have done much to soothe her sorely-
wounded spirit. The religious experiences of Lady
Warwick, whom we have seen in her worldly days as
Mary Boyle, belong, strictly speaking, to a rather later
day, but they are valuable as showing the type of religion
which was called Evangelical, and doubly so because such
records on the Puritan side are very scanty. She, too,
abounded in good works and charity to the poor, but her
goodness was, if we may be allowed the expression, of a
more individualistic type; of corporate church life she
seems to have no conception. She would drive any
distance to hear noted preachers, but beyond that was
satisfied with her own private prayers and meditations,
and in intercourse with her friend and vicar, Dr. Walker,
gave quite as much advice as she received. Her meditations show a sensitive, conscientious soul, and great
devotion; but her idea of God is of an angry deity on the
look-out for the smallest lapse, and visiting her for it with
some appropriate punishment.[1] She makes one think of
those eighteen on whom the Tower of Siloam fell.

On the religious side Mrs. Hutchinson's *Memoirs* are
disappointing. Invaluable as they are for the light they
throw on the inner workings of the Presbyterian and
Independent factions, it is difficult to gather from them
any idea of what the religious practices of the Puritans
were. Daily worship in the churches and the use of the
Book of Common Prayer was put down with a strong
hand so soon as they got the power, so it is not likely
that they attended daily service in the preceding years.
The Lord's Day or Sabbath, as they called it, was very

[1] *Mary Rich, Countess of Warwick*, by Constance F. M. Smith.

+ That is what God is if the ordinances of the Church
to placate him are necessary —

strictly observed among them, but rather as a day of
humiliation than a festival. The service on that day
consisted of long extempore prayers, metrical psalms sung
without accompaniment and with each line read aloud
before being chanted, and very long sermons, lasting
sometimes over two hours, which were listened to with
great enthusiasm. Some of the Puritans, as we saw in
Lady Brilliana Harley's letters, fasted, but we do not read
of any such observance by Lady Warwick nor in the
Hutchinson household. Private prayer, meditation, reading of the Bible and good books, as well as charity to the
poor, were practices common to all religious women, and
no instance is to be found among the Puritans which
reaches the high perfection of the family at Little Gidding.

The idea which animated their practice—or want of
practice—seems to have been that religion might be more
spiritual, independent of forms or of priesthood, and the
ultimate outcome was that when the spirit evaporated
the forms were gone too, and laxity took the place of the
first fervour.[1]

It would hardly be fair to take Mrs. Hutchinson as
a type of the religious life of her party. The little girl
who could repeat long sermons correctly at four years
old, who lectured her small playfellows and scornfully
pulled their dolls to pieces, retained all her life the
conviction that the first of religious duties was to preach
to her neighbours, and her vocabulary of abusive epithets
rivals that of Milton himself. She does not even spare
her own side ; of the ladies of Cromwell's family she

---

[1] Certainly we may gather from the swarms of petitions from parishioners
against their parsons, addressed to the Parliament when in power, that the
spirit animating the rank and file of the Puritan party was far more hostility
to certain forms than zeal for religion itself. The immense number found
among the papers of Sir Edward Dering, and published by the Camden Society,
are nearly all in complaint of the altar having been placed at the east end and
railed round (according to the archbishop's desire), and the parson bowing
towards it or at the name of Jesus. Occasionally a lack of preaching and
plurality of cures are complained of, in some few cases drunkenness and
quarrelsomeness, immorality in only one.

Q

*Those outward forms represented an idea of the
character of God entirely contrary to the teaching
of Jesus.

remarks that 'they were setting up for principality, which
'suited no better with any of them than scarlet on an
'ape. His daughter Fleetwood,' she observes, 'was
'humbled and not exalted with these things, but the rest
'were insolent fools. Claypole, who married his daughter,
'and his son Henry, were two debauched, ungodly
'cavaliers.' Then, after deploring the decay of religion,
she goes on : 'Almost all the ministers everywhere fell in
'and worshipped this beast (Cromwell), and courted and
'made addresses to him.' Since this is the style in which
she describes 'the godly,' the reader is not astonished at
her picture of the Court of James I., nor at this sketch of
the general condition of the country in his time : 'The
'generality of the gentry of the land soon learned the Court
'fashion, and every great house in the country became a sty
'of uncleanness. To keep the people in their deplorable
'security till vengeance overtook them, they were enter-
'tained with masks, stage plays, and various sorts of ruder
'sports. Then began murder, incest, adultery, drunken-
'ness, swearing, fornication, and all sorts of ribaldry, to be
'no concealed but countenanced vices, because they held
'such conformity with the Court examples.' Of the
mixed marriages which especially excite her ire, she
writes, 'I have observed that there was not one house in
'ten, where such a marriage was made, but the better
'party was corrupted, the children's souls sacrificed to
'devils, the worship of God was laid aside in that family
'for fear of distasting the idolater.' Later in the same
paragraph she speaks of 'the general apostasy from
'holiness and defection to lewdness.' It is well to
remember that in Puritan phraseology 'the godly' are
those belonging to the speaker's own party, or rather to
his own particular section of it ; 'the malignants' are
those of the other side, whatever their personal character
may be. Frequently, when in her memoirs Mrs. Hutchinson speaks of the doings of 'wicked and lewd' persons, a
little inquiry reveals the fact that the lewdness only

* Is it not so likewise. as a rule. in the phras-
iology of Episcopalians & Papists ?

consisted in opposition to Colonel Hutchinson's views or merely in taking up arms for the king. We must do her the justice, however, to remember that her deeds were better than her words, and she treated wounded prisoners of war with great humanity.

She speaks of Charles with more respect than of his father, observing that he was temperate, chaste, and serious, but declares, 'his firm adherence to prelacy was ' not for conscience of one religion more than another, ' for it was his principle that an honest man might be ' saved in any profession ; but he had a mistaken prin- ' ciple that kingly government in the state could not ' stand without episcopal government in the Church ; and ' therefore as the bishops flattered him with preaching up ' his sovereign prerogative, and inveighing against the ' puritans as factious and disloyal, so he protected them ' in their pomp and pride, and insolent practices against ' all godly and sober people in the land.' She goes on to insinuate that the Duke of Buckingham had poisoned King James, and that Charles had been privy to it ! Truly, with all their esteem for the Ten Commandments, the Puritans must surely have thought the ninth was not intended to apply to persons in public life.

Compared with her expressions of candid opinion, Bishop Earle's light raillery of a she-precisian reads playfully ; and indeed it is difficult in the utterances of the Royalists to find any epithet harsher than 'round- ' head,' 'rebel,' or 'crop-eared knave.' This is the way Dr. Earle sketches the 'she precise hypocrite' :—

'She is one that hath taken a toy at the new fashion ' of religion, and is enamoured at the new fangle. She ' is a nonconformist in a close stomacher and ruff of ' Geneva print (*i.e.* a small plait affected by the Puritans, ' called after the minute print in use at Geneva). She ' rails at the Whore of Babylon as a very naughty ' woman. She has left her virginity as a relic of popery, ' and marries in her tribe without a ring. Her devotion

' at Church is much in the turning up of her eye ; and
' turning down the leaf of her book when she hears
' named chapter and verse.   When she comes home she
' commends the sermon for the scripture, and two hours.
' She loves preaching better than praying, and of preachers
' lecturers ; and thinks the week-day's exercise far more
' edifying than the Sunday's.   Her oftest gossipings are
' Sabbath-day's journeys, where (tho' an enemy to super-
' stition) she will go on pilgrimage five miles to a silenc'd
' minister, when there is a better sermon in her own
' parish.   She doubts the Virgin Mary's salvation, and
' does not saint her, but knows her own place in Heaven
' as perfectly as the pew she has a key to.   She is so
' taken up with faith she has no room for charity, and
' understands no good works but what are wrought on
' the sampler.   She accounts nothing vice but superstition
' and an oath, and thinks adultery a less sin than to
' swear by my truly.   She rails at other women by the
' names of Jezebel and Dalilah ; and calls her own
' daughters Rebecca and Abigail and, not Ann, but
' Hannah.   She suffers them not to learn the virginals
' because of their affinity with organs. . . . It is a question
' whether she is more troubled with the Devil or the
' Devil with her. . . . Nothing angers her so much as
' that women cannot preach, but what she cannot do in
' church she does at the table, where she prattles more
' than any against sense and anti-christ, till a capon's
' wing silence her.   She expounds the priests of Baal
' reading ministers, and thinks the salvation of that parish
' as desperate as the Turks'. . . . She is one that thinks
' she performs all her duties to God in hearing, and
' shows the fruit of it in talking.   She is more fiery than
' her husband against the May-pole, and thinks she might
' do a Phineas act to break the pate of the fiddler.   She
' is an everlasting argument, but I am weary of her.' [1]

The reader may well be so too, and will turn with

[1] *Microcosmography.*

a sense of refreshment to the wide-minded and tolerant
religion of a layman, the religion of a doctor, set forth in
a little book of meditative essays—the *Religio Medici* of
Sir Thomas Browne.   If so far this chapter has been
chiefly concerned with the religion of women, it is because
it is the private and personal life with which it has to do,
and that of men was more manifested in public affairs.
But this little book of the Norwich doctor's, though
thoroughly masculine, is essentially personal, and deals
with his inner life and thoughts upon the much-vexed
topic of religion.   It has a peculiar interest, inasmuch as
it reflects the transitional life of the period ; he stands,
as it were, holding with one hand to the traditional
credulousness of the age which was passing, grasping
with the other at the inquiring and scientific spirit of
that which was coming over the hills of time.

Even in those and still earlier days the study of
medicine was prone to lead to agnosticism or materialism,
as he acknowledges, quoting the old proverb, ' Three
' doctors, two atheists ' ; but he himself had escaped those
tendencies, as well as the more subtle one to indifferentism
—not easy to avoid for a man who had travelled much, and
studied first at Padua and then at Leyden, changing, as
his biographer remarks, from the most bigoted Roman
Catholic to the most bigoted Protestant atmosphere, and
no doubt finding friends and conscientious men in both
communities.   The effect on his own opinions let him
tell in his own words :—

' But because the name of a Christian is become too
' general to express our faith,—there being a geography
' of religion as well as lands, and every clime distinguished
' not only by their laws and limits, but circumscribed by
' their doctrines and rules of faith,—to be particular, I
' am of that reformed new-cast religion, wherein I dislike
' nothing but the name ; of the same belief our Saviour
' taught, the apostles disseminated, the fathers authorized,
' and the martyrs confirmed ; but by the sinister ends of

' princes, the ambition and avarice of prelates, and the
' fatal corruption of the times, so decayed, impaired and
' fallen from its native beauty, that it required the careful
' and charitable hands of these times to restore it to its
' primitive integrity.' In the next section he continues:
' Yet have I not so shaken hands with those desperate
' resolutions who had rather venture at large their decayed
' bottom than bring her in to be new-trimmed in the
' dock,—who had rather promiscuously retain all than
' abridge any, and obstinately be what they are than
' what they have been,—as to stand in diameter and
' sword's point with them. We have reformed from
' them, not against them : for omitting those impropera-
' tions and terms of scurrility betwixt us, which only
' difference our affections and not our cause, there is
' between us one common name and appellation, one
' faith and necessary body of principles common to us
' both ; and therefore I am not scrupulous to converse
' and live with them, to enter their churches in defect of
' ours, and either pray with them or for them. I could
' never perceive any rational consequence from those
' many texts which prohibit the Children of Israel to
' pollute themselves with the temples of the heathens ;
' we being all Christians, and not divided by such detested
' impieties as might profane our prayers, or the place
' wherein we make them ; or that a resolved conscience
' may not adore her Creator anywhere, especially in
' places devoted to His service ; if their devotions offend
' Him, mine may please Him : if theirs profane it, mine
' may hallow it. Holy water and crucifix (dangerous to
' the common people) deceive not my judgment, nor
' abuse my devotion at all. I am, I confess, naturally
' inclined to that which misguided zeal calls superstition :
' my common conversation I do acknowledge austere, my
' behaviour full of rigour, sometimes not without morosity ;
' yet at my devotion I love to use the civility of my knee,
' my hat, my hand, with all those outward and sensible

'motions which may express or promote my invisible
'devotion.   I should violate my own arm rather than a
'church; nor willingly deface the name of saint or
'martyr.   At the sight of a cross or crucifix, I can
'dispense with my hat, but scarce with the thought or
'memory of my Saviour.   I cannot laugh at, but rather
'pity the fruitless journeys of pilgrims, or contemn the
'miserable condition of friars; for, although misplaced
'in circumstance, there is something in it of devotion.
'I could never hear the Ave-Mary bell without an
'elevation, or think it sufficient warrant, because they
'erred in one circumstance, for me to err in all,—that is
'in silence and dumb contempt.   Whilst, therefore, they
'direct their devotions to her, I offer mine to God;
'and rectify the errors of their prayers by rightly ordering
'mine own. . . . As there were many reformers, so like-
'wise many reformations; every country proceeding in a
'particular way and method, according as their natural
'interest, together with their constitution and clime,
'incline them: some angrily and with extremity; others
'calmly and with mediocrity, not rending but easily
'dividing the community, and leaving an honest possi-
'bility of reconciliation;—which, though peaceable spirits
'do desire, and may conceive that revolution of time and
'the mercies of God may effect, yet that judgment that
'shall consider the present antipathies between the two
'extremes,—their contrarieties in condition, affection, and
'opinion,—may with the same hopes expect a union of
'the poles of heaven.'

He confesses that the Church of England squares
most closely with his particular devotion; in points
indifferent he is guided by his own reason.   'I condemn
'not all things in the Council of Trent,' he says, 'nor
'approve all in the Synod of Dort.   In brief, where the
'Scripture is silent, the Church is my text; where that
'speaks 'tis but my comment; where there is joint silence
'of both, I borrow not the rules of my religion from

' Rome or Geneva, but from the dictates of my own
' reason. It is an unjust scandal of our adversaries, and
' a gross error in ourselves, to compute the nativity of our
' religion from Henry the eighth ; who, though he rejected
' the Pope, refused not the faith of Rome, and effected
' no more than what his own predecessors desired and
' essayed in ages past, and it was conceived the state of
' Venice would have attempted in our days.'

It would need far too large a disquisition in this place
to go into his utterances on all the mysteries of religion,
especially those that were vexing men's minds in that
day of questionings. In many things he is the mouth-
piece of his own times ; in some the forerunner of ours.
The great mysteries of faith he holds to be beyond the
province of reason, not against it. ' Many things are
' true in divinity, which are neither inducible by reason
' nor confirmable by sense ; and many things in philo-
' sophy confirmable by sense yet not inducible by
' reason.' And in an earlier passage, ' I can answer all the
' objections of Satan and my rebellious reason with that
' odd resolution I learned of Tertullian, " *Certum est quia*
' " *impossible est*." I desire to exercise my faith in the
' difficultest point ; for to credit ordinary and visible
' objects is not faith but persuasion.'

The whole book has to do with thoughts and beliefs,
not with practices, but incidentally we gather that those
he observed were what the Church of England in his day
enjoined. The sum of all his meditations is that happiness
is to be found in God alone : ' Whatsoever else the world
' terms happiness is to me a story out of Pliny, a tale of
' Boccace or Malizspini, an apparition of neat delusion,
' wherein there is no more of happiness than the name.
' Bless me in this life with but the peace of my conscience,
' command of my affections, the love of Thyself and my
' dearest friends, I shall be happy enough to pity Cæsar.'

In the same spirit wrote the King in his captivity and
in the near prospect of a violent death :—

A quiet conscience in the breast
Has only peace, has only rest,
The music and the mirth of kings
Are out of tune unless she sings ;
Then close thine eyes and sleep secure.

The *Eikon Basilike*, or Portraiture of the King by his own hand, from which these lines are taken, can in one sense hardly be said to belong to home life, written by a king, first in camp, then in captivity ; yet since it concerns not merely his actions but his private reflections and devout meditations, it may fitly be compared with similar utterances of the most devout minds of the time. The question of the authenticity of the book, so ably disposed of by Dr. Wordsworth, belongs to history ; for us the internal evidence should be enough. To say nothing of the close similarity in style, phrase, turn of thought, to the King's own utterances, whether recorded in Clarendon or in his letters, it is impossible that any man, especially any unprincipled man writing with intent to deceive, could so have counterfeited the sincerest penitence, patience, faith. The book is half an Apologia— a setting forth of his own view of the difficulties in which he found himself, with the motives which induced him to act as he did ; the other half is composed of the meditations and prayers which flowed from the circumstances, couched often in the words of the gospels or of his favourite psalms. Sir Thomas Herbert, who was in attendance on the King throughout his long imprisonment, testified how regular he was in the observance of his hours for prayer, meditation, and reading the Bible, and how much consolation he found therein, although deprived by order of the Parliament of the ministrations of his chaplains.

The reality of these devotions and the absence of all hypocritical parade are manifest in their simplicity, and were sufficiently proved by the spirit they wrought in him. Here are neither fretful repinings nor morbid self-

accusations; only the quiet committing of his cause into
the hands of a righteous Judge :—

' If Thou, Lord, wilt be with me, I shall neither fear
' nor feel any evil, though I walk through the valley of
' the shadow of death.'

And these words which echo those not only of the
first martyr but of a greater Example :—

' And when Thou makest inquisition for my blood, O
' sprinkle their polluted, yet penitent souls, with the
' Blood of Thy Son, that the destroying angel may pass
' over them.

' Though they think my kingdoms on earth too little
' to entertain at once both them and me, yet let the
' capacious kingdom of Thy infinite mercy at last receive
' both me and my enemies.'

Memorial Medal of King Charles I.

CHAPTER XVI

IN TIME OF TRIAL

FROM nursery rhymes and baby games to arranged marriages, from the horn-book to university studies, from dress, amusements, everyday occupations to the most serious concerns, we have taken a general, if only a bird's-eye view of the life led by the cultivated classes during the half century that preceded the great Civil War. The test of that life came in blood and fire. How had those pleasant country homes, with their old traditions, their religious customs, fitted their sons and daughters to play their parts when the unlooked-for, the impossible, happened?

The men went forth to their posts in council or in camp, but what of the women who remained at home, who knew their husbands and sons in danger, their homes threatened, who went in constant fear of attack, or, at the least, of the quartering of troops upon them, and the destruction of all the little personal possessions which mean home to most women? The note of the day amongst them is heroism; not only the heroism of deeds which find a record in history, but that of the cheerful, uncomplaining patience with which they took the spoiling of their goods, the personal hardships, the poverty, the daily miseries which the war involved.

It was not always a passive heroism that was shown; the home of Sir John Killigrew, near Falmouth, was not the only one whose owners were ready themselves to commit it to the flames sooner than that it should fall into the hands of the enemy and be a base for further operations. Many a woman even, left to herself, with none but her servants and young children with her, whose training had been only the ordering of a large household, found herself competent to provision, man, and hold her husband's castle for the King, even in some cases commanding the troops herself. Among the valiant ladies who thus won for themselves renown in the pages of history the names of Dame Mary Bankes and of Charlotte de la Tremouille, Countess of Derby, spring at once to remembrance.

Corfe Castle, which stands in a strong position on the chain of hills which cut off the Isle of Purbeck from the rest of Dorsetshire, must have been not only a fortress, but a luxurious home full of beautiful things, many of which were described in the former volume, and it was so well fortified as to defy menace for a long time.[1] When in 1642 Sir John Bankes, who was Chief Justice of the Common Pleas and one of the Privy Council, was summoned to attend the King at York, he sent Lady Bankes and her children to his Dorsetshire castle, no doubt believing that there they would be in perfect safety. During the winter, the first winter of the war, she remained there undisturbed, but the spring of 1643 saw matters growing more serious as the enemy drew nearer and nearer. By May the rebels, under the command of Sir Thomas Trenchard and Sir Walter Erle, were in possession of Dorchester, Lyme, Melcombe, Weymouth, Wareham, and Poole, Portland Castle having been delivered to them by treachery, and only Corfe Castle remained in obedience to the King. It was, of course, of the utmost importance to them that they should gain this, and so put themselves in possession of the whole of the sea-coast of Dorset, and, no doubt, thinking they had only a woman to deal with, Sir John being now on circuit, they promised themselves an easy victory.

Dame Mary, however, who was a Hawtrey of Rislip,

[1] *The Story of Corfe Castle*, by the Right Hon. George Bankes.

Corfe Castle in 1643.

Plate XVII.

of ancient lineage and honourable traditions, and moreover
a woman of great good sense and courage, was in no wise
disposed to yield tamely, but resolved to do the best she
could in the difficult position in which she found herself.
The account of the defence she made is given very fully
in *Mercurius Rusticus*, one of the 'Diurnalls' on the Royalist
side, and this description, being the most circumstantial,
we will follow.

'There is an usage,' begins this chronicle, 'that the
' Mayor and Barons, as they call them, of Corfe Castle
' (meaning the small town that surrounds the castle),
' accompanied by the gentry of the Island (the so-called
' Isle of Purbeck), have permission from the lord of the
' castle, on May-day, to course the stag, which every year
' is performed with much solemnity and great concourse
' of people. On this day some troops of horse from
' Dorchester and other places came into the island,
' intending to find other game than to hunt the stag,
' their business being suddenly to surprise the gentlemen
' in the hunting, and to take the castle ; the news of their
' coming dispersed the hunters and spoiled the sport of
' that day, and made the Lady Bankes to give order for
' the safe custody of the castle gates, and to keep them
' shut against all comers. The troopers having missed
' their prey on the hills (the gentlemen having with-
' drawn themselves), some of them came to the castle
' under a pretence to see it, but entrance being denied
' them, the common soldiers used threatening language,
' casting out words implying some intentions to take
' the castle ; but their commanders (who better knew
' how to conceal their resolutions) utterly disavowed any
' such thought, denying that they had any such commission ;
' however, the Lady Bankes very wisely, and like herself,
' hence took occasion to call in a guard to assist her, not
' knowing how soon she might have occasion to make use
' of them, it being now more than probable that the rebels
' had a design upon the castle.'

The narrative may now be condensed a little. This measure, of course, made Lady Bankes's intentions suspected, the more so as she was getting in considerable supplies, even more than seemed necessary for the needs of her large household, and rumour quickly got about that she was provisioning the castle for a siege. The possible need for this was no doubt in her thoughts, and she got in as much as she prudently could, while abstaining from any overt act of defiance. Quietly as she went about it the mere rumour provoked a proclamation in the market-place at Wareham that no beef, beer, or other provisions should be sold to Lady Bankes for her use.

The cruelty of her position must have been greatly aggravated by the fact that those who were concerting measures against her were not invaders or foreign foes, but old neighbours and former friends, who had sat at her table many a time and enjoyed her hospitality ; for among the sequestrators for the county of Dorset were the owners of neighbouring estates—Sir John Bingham of Bingham's Melcombe, into whose hands subsequently many of the treasures of Corfe Castle fell ; Sir Thomas Tregonwell ; Sir Walter Erle, and Sir Thomas Trenchard of Wolverton, near Dorchester ; and Sir John Bankes, having already subscribed largely to the King's necessities, had incurred sequestration.

Lady Bankes was next summoned to deliver four small pieces of cannon, and on her refusal forty seamen came very early in the morning to demand the pieces. To quote again from *Mercurius:* 'The lady in person (early 'as it was) goes to the gates and desires to see their 'warrant; they produced one under the hands of some 'of the commissioners ; but instead of delivering them, 'though at the time there were but five men in the castle, 'yet these five, assisted by the maid-servants, at their 'lady's command, mount these pieces on their carriages 'again, and loading one of them they gave fire, which 'small thunder so affrighted the seamen that they all

' quitted the castle and ran away. They being gone, by
' beat of drum she summons help into the castle, and upon
' the alarm given a very considerable guard of tenants and
' friends came in to her assistance, there being withal some
' fifty arms brought into the castle from several parts of
' the island : this guard was kept in the castle about a
' week. During this time many threatening letters were
' sent to the lady, telling her what great forces should be
' sent to fetch them if she would not by fair means be
' persuaded to deliver them ; and to deprive her of her
' auxiliaries, all or most of them being neighbours there-
' abouts, they threaten that if they oppose the delivery of
' them, they would fire their houses : presently their wives
' come to the castle, there they weep and wring their
' hands, and with clamorous oratory persuade their
' husbands to come home, and not by saving others to
' expose their own homes to spoil and ruin.'

Thus hard pressed, Lady Bankes found herself compelled to come to a composition and deliver her four
small pieces, after which, the rebels no longer fearing, and
becoming remiss in their watches, she was able to ' lay
' hold of the present opportunity,' and furnish the castle
with provisions. Moreover, hearing that the royal troops
under Prince Maurice and the Marquis of Hertford were
marching towards Blandford, she contrived to get a
message to them, representing the importance to the
King's cause of holding the castle, and asking for assistance and a commander. They sent a small force under
Captain Lawrence and Captain Bond, and presently the
siege began in earnest. The besiegers, under Sir Walter
Erle, first possessed themselves of the town, and assaulted
the castle on all sides at once. They had two engines
of assault, the 'sow' and the 'boar,' but the defenders
were such excellent marksmen that they shot at the legs
of those under the sow with such good effect that they
completely disabled her. After a time, making no way,
the assailants obtained from the Earl of Warwick a

supply of petards, granadoes, and scaling-ladders, together with a hundred and fifty mariners, with whose aid they attempted to storm the place. *Mercurius* is sarcastic about the courage of Sir Walter Erle, a quality with which he was not well equipped. The watchword given was Old Wat, 'a word ill chosen by Sir Watt Erle, and 'considering the business in hand, little better than 'ominous, for if I be not deceived, the hunters that beat 'the bushes for the fearful timorous hare call him Old 'Watt.' He justified the comparison, being seen to creep on all fours on the side of the hill to avoid danger.

The middle ward was defended by Captain Lawrence, the upper ward by Lady Bankes herself with her daughters, women, and five soldiers, and bravely did these women bear themselves, for by heaving over stones and hot embers they repelled the assailants and kept them from climbing the ladders. 'Being repelled, and having in this 'siege and assault lost and hurt an hundred men, old Sir 'Watt, hearing that the King's forces were advancing, 'cried, and ran away crying, leaving Sydenham to 'command in chief, to bring off the ordnance, ammunition, 'and the remainder of the army, who, afraid to appear 'abroad, kept sanctuary in the church till night, meaning 'to sup and run away by starlight; but supper being 'ready and set on the table, an alarm was given that the 'King's forces were coming. This news took away all 'Sydenham's stomach; all this provision was but messes 'of meat set before the sepulchres of the dead: he leaves 'his artillery, ammunition, and (which with these men is 'something) a good supper, and ran away to take boat 'for Poole, leaving likewise at the shore about an hundred 'horse to the next takers, which next day proved good 'prize to the soldiers of the castle. Thus, after six weeks' 'strict siege, this castle, the desire of the rebels, the tears 'of old Sir Watt, and the key of those parts, by the 'loyalty and brave resolution of this honourable lady,

' the valour of Captain Lawrence and some eighty soldiers
' (by the loss of only two men), was delivered from the
' bloody intentions of these merciless rebels on the fourth
' of August, 1643.'

Allowing for the exaggerations of partisan journalism,
the reputation of Sir Walter for courage cannot have stood
very high, and is in marked contrast to the behaviour not
only of Lady Bankes herself and her daughters, but of
her maid-servants also, who valiantly helped to repel the
enemy.

Unhappily this was not the end : through the varying
fortunes of the war Corfe Castle kept up its reputation,
and was one of the last places that held out for the King.
The final siege began June 20, 1645, and lasted to
near the end of the following February.   In December
Fairfax sent a regiment of horse and two of foot against
it, the whole of the West being by that time in the hands
of the rebels.   During this siege a chivalrous attempt
was made by a young officer named Cromwell, with a
troop of a hundred and twenty men, to come to the aid
of the now widowed lady and her daughters, straitly shut
up as they were in the closely invested castle.   His
forcing his way through the besiegers and tendering his
service to the lady reads like a page of old romance.
Even now it needed treachery to reduce the castle ; the
intrepid Dame Mary was as resolute as ever, but some of
those within, weary of holding out against odds, betrayed
it to Colonel Bingham, who, being an old friend and
neighbour of Lady Bankes, and moreover struck with the
fortitude she had displayed, obtained for her the lives of
her garrison.   In any case the defence could not have
been long protracted ; the King's cause was by this time
desperate, and the whole surrounding country in the
hands of the enemy.   Where Dame Mary and her
daughters went when they found themselves despoiled of
their home and nearly all their possessions, we are not
told, but later there is mention of an attempt to rob her

R

of the jointure that remained to her on the sequestration of her husband's estate. For a long time the question was unsettled, but when Cromwell had disposed of the Long Parliament and made himself master of the realm, he allowed her, on the payment of a large composition, to receive her jointure annually. He had the reputation of one who never made war upon women, and without doubt respected her as a courageous and worthy foe. She only outlived the Restoration one year.

Another brave lady who nobly maintained her husband's honour at home while he was fighting for the King was Charlotte, Countess of Derby.[1] Lathom House is described by the writers of the day as a princely mansion capable of entertaining three kings and their suites; it was strongly fortified with no less than eighteen towers. In May 1643 the Governor of Manchester called upon the Countess, the Earl being in the Isle of Man, to subscribe to the propositions of Parliament or deliver the castle, but she would neither tamely give up her house nor purchase her peace at the price of honour. For long she was practically in a state of siege, being closely confined within her own gardens and grounds, though for nearly a year no attack was made, and continual letters with fresh proposals for surrender kept coming from the Parliament, to which she sent most spirited answers, the last being 'that she judged it more noble whilst she could ' to preserve her liberty with her arms than to buy a ' peace with slavery,' adding, ' What assurance have I of ' liberty, or of the performance of any condition when my ' strength is gone? I have received under the hands of ' some eminent personages, that your general is not very ' conscientious in the performance of his subscriptions, so ' that from him I must expect an unsinewed and faithless ' agreement. It is dangerous treating when the sword is ' given into the enemy's hand;' therefore she declared ' not a man should depart from her house, but she would

---

[1] *Siege of Lathom House.* Bohn Library.

'keep it, while God enabled her, against all the King's
'enemies.' And the next day, to second and confirm her
answer, a hundred foot under Captain Farmer, and her
whole force of cavalry, which was but twelve horse, sallied
out upon the enemy, slew about thirty men, took forty
arms, one drum, and six prisoners, with not one man of
their own slain or wounded. From the prisoners they
learned the intention of the enemy to starve the house,
'the commanders having courage to pine a lady, not to
'fight with her.'

Both sides called upon the sanctions of religion for
their designs. The besiegers sent out a notice 'to all
'Ministers and Parsons in Lancashire, well-wishers to our
'successe against Lathom House, theise.

'Forasmuch as more than ordinary obstructions have
'from the beginning of this present service agaynst
'Lathom House interposed our proceedings, and yet still
'remaine, which cannot otherwise be removed, nor our
'successe furthered, but onely by devine assistance ; it is
'therefore our desires to the ministers, and other well-
'affected persons of this county of Lancaster, in publike
'manner, as they shall please, to commend our case to
'God, that as wee are appoynted to the said imploy ment,
'soe much tending to the settleing of our present peace
'in theise parts, soe the Almighty would crowr our
'weake endeavours with speedy successe in the said
'designe.   RAPH ASHTON.
                                   JOHN MOOR.

'ORMSKIRK, *April* 5, 1644.'

Meanwhile one of their preachers, Bradshaw, 'to the
'dishonour of that house (Brasenose) which had given
'him more sober and pious foundations, took occasion
'before his patrons in Wigan, to profane the fourteenth
'verse of the fiftieth chapter of Jeremiah, from thence by
'as many marks and signs as ever he had given of
'antichrist, proving the Lady Derby to be the scarlet

' whore and the whore of Babylon, and Lathom to be
' Babel itself, whose walls he made as flat and thin as his
' discourse. Indeed before he despatched his prophecy,
' he thumped them down, reserving the next verse to be
' a triumph for the victor.'

Nor were the besieged neglectful of their religious
observances. 'Her ladyship commanded in chief; whose
' first care was the service of God, which in sermons and
' solemn prayers she saw duly performed. Four times
' a day was she commonly present at public prayer,
' attended by the two little ladies her children, the Lady
' Mary and the Lady Katherine, for piety and sweetness
' truly the children of so princely a mother : and if daring
' in time of danger may add anything to their age and
' vertues, let them have this testimony, that though truly
' apprehensive of the enemy's malice, they were never
' startled by any appearance of danger.'

The chatelaine's prudent care is shown in the following
note : 'The provisions would have lasted two months
' longer, notwithstanding the soldiers had always sufficient,
' whom her ladyship took care oftentimes to see served
' herself.'

A very full and precise journal of the siege day by
day was kept by one of the defenders. Two MS. copies
of this exist, one in the British Museum, one in the
Bodleian ; the latter ends thus : 'Finis of a brief Journal
' of the Siege against Lathom House'; and on the fly-leaf
is written in the same hand as the MS, 'wherein I was
' wounded, Edward Halsall.'

It would take too long to go through the daily account
of attack and repulse : it lasted not much less than three
months, the first sally having taken place on March the
12th, and relief not arriving till near the end of May,
when Prince Rupert appeared, together with the Earl of
Derby, and put the besiegers utterly to rout.

'May 29'—to quote from the journal—'The Prince
' this day not only relieved but revenged the most noble

' lady his cousin, leaving 1600 of her besiegers dead in
' the place, and carrying away 700 prisoners. For a
' perpetual memorial of his victory, as a brave expression
' of his own nobleness, and a gracious respect to her
' ladyship's sufferings, the next day he presented her
' ladyship, by the hands of the valiant and truly noble
' Sir Richard Crane, with twenty-two of those colours,
' which three days before were proudly flourished before
' her house, which gift will give honour to his Highness
' and glory to the action, so long as there lives one
' branch of that ancient and princely family which his
' Highness that day preserved.'

Like every other stronghold, Lathom House was
eventually surrendered. On the 8th of December
1645, the *Perfect Diurnall*, a newspaper of the day,
gave the following intelligence of its fall : ' On Saturday,
' December 6, after the House was up, there came letters
' to the Speaker of the Commons' House of the surrender
' of Lathom House in Lancashire, belonging to the Earl
' of Derby, which his Lady, the Countess of Derby,
' proving herself the better soldier of the two, hath above
' these two years kept in opposition to our forces.'

The Earl and Countess retired to their little kingdom
in the Isle of Man, where they could bid defiance to the
Parliament. ' On the faith of a safe conduct from Fairfax,
' they sent their children into England for education ;
' who, however, were seized and sent as prisoners to
' Liverpool. Though repeated offers were made to
' restore them, and the whole of his estates, if the Earl
' would give up his island,' he remained firm in his loyalty
and boldly replied, ' That he was greatly afflicted at the
' sufferings of his children ; that it was not in the nature
' of great and noble minds to punish innocent children
' for the offences of their parents ; that it would be a
' clemency in Sir Thomas Fairfax either to send them
' back to him, or to their mother's friends in France and
' Holland ; but if he would do neither, his children must

' submit to the mercy of Almighty God, but should never
' be released by his disloyalty.'

After the battle of Worcester, the Earl, 'having nobly
' provided for the safety of his young sovereign at the
' expense of his own,' had the honour of dying on the
scaffold, and meeting his fate in the same spirit as his
royal master, he made request that the block might be
moved so as to face the church, saying 'I will look
' towards Thy sanctuary while here, as I hope to live in
' Thy heavenly sanctuary for ever hereafter.'

His widow, having been betrayed with her children
into the hands of her enemies, remained in prison—where
two of her children died of the smallpox—until the
Restoration, when she returned to Knowsley Hall in the
neighbourhood of Lathom House, and there she died
in 1663.

To tell of half the stories of womanly courage and
womanly resource which the exigences of the war called
out would require a volume rather than a chapter. The
part played by Mrs. Lane in the escape of Charles II.
after the battle of Worcester is well known and belongs
to a slightly later date ; but a not less devoted, if a less
important service, was rendered by Lady Morton, one of
the Queen's ladies, to whose care the youngest princess,
Henrietta, was committed at a fortnight old, and who
contrived to spirit the baby away to France to her
mother when ordered to give her up to the custody of
the Earl of Northumberland when the other children were
placed by Parliament in his care.

Lady Morton had remained at Exeter with the infant
princess when the Queen was compelled to take flight,
and when the city was relieved by the royal troops she
was able to lay the child in its father's arms. By his
desire it was at once baptized by the name of Henrietta
Anne, and was then taken by Lady Morton to Oatlands
until the order came for her to be given over to the
Countess of Northumberland. Lady Morton at once

'1648, in the evening, was the time resolved on for the
'Duke's escape. And in order to that, itt was designed
'for a week before every night as soon as ye Duke had
'suped hee and those servantts that attended his Highnese
'(till the Earle of Northumberland and ye rest of ye
'howse had suped) wentt to a play called hide and seek,
'and sometimes hee would hide himselfe so well that in
'halfe an hower's time they could not find him. His
'Highnese had so used them to this, that when he wentt
'really away they thought hee was butt att the usual
'sport. A little before the Duke wentt to super that
'night hee called for the gardiner, who only had a treble
'key besides that wch ye Duke had, and bid him give
'him that key till his owne was mended, wch hee did.
'And after his Highnese had suped, hee imeadiately
'called to goe to the play, and wentt downe the privy
'staires into the garden, and opened the gate that goes
'into the parke, treble locking all the doores behind him.
'And at the garden gate C. B. waited for his Highnese,
'and putting on a cloake and periwig hurried him away
'to the parke gate, where a coach waited yt carried
'them to ye watter side, and taking the boate that was
'apoynted for that service, they rowed to the staires next
'the bridge where I and Miriam waited in a private
'howse hard by that C. B. had prepared for dressing his
'Highnese, where all things were in a readinese.

  'Butt I had many feares, for C. B. had desired mee,
'if they came nott there precisely by ten a'clocke, to
'shift for my selfe, for then I might conclude they were
'discovered, and so my stay there could doe noe good,
'but prejudice my selfe. Yett this did not make mee
'leave the howse, though ten a'clocke did strike, and hee
'that was intrusted offten wentt to the landing place and
'saw noe boate comming & was much discouraged, and
'asked me what I would doe. I told him I came there
'with a resolution to serve his Highnese, and I was fully
'determined nott to leave that place till I was outt of

' hopes of dooing what I came there for & would take
' my hazard. And while I was thus fortifying my selfe
' against what might arive to mee, I heard a great noise
' of many as I thought comming up the stairs wch I
' expected to be soldiers to take mee, butt itt was a
' pleasing disappointment, for ye first that came in was
' the Duke, who with much joy I took in my armes &
' gave God thankes for his safe arrivall. His Highnese
' called " Quickely, quickely dress mee " ; and putting of
' his cloaths I dresed him in the wemens habitt that was
' prepared, wch fitted his Highnese very well and was
' very pretty in itt. Affter hee had eaten something I
' made ready while I was idle lest his Highnese should
' bee hungry, and having sentt for a Woodstreet cake
' (wch I knew hee loved) to take in the barge, with as
' much hast as could bee, his Highnese wentt crose the
' bridge to ye staires where the barge lay, C. B. leading
' him ; & imediately the boatmen plied the oare so well
' that they were soon out of sight, having both wind and
' tide with ym. Butt I affterwards heard that the wind
' changed & was so contrary that C. B. told me he was
' terribly afraid they should have been blowne back
' againe. And the Duke, " Doe anything with me rather
' " than let me goe back againe," which put C. B. to
' seeke helpe where itt was onely to be had, & affter hee
' had most fervently supplicated assistance from God,
' presently the wind blewe faire, & they came safely to
' their intended landing place. Butt I heard there was
' some defeculty before they gott to ye ship at Graves
' End, which had like to have discovered them, had not
' Collonell Washington's lady assisted them.
' Affter the Duke's barge was out of sight of ye bridge
' I and Miriam went where I apointed ye coach to stay
' for mee, and made drive as fast as ye coachman could to
' my brother's howse where I staid. I mett none in the
' way that gave mee any aprehension that the designe
' was discovered, nor was itt noised abroad till the next

'day, for (as I related before) ye Duke having used to
'play att Hide & Seeke, and to conceal him selfe a long
'time, when they mist him att the same play, thought he
'would have discovered himselfe as formerly when they
'had given over seeking him. Butt a much longer time
'beinge past then usually was spentt in that divertisse-
'ment, some began to aprehend that his Highnese was
'gone in earnest past their finding, wch made the Earle
'of Northumberland (to whose care hee was committed)
'afster strict search made in the howse of St. James & all
'thereabout to noe purpose, to send & acquaint the Speaker
'of the House of Commons that the Duke was gone, butt
'how or by what meanes hee knew nott, butt desired that
'there might bee orders sent to the Cinque Ports for
'stoping all ships going outt till the passengers were
'examined & search made in all suspected places where
'his Highnese might bee concealed.

'Though this was gone aboutt with all the vigillancy
'immaginable, yett itt pleased God to disapointt them of
'there intention by so infatuating those severall persons
'who were imployed for writing orders that none of them
'were able to writt one right, butt ten or twelve of ym
'were cast by before one was according to their minde.
'This account I had from Mr. N., who was mace-bearer
'to the Speaker all that time & a witnese of itt. This
'disorder of the clarkes contributed much to the Duke's
'safety, for hee was att sea before any of the orders came
'to the ports, & so was free from what was disigned if
'they had taken his Highnese.

'Though severalls were suspected for being accesory
'to the escape, yett they could nott charge any with itt
'butt the person who wentt away, & hee being outt of
'there reach, they took noe notice as either to examine or
'imprison others.'

This narrative properly belongs to the pages of history;
indeed, Anne Murray well deserves her little niche there
for the hand she had in it; but her story is so full of

little womanish touches, with its naïve description of the mohair suit and the tailor's perplexity at the measurements, the Woodstreet cake, too, which her thoughtful kindness prepared to solace the boy on his hazardous journey, that it seems not out of place among the things which women did in their own feminine fashion. It is sad that poor Anne's own romance, thus strangely begun, should have ended so unhappily as has been related in the previous volume.

CORFE CASTLE IN 1660.

PLATE XVIII.

CHAPTER XVII

WHAT WAS LEFT

THE last ten years of the half century which has formed the subject of this study brought about a complete change, not only in the political constitution, but in the whole life of the country ; not alone laws and religion were overturned, but society as a whole was more entirely and abruptly altered than has ever been the case at any other period. Having gleaned from their own pens some notion of the life led by the cultivated classes either in town or country, we may, without going into the question of political gain or loss, inquire how that life was affected by the changes.

As to material comfort, that was in many cases exchanged for utter ruin. The great strongholds which had stood siege, such as Corfe Castle, Lathom or Basing House, were 'slighted,' that is, blown up, having been plundered of all their contents, and their ruins still stand as gaunt reminders of the strength of an earlier day. But these belong to the fortunes of war and the glory of it ; what comes more closely home to our sympathies are the pitiful accounts of waste, loss, and desolation which were the lot of hundreds of modest, comfortable, well-furnished houses. These quiet homes, which were not strongholds and were never besieged, have no glory in history, but they suffered ; they were plundered, many of them first by one side and then by the other ; they were wasted and their resources overtaxed by the continual quartering of troops ; they were sequestrated or impoverished by fines and compositions; they were left to neglect and decay while the master and all sons and servants able to bear arms were away fighting; and in many cases they were despoiled by their owners of everything of value, in order to lend aid to the King.

From the many letters, diaries, inventories which were quoted in the former volume, a fair notion may have been gained of the comfort, of the furniture, books, pictures, musical instruments, of the domestic resources, the gardens, farm-yards, orchards of these country homes. What a contrast was their condition when civil war had stalked through the land! What the troops had spared, moth and rust had consumed; there was no one to take care of anything; indeed, to appear more prosperous than your neighbours was to invite plunder on one pretext or another. Poor Mary Verney's description of how she found matters at Claydon after four years in exile is but a typical instance.

'The house is most lamentably furnished, all the linnen
'is quite worne out . . . the feather bedds that were
'waled up are much eaten with ratts . . . the fire-irons,
'spitts, and other odd things are so extremely eaten with
'Rust that they canot be evor of any use againe. . . . The
'cloath of the Musk-coloured stooles is spoyled and the
'diningroome chaires in Ragges.' Her husband, who took as much interest in the minor things of life as a woman, was in great anxiety lest 'Moathes' should have destroyed the 'Turkie Worke cushions,' and also for the 'greate churche cushions and the purple satten ones.'[1]

But there were more unhappy results of neglect than cushions and fire-irons: the children, left to servants, and exposed, no doubt, to seeing a good deal of rude and insolent behaviour when troops came down upon them, were growing up like wild colts. In such times all discipline was relaxed, and the younger girls of the Verney family suffered in manners and morals. How rude they were,

[1] *Verney Memoirs.*

how quarrelsome, how 'extream clownish,' has already been quoted from their sister-in-law's letters ; and theirs was no isolated case, to judge by the many instances of children of excellent parents who turned out badly.   Not in Claydon only, but in many another home we may be sure, though its annals may be unrecorded, the children, hitherto so carefully nurtured, were growing up neglected like these poor little Verney girls, and moreover sharing, as children always will share, in the sense of anarchy and the loosening of all authority which was abroad.

Hillesden, the home of Dame Margaret Verney, where her brother, Sir Alexander Denton, lived with his large family and his two sisters, met with a cruel fate.   It was at no great distance from Claydon, and must have been like a second home to the young Verneys, especially in the lifetime of their grandmother, old Lady Denton. Although Sir Alexander had married a cousin of John Hampden, and, like many Buckinghamshire squires, was in sympathy with the reforming views of the Long Parliament in its early days, when war broke out he remained loyal, and fortified his house, which was in an important position, lying between Oxford and Newport Pagnell.   It was besieged by Sir Samuel Luke and Colonel Cromwell, and being unable to offer a protracted resistance, surrendered on promise of quarter.   It was plundered and burnt to the ground, and the ladies, including Pen Verney, who was on a visit there, were robbed of everything they possessed, though not personally molested, and were obliged to take refuge at Claydon.

Sir Alexander was carried off to the Tower.   He displayed great fortitude as to the loss of his liberty and all his property ; but another blow which soon fell on him in the death of his eldest son, John, a most promising young man, who fell at Abingdon, lamented by his very enemies, broke him down completely, and he died in prison.

The siege gave occasion to two curious little romances

which led to two marriages in the family. Colonel Smith, who was in command of the defence, fell in love with Margaret Denton, and married her not long after. The other affair was more amusing : one of the aunts was a middle-aged spinster, and during the course of the siege one of the attacking party, Jaconiah Abercrombie by name, contrived to find opportunity for paying his addresses to her, and, in spite of belonging to the enemy's side, was accepted. Possibly Mistress Susan was really attracted by her Puritan lover, or possibly, as the old saying is, she felt it was getting late in the afternoon, for we must remember that in those days to be an old maid was something of a reproach. They were married very shortly after, but her wedded bliss was not of long duration ; next year Henry Verney wrote to his brother, 'Your ante's husband was killed this week by a party ' from Borestall and buried at Hillesden.'

The most painful feature of all that sad time, and the one that cut the deepest into family life, was the dividing of households—characteristic of all civil war, but more especially of this, where there were so many shades of opinion that it was hard to tell where the dividing line would run ; and indeed in many cases the most honest man found his conscience would not suffer him to remain attached to the side he had first chosen. Affectionate households were split into opposing factions ; brother arrayed against brother, father against son. And it was amongst the best that these cruel divisions came.

Happiest were the extreme men who could see only one side ; such, for instance, as Colonel Hutchinson, who never wavered for one moment in his conviction that 'popery and prelacy' were practically the same thing, and both were of the devil, and therefore naturally regarded all who thought as he did as 'the godly,' and all others as 'malignants,' bent on the destruction of their country. It gave an entire simplicity to his view of his duty, and he never faltered, either before the event nor after it, in his belief that in condemning an innocent man to death, by a tribunal which had no jurisdiction over him, he was fulfilling his duty to God.   He died in prison calmly, courageously, absolutely unrepentant, having never swerved from the course he had laid down for himself, and believing to the last that he had the support of a good conscience.

The same undoubting faith in a good cause, untroubled by any questionings as to the balance of right that might be on the one side or on the other, is shown in the letter which the King's faithful servant, Endymion Porter, wrote to his wife on the outbreak of the war :—

'MY DEAREST LOVE—As for monies, I wonder that
' you can imagine that I should help you, but you always
' look for impossibilities from me, and I wish it were a
' time of miracles, for then we might hope for a good
' success in everything ; whither we go and what we are
' to do I know not, for I am none of the Council ; my
' duty and loyalty have taught me to follow my King
' and Master, and by the grace of God nothing shall
' divert me from it ; I could wish you and your children
' a safe place, but why Woodhall shall not be so I cannot
' yet tell ; I could likewise wish my cabinets and other
' things were at Mr. Courteen's, but if a very discreet
' man be not there and take the advice of the Joiner to
' convey them thither, they will be as spoiled in the
' carriage as with the rabble ; dearest Love, to serve God
' well is the way in everything that will lead us to a
' happy end, for then He will bless us and deliver us out
' of all our troubles.   I pray you have a care of yourself
' and make much of your children, and I presume we
' shall be merry and enjoy one another ere long.   I writt
' to you and sent the letters by Nick on Tuesday, but the
' rogue is drunk, and I hear not of him.   If you remember
' my service to Mrs. Eure and tell her that I am her
' faithful servant, I will give you leave to kiss Mrs. Marie
' for me ; I wish sweet Tom with me, for the King and

+ King Charles was not innocent — s If any man ever deserved hanging as a traitor he did.

' Queen are forced to lie with their children now, and I
' envy their happiness. I pray you let this bearer come
' to me again when you hear where we rest, and so Good-
' night sweet Noll.—Your true friend and most loving
' husband, ENDYMION PORTER.

' WINDSOR, *thes* 14*th of January* 1642.[1]

The case of Sir Edmund Verney, the royal standard-
bearer, was typical of many: liberal in politics, and a
religious man of strongly Protestant views, he had, with
many of the best and wisest men of the time, such as
Hyde and Falkland, sided with the popular party in their
earlier demands for certain measures of reform, and in
their resistance against encroachments of royal prerogative
on the liberties of the people. When, however, constitu-
tional resistance passed into rebellion he doubted no
longer where his duty lay, and followed the King whom
he had served faithfully his whole life. At the same
time, he neither understood nor sympathised with his
policy ; he saw no reason why fatal concessions should
not be made on the religious question, and would have
been quite willing to see the Church of England sever her
continuity with the primitive Catholic Church, and become
as one of the Protestant sects. Feeling that the side he
fought for was in many points in the wrong, he suffered
greatly, and in nothing more bitterly than in finding his
eldest son taking up arms against the King. His mind
on the matter is very graphically set forth in a conversation he had with Mr. Hyde, which is thus related in the
latter's Life :—

' Mr. Hyde was wont often to relate a passage in that
' melancholick Time, when the Standard was set up at
' Nottingham, with which He was much affected. Sir
' Edmund Verney, Knight-Marshall, who was mentioned
' before as Standard Bearer, with whom He had a great
' Familiarity, who was a man of great Courage, and

[1] *Letters of Mr. Endymion Porter*, by Dorothea Townshend.

‘ generally beloved, came one Day to him and told him,
‘ “ He was very glad to see him, in so universal a Damp,
‘ “ under which the Spirits of most Men were oppressed,
‘ “ retain still his natural Vivacity and Cheerfulness ; that
‘ “ He knew that the Condition of the King, and the
‘ “ Power of the Parliament, was not better known to any
‘ “ Man than to him ; and therefore He hoped that He
‘ “ was able to administer some Comfort to his Friends,
‘ “ that might raise their Spirits, as well as it supported
‘ “ his own.”   He answered, “ that He was in Truth
‘ “ beholden to his Constitution, which did not incline him
‘ “ to Despair ; otherwise He had no pleasant Prospect
‘ “ before him, but thought as ill of Affairs as most Men
‘ “ did ; that the other was as far from being melancholick
‘ “ as He, and was known to be a Man of great Courage
‘ “ (as indeed He was of a very cheerful, and a generous
‘ “ Nature, and confessedly valiant), and that they could
‘ “ not do the King better Service than by making it their
‘ “ Business to raise the dejected Minds of Men; and root
‘ “ out those Apprehensions that disturbed them, of Fear
‘ “ and Despair, which could do no Good, and really did
‘ “ much Mischief.”   He replied smiling, “ I will willingly
‘ “ join with you the best I can, but I shall act it very
‘ “ scurvily.   My Condition,” said He, “is much worse than
‘ “ yours, and different I believe from any other Man’s,
‘ “ and will very well justify the Melancholick that, I con-
‘ “ fess to you, possesses me.   You have Satisfaction in
‘ “ your Conscience that you are in the Right ; that the
‘ “ King ought not to grant what is required of him ; and
‘ “ so you do your Duty and your Business together :
‘ “ but for my Part, I do not like the Quarrel, and do
‘ “ heartily wish that the King would yield and consent
‘ “ to what They desire ; so that my Conscience is only
‘ “ concerned in Honour and in Gratitude to follow my
‘ “ Master.   I have eaten his Bread, and served him
‘ “ near thirty Years, and will not do so base a Thing
‘ “ as to forsake him ; and chuse rather to lose my Life

' " (which I am sure I shall do) to preserve and defend
' " those Things which are against my Conscience to
' " preserve and defend. For I will deal freely with you,
' " I have no Reverence for the Bishops, for whom this
' " Quarrel subsists." It was not a Time to dispute ; and
' his Affection to the Church had never been suspected.
' He was as good as his Word ; and was killed in the
' Battle of Edgehill, within two Months after this Dis-
' course. And if those who had the same and greater
' Obligations, had observed the same Rules of Gratitude
' and Generosity, whatever their other Affections had
' been, that Battle had never been fought, nor any of that
' Mischief been brought to pass, that succeeded it.'

Sir Edmund died grasping the standard, and the
hand that held it, wearing the ring with an engraved
portrait that King Charles had given him, was chopped
off in witness to his loyalty to his trust.

That his eldest son took a different view of his duty
must have been a great grief to such a man, for they had
been more to each other than most fathers and sons.
Ralph seems never to have caused his parents anxiety
or trouble from his boyhood, and as he grew up became
his father's trusted counsellor and deputy ; to find his
favourite son siding with the King's enemies must have
been a crushing blow to the loyal old man. One consolation remained : no one who knew Ralph Verney
could doubt for a moment that he acted in sincerity and
from conscientious motives. Certainly self-interest never
swayed him, for, unlike many half-hearted ones who
changed with the fortune of the day, Ralph went always
with the weaker side and cast in his lot just where it
was to his disadvantage. At the beginning of the war,
when the King's party was the strongest and far the
most experienced in warfare, and it seemed likely they
would gain the day, Ralph gave his support to the
Parliament, and was only eager to secure those liberties
which he conceived were threatened ; but when Cromwell's

Ironsides were showing what the people could do, and he was gradually usurping all power, he at last perceived whither their aims were tending, and went into exile sooner than sign the Covenant, finding that liberty of conscience was but an empty name. His mistakes were bitterly punished by the sorrows and losses he brought on himself and his family, suffering fines and sequestrations on both sides. A good man, but of no great strength of mind or character, he wins respect by his entire absence of self-seeking ; but he was not clear-sighted nor firm enough for his adhesion to be of much value to either side.

Of a very different temper were his two brothers : Edmund the Wykehamist giving himself to the Royalist cause with whole-hearted devotion, and, like his father, laying down his life in it ; while Henry, of a light and frivolous disposition, fonder of racing and betting than of any serious occupation, hesitated long to which side to offer his sword, and apparently decided at last for the King's party because it was supported by more men of fashion. He writes to his brother a few days after he had joined the royal forces, 'The King's hand I have ' kist ; a lookt earnestly uppon mee, but spake not to ' mee.' On this the editor of the Letters comments : ' Surely a cold reception for Charles to give the son of ' his faithful servant, slain in his service at Edgehill, not ' four months before ; and himself a soldier who only ' asked to be allowed to serve him.' In all probability the King was aware that the young man had been equally ready to accept a commission in the Parliamentary army, and that his elder brother was at the moment in the service of his enemies. That he 'looked ' earnestly upon him' showed that Charles had not forgotten Sir Edmund.

The letter written by young Edmund, the King's loyal servant, to his eldest brother on learning the line he had taken, is among the most beautiful of the many beautiful letters written at that time :—

'BROTHER—what I feared is prooved too true, which
'is your being against the King; give me leave to tell
'you in my opinion tis most unhandsomely done, and it
'greeves my hearte to thinke that my father allready and
'I, who soe dearly love and esteem you, should be bound
'in consequence (because in duty to our King) to be
'your enemy. I heare tis a greate greife to my father.
'I beseech you consider that majesty is sacred; God
'sayth, " Touch not myne anointed " ; it troubled Davyd
'that he cutt but the lapp of Saul's garment; I believe
'yee will say yee intend not to hurt the King, but can
'any of yee warrant any one shott to say it shall not
'endanger his very person? I am soe much troubled to
'think of your being of the syde you are that I can
'write no more, only I shall pray for peace with all my
'hearte, but if God grant not that, yet that He will be
'pleased to turn your hearte that you may soe express
'your duty to your King that my father may still have
'cause to rejoice in you.'

This letter arrived just after Sir Edmund had fallen
at Edgehill; it must have cut Ralph to the quick, but he
left it long unanswered, and the next February Edmund
wrote again: 'I believe you have written too and that
'it is only your heats one way and myne the other
'that have occasioned the miscarryage of our letters. I
'beseeche you let not our unfortunate silence breede the
'least distrust of each other's affections, although I would
'willingly lose my right hand that you had gone the
'other way, yet I will never consent that this dispute
'shall make a quarrel between us, there be too many
'to fight with besides ourselves. I pray God grant a
'suddaine and firme peace that we may safely meete in
'persone as well as in affection. Though I am tooth
'and nayle for the King's cause, and endure soe to the
'death, whatsoever his fortune be, yet sweete brother,
'let not this my opinion (for it is guyded by my con-
'science), nor any report which you can heare of me,
'cause a diffidence of my true love to you.'

Sic!

After some delay Ralph replied coldly :—

'BROTHER—I know not how saifly this letter may
' come into your hands, therefore I shall only tell you
' that in October I received your letter dated September
' 14, which was soe full of sharpnesse that I rather chose
' to forbeare answering it (being willing to avoyde all
' matter of dispute) then returne such a reply (as that
' language did deserve) to a brother I love soe well. I
' have now received another from you in another straine
' by Mr. Rogers, for which I thanke you, and let me
' intreate you to stick to the resolution you have taken
' concerning mee, and I shall promise to doe the like to
' you. I will send you noe newes least it cause the letter
' to miscarry. . . Your truly affectionat Brother to serve
' you, R.V.'[1]

Here was a father and three sons, each taking his own
line, and no two feeling exactly alike, for the younger
Edmund, though he could not outdo his father in personal
loyalty, was in conviction far more whole-heartedly for
the King, and Ralph's conscientious vacillations had
nothing in common with Henry's easy-going indifference
to one side or the other. They were but typical of the
divided counsels in many another family throughout the
country, and those, too, amongst the worthiest ; for the
larger minded a man was, the more likely to see how much
was to be said for the opponent's point of view, how great
were the shortcomings on his own side. For years the
questions at issue had been debated with more or less
heat, and it was inevitable that men of different tempera-
ments should take different views of what their conscience
demanded, especially in the beginning, when few thought
the struggle would have gone so far, not reflecting how
much easier it is to draw the sword than to sheathe it,
when every victory has exasperated the situation more
and more.

[1] *Verney Memoirs.*

Another instance of a divided family was that of the Sidneys. The Earl of Leicester himself had no more doubt than had Sir Edmund Verney which side honour and duty called him to support, but he was a man of very different temper, and his adhesion was so uncertain and wavering that it was impossible to trust him with any important position, which want of confidence offended and estranged him. His second and cleverest son, Algernon, was what in later times would be called a radical of a visionary type, and he carried his elder brother with him, while Dorothy's husband, young Lord Sunderland, was among the king's most devoted adherents, and Lady Leicester showed her loyalty when the Royal children were entrusted to her charge by insisting, against the desire of the Parliament, that they should be treated in her household with the respect due to their rank.

Although it is chiefly amongst these distinguished people that the records have come down to us, the same thing must have been taking place in many quiet homes throughout the country. Everywhere were friends estranged, families separated, suspicions engendered. Another cause which made for the destruction of family life for the next generation or two was the exile which was the lot of so many. Either the children were separated from their parents, or they were brought up in foreign homes with foreign ideas and habits. It was not only the sorrow of exile but its results that were to be deplored.

The condition of the Church too was lamentable ; the iconoclastic rage of the Puritans exceeded even that at the time of the Reformation, and not only spared neither statue nor painted window, but broke up all organs and committed to the flames piles of ancient music-books containing unpublished treasures of old Church music which could never be recovered. Many churches were utterly wrecked, and so terrible was the destruction wrought by Waller's troops in Winchester Cathedral that it was seriously debated whether it would not be best to pull the old building down and use the material. It was only saved by a representation made by the townsmen to the Protector that its long nave was the best place in the town where large numbers might hear sermons. The use of the Book of Common Prayer was interdicted—so much for freedom of conscience—and all priests who adhered to their ancient laws and canons, or who had given any aid to the king in his distress, were turned out of their livings, and their places supplied by Independent or Presbyterian preachers—'godly ministers' in the phraseology of the day. Daily service in the churches was entirely discontinued, the only week-day worship consisting of the Wednesday evening lecture with a long extempore prayer. With that exception public worship was entirely relegated to 'the Sabbath,' which was observed as a day of mortification and gloom, not only all games and sports being forbidden, but even the innocent recreation of a country walk. Taylor relates how in the village of Barnsley 'little children were not suffered to walk or ' play : and two women who had been at Church before ' and after Noone, did but walke in the fields for their ' recreation, and they were put to their choice either to ' pay sixpence apiece (for prophane walking) or to be ' laid one houre in the stocks ; & the peevish willfull ' women (though they were able enough to pay) to save ' their money & jest out the matter, lay both by the ' heeles merrily one houre.' [1]

And this was what took the place of the godly discipline of *The Country Parson ;* no fancy picture be it remembered, for it was exemplified not only in the life of the writer, but in that of many another, such as Hammond, Vaughan, Owen, Cosins, Morley. For it was the best men who were driven out ; the careless and self-seeking, the time-servers and indifferent, could easily secure their peace by violating their conscience and so

[1] *A Short Account of a Long Journey*, by John Taylor, the Water-Poet.

retain their livings.   Great numbers preferred penury and
exile, some taking refuge abroad, some living in retirement in England and ministering privately whenever
occasion served.   Evelyn has this entry for March 5,
1649 :—

    ' Mr. Owen, a sequestr'd & learned minister, preached
' in my parlour, and gave us the Blessed Sacrament now
' wholly out of use in the Parish Churches, which the
' Presbyterians & Fanaticks had usurped.'

    Thus religion, banished in the name of religion, kept
on its hidden way.   When the storm had passed it was
found how many had kept the lamp of faith alight, and
these came back to plant once more the old waste places :
Ken and Morley, Hammond and Hall, did their utmost
to rebuild the churches and to restore the ancient godly
customs, but it was hard work to form again the religious
habits, the broken traditions of a whole people ; it would
have been easier to rebuild a ruined cathedral than to
bring back the scattered congregations to the ways they
had once walked in.

    When the Restoration came a new order began ; the
old could never be brought back ; there were many
things no Restoration could restore.   Monarchy was set
up again, and the Church was reinstated, but the scaffold
at Whitehall saw the end of more things than one man's
life.

INDEX

THE END

T